THE EARLY YEARS OF THE FA CUP

THE EARLY YEARS OF THE FA CUP

**HOW THE BRITISH ARMY HELPED
ESTABLISH THE WORLD'S FIRST
FOOTBALL TOURNAMENT**

James W. Bancroft

FRONTLINE
BOOKS

First published in Great Britain in 2021
FRONTLINE BOOKS
an imprint of Pen & Sword Books Ltd,
47 Church Street, Barnsley, S. Yorkshire, S70 2AS

ISBN: 978-1-39909-991-2

CIP data records for this title are available from the British Library

For more information on our books, please visit
www.frontline-books.com, email info@frontline-books.com
or write to us at the above address.

Printed and bound by CPI Group (UK) Ltd, Croydon, CR0 4YY
Typeset by Concept, Huddersfield, West Yorkshire
Pen & Sword Books Ltd incorporates the imprints of Pen & Sword
Archaeology, Atlas, Aviation, Battleground, Discovery,
Family History, History, Maritime, Military, Naval, Politics,
Social History, Transport, True Crime, Claymore Press,
Frontline Books, Praetorian Press,
Seaforth Publishing and White Owl

For a complete list of Pen and Sword titles please contact
PEN & SWORD LTD
47 Church Street, Barnsley, South Yorkshire, S70 2AS, England
E-mail: enquiries@pen-and-sword.co.uk

Or

PEN AND SWORD BOOKS
1950 Lawrence Rd, Havertown, PA 19083, USA
E-mail: Uspen-and-sword@casematepublishers.com

Contents

Introduction

The 2021–22 football season marks the 150th anniversary of the Football Association Challenge Cup competition, the oldest football tournament in the world. Members of the British Army took a prominent part in its formation and establishment, and they helped to put the sport on the road to national and international status.

My first introduction to football was a sad one. On the late afternoon of 6 February 1958, news came of the Munich Air Disaster, as a result of which many people associated with Manchester United lost their lives, including several of the immortal Busby Babes. These included Geoff Bent and Eddie Colman from my own city of Salford. I remember crowds of people lining the streets to watch the funeral processions of the two local victims, and the tragedy left a dark cloud of grief over the district for many months afterwards. As time went by I witnessed what passion the game of football itself can stir up, while watching Best, Law and Charlton at Old Trafford, and Lee, Bell and Summerbee at Maine Road; and especially during that one match of the year known as the FA Cup final. Little did I realise the proud history that competition has, and how 'cup fever' would fascinate me for most of my life. As a domestic competition it has not and will never be rivalled anywhere in the world.

At the same time as I began watching football and getting to know the game, another event stirred something inside me. Because of films like *The Alamo* with John Wayne and *The Magnificent Seven* with Steve McQueen, I was coming to the conclusion that all heroes were American. However, in 1964 I saw a film called *Zulu* with Stanley Baker and Michael Caine, which depicts the battle at Rorke's Drift during the Zulu War of 1879, when a company of British soldiers held off ferocious attacks by as many as 3,000 warriors. They fought with such bravery that the Zulus gave up and retreated, and fifteen gallantry medals were awarded to the survivors. I was in awe!

As my interest in British military history and the history of British football has developed, particularly during the reign of Queen Victoria,

I have spent more than forty years learning about the subjects and collecting information to build up quite a comprehensive archive. Using this information I wrote *Rorke's Drift: The Zulu War, 1879*, which has been reprinted seven times, and I am told inspired other people to become interested in the subject. Its success prompted me to write further on aspects concerning the history of Victorian Britain, and this project has allowed me to use my combined knowledge of the two subjects I have the most interest in – the military and football; and this work brings together the heroes of both.

I have produced biographical tributes to three Royal Engineer officers who I believe played some part in the 1872 FA Cup final but have not previously been given recognition, and the reasons for doing so are explained in the text.

Most of the military men who took part in the early FA Cup competitions went on to have distinguished military careers and saw active service in most of the campaigns throughout the British Empire. One was recommended for the Victoria Cross for valour in Afghanistan, and some of them gave their lives in famous battles such as Tofrek in the Sudan, on Spion Kop in South Africa and on the Western Front during the Great War.

The narratives of the Royal Engineers' Cup finals are my interpretation of the reports written by the Engineers' secretary in their 'old Club Book', which I have enhanced by including one newspaper report for each Royal Engineers game. A list of publications and institutions I used for further information or to cross-reference with my archive is provided in the Bibliography, and I have presented the biographical tributes in a chronological narrative form as much as possible, as opposed to lists of facts and figures.

It was an amateur game – officially – and most grounds were not enclosed. At a time when there has been talk of a financially motivated breakaway European Super League, imagine going to Hackney Marshes in London or Hough End playing fields in Manchester, or any such area in the country, and having the choice of watching three FA Cup ties completely free; and what if two of the games included former winners of the trophy? That was possible at the Great Lines at Chatham on 31 October 1885. On that day the Royal Engineers (winners in 1875) played Old Foresters; Chatham FC played Old Carthusians (winners in 1881); and Rochester played Reading.

This publication gives the opportunity to look back at a time when football was played for the sport itself.

James W. Bancroft

Chapter 1

Little Tin Idol

People continue to discuss, even argue, about the laws of the game, and there was disagreement over the laws between football and rugby soon after the establishment of the Football Association in 1863. Blackheath representatives favoured the retention of hacking, tripping and catching the ball, while the Cambridge University people championed the dribbling game and forbade most of the dangerous play. The Blackheath set eventually resigned from the Association and took up the handling code as played at Rugby School. The Football Association adopted the Cambridge rules, football and rugby went their separate ways, and modern organised soccer began.

The move that did most to broaden and strengthen the influence of the FA came on Thursday, 20 July 1871. A young officer of the Royal Engineers by the name of Francis Marindin joined another six members of the Football Association at a special meeting at the *Sportsman* office in London, requested by the secretary, Sunderland-born Charles William Alcock (1842–1907), of the Wanderers FC, one of the early leading lights of football. Also at the meeting was the honorary treasurer to the Football Association Committee, Alfred Stair (1845–1914) of Upton Park; John Hardinge Giffard (1847–1903) of the Civil Service Club; Douglas Allport of Crystal Palace FC; Morton Peto Betts (1847–1914) of Harrow School; and Charles William Stephenson (1853–1924) of Westminster School.

The year 1871 had a particularly cold and wet summer. Any talk of sport would have been W.G. Grace's excellent batting averages at Kennington Oval, and Derbyshire CCC had begun to play its inaugural first-class cricket season. The British Open Golf Championships had been postponed because of a dispute about who should administer the competition, and it would not be cancelled again for any reason other than war until the Covid pandemic caused the cancellation of the 2020 tournament. Baron Mayer de Rothschild's horse Hannah, named after his only daughter, had won the filly triple crown, and another of his horses won the Epsom Derby. Other topics of discussion might have been relief that Europe had been at peace since the Treaty of Frankfurt had been signed in May to end hostilities in the Franco-Prussian War. However, reports that the transport of humans was still going on in areas of Egypt and the Sudan caused the British Government to begin the conquest of the Upper Nile and the suppression of the slave trade in the region. The Welsh reporter and explorer Henry Morton Stanley had begun his expedition to Africa to try to find out what had happened to the Scottish missionary and anti-slavery crusader Dr David Livingstone.

Eventually it was down to the business at hand, as the members were curious to know why such a special meeting had been arranged. The room came to order, the tall and athletic-looking Alcock got to his feet and put forward the proposal: 'That it is desirable that a Challenge Cup should be established in connection with the Association for which all clubs should be invited to compete.'

Alcock had been educated at Harrow School, where he had taken part in the 'Cock House' competition; a system of house matches based on the knockout principle. Most of the other men sat in the room had attended public schools and had experienced the tradition and excitement created by the tournament, so the principle of the competition took little explaining. The idea met with favour and Alcock intended to make his vision a reality. The Football Association Challenge Cup was established, and its inception was the beginning of the modern game as we know it.

The season was already under way so there was no time to waste and 15 August was the date agreed that every club that wanted to take part in the competition must make their wishes known. Fifteen clubs responded in time. On 16 October 1871 a second special meeting was held, and eleven member clubs were represented. Major Marindin and all those who attended the first meeting returned except Westminster School, and in addition there were members of Barnes FC, Clapham Rovers, Hampstead Heathens, Windsor Home Park and Lausanne FC. The first date was agreed when all fifteen clubs could muster a team; and that historic date was 11 November 1871. It is unlikely that those eleven men knew quite what they were starting.

The Wanderers FC was originally formed in 1859 as Forest FC by Charles Alcock and a number of other pupils of Harrow School. The Forest Club played their early matches at Leytonstone and was represented by Alcock at the inaugural meeting of the Football Association, held at the Freemason's Tavern on Great Queen Street, Lincoln's Inn Fields,

London, on 26 October 1863. The club gradually changed its name to the Wanderers in the mid-1860s, and they played their matches at Kennington Oval.

Harrow School/Chequers entered the FA Cup for several seasons but never fulfilled any of the fixtures, until they changed their name to Old Harrovians in 1876. However, as stated, it was the inter-house football tournament that Alcock played while he was at the school that planted the idea in his mind for a knockout competition between the clubs of the Football Association.

Upton Park was formed out of the local cricket club in 1867, and played their home games at West Ham Park. They reached the FA Cup quarter-finals in 1877, 1878, 1882 and 1884. They became stalwarts of the amateur game; being directly involved in a showdown over 'Shamateurism' after a 1-1 draw with Preston North End during a fourth-round FA Cup match in 1884. The Football Association disqualified Preston from the competition. However, matches played against Preston North End drew large attendances, which eventually led to the legislation allowing professionalism in July 1885. They are believed to have been the first-ever Olympic football champions when they represented Great Britain in Paris in 1900; however, modern research suggests that this was a completely different club.

The Civil Service Club, based at Richmond Park, was represented at the first meeting of the Football Association in 1863 by George Warne, a clerk at the War Office who played full-back for them. They can claim to be one of only two founder members of both the Football Association and the Rugby Football Union, which was established in 1871; the other being Blackheath. Two of its players represented Scotland in the unofficial international match against England in November 1870, despite one of them being English. One of their players, William Lindsay, helped the Wanderers to win the FA Cup in 1876, 1877 and 1878. They made a name for themselves while touring across Europe over a twenty-five-year period from 1901; twice beating Real Madrid and Barcelona.

Crystal Palace were founded in 1861 by the cricket team of the same name to give them something to do in the winter months to keep fit. They played their home matches on Clapham Common, and Frank Day represented the club at the inaugural Football Association meeting. They provided four international players for England from 1873 to 1876. They are the only surviving League club to have taken part in the first FA Cup competition, but they stopped playing organised matches from 1875 until they built a new Sports Arena at Crystal Palace Park in Penge. The FA Cup finals were played there from 1895 to 1914 after

3

the Kennington Oval committee banned football matches because they were ruining the pitch.

After Charles Stephenson had represented Westminster School in the FA meeting in July 1871 the school does not appear much in records in connection with the competition afterwards. However, the school provided several players who appeared in FA Cup finals. They played their home matches at Vincent Square, also known as Westminster School Playing Fields. Six former pupils of the school have been awarded the Victoria Cross for valour. The Old Westminsters entered the FA Cup from 1882 to 1894. They played at the Limes Ground in Barnes and do not seem to have been associated with the school.

Barnes had been formed by Ebenezer Cobb Morley in 1862. Morley was one of the eleven members represented at the inaugural meeting of the Football Association, and he became the first secretary of the FA. They played their home games on Barnes Green near a pub called the White Hart, which still exists on the banks of the River Thames. They played in the first-ever match under FA rules – a goalless draw against Richmond. Barnes continued to enter the competition until 1886.

Formed in 1869, the Clapham club played most of their early games on Clapham Common. After losing the 1879 FA Cup final to Old Etonians, they finally won the trophy in the following year by beating Oxford University. They continued to enter the competition until 1887.

Hampstead Heathens were formed in 1868. The club existed until 1872, and the 1871–72 FA Cup was the only competition they entered. They played regular fixtures with the Wanderers at The Oval, the first one being on 4 December 1869. They lost all the games in Kennington, but the one occasion when they played the fixture in Hampstead, on 17 December 1870, they won 5-0.

A cricket ground had opened at Windsor in 1850, and according to the *Windsor and Eton Express*, the local club played their first match at Home Park in December 1870. The club began to appear on known fixture lists during the season of the first FA Cup competition. They entered the FA Cup in 1872–73 and 1874–75, and again in 1881–82. They played regular matches with Maidenhead and Great Marlow. However, in September 1882, they amalgamated with local rivals Grosvenor FC to form the Windsor Football Club.

Lausanne FC was founded by about sixty members in the Peckham and Dulwich area of London in 1867. In its early days the club played twenty-a-side rugby and became loosely interested in the Association game, although they never played in the FA Cup. On 26 January 1871, they were one of the twenty-one clubs who sent representation to the Pall Mall Restaurant on Regent Street in London for the meeting that established the formation of the Rugby Football Union, and they decided to join that establishment. They played on the Rosemary Branch Grounds in Peckham, when they changed into their colours of violet with an amber stripe on the left arm at the Rosemary Branch pub on Southampton Street. They moved to New Cross Gate in 1874 and then to Dulwich the following year, where they were known to change at the Greyhound pub in Dulwich village. The club disbanded in 1881.

On 1 February 1872 a sub-committee consisting of Charles Alcock, Alfred Stair and Douglas Allport was appointed to select and purchase an appropriate trophy. It was made of silver, stood on an ebony plinth and measured about 18in high. It cost twenty pounds, a guinea of which was generously donated by Queen's Park of Glasgow from their annual income of six pounds. With it eventually becoming so coveted, it was known as 'The Little Tin Idol'. The FA decided to present the eventual winners with 'eleven medals or badges of trifling value'. The committee could exempt or zone provincial clubs. In the first two rounds the respective captains tossed a coin for the choice of venue, but after the second round all matches were to be played at Kennington Oval, or as instructed by the committee.

Under the headline 'Association Challenge Cup – final tie' the *Morning Post* of 16 March 1872, the morning of the first FA Cup final, published an interesting leading article, which gives an insight into how the FA Cup and football in general was viewed by the British press before the first final had been played. It reflects the mood of the time, and makes some interesting points concerning the differences between Association football and rugby football; even suggesting that the two codes might find a compromise of the rules and remain as one institution.

The secretary of the Royal Engineers thought the piece was significant enough to keep for posterity in the previously mentioned 'old Club Book'. In his article for the 1928 *Royal Engineers Journal*, Richard Ruck states: 'All the RE matches from 1871 to 1875 were recorded in the old Club Book, which I have by my side; therein are descriptions of most of the games, together with extracts from various newspapers.' It has been my privilege to have the same book at my side several times over the years. The second part of the newspaper article states:

> It should be remarked that in one respect this match will be unsatisfactory. The Association does not represent half of the Football Clubs in the country, and therefore the contest between the Association Clubs can only determine which among those

clubs is the strongest, and not which is the strongest club in the whole country. The contest, in fact, is of a limited nature. It is true that the Association is now very large, extensive, and powerful; that it is the leading football institution. But it is no less true that the devotees of the Rugby game, and its modifications, are extremely numerous, and that the players of this description of the game are just as brilliant, as noted, and as important as the members of the Association.

Possibly next year we may have a Rugby Cup to be competed for by the clubs playing this game. If so, we may, perhaps, have to compare the one contest to the St Leger and the other to the Derby. It would be more satisfactory, however, if all the clubs in the country could agree – as in the case of cricket – to play identically the same game. Then the rivalry would assume a very different and much more interesting aspect. The trial of strength and skill would be for the football premiership absolutely. The excitement in such case can readily be imagined. We fear that such a result can as yet scarcely be hoped for.

It is true that the Association have recently modified their rules somewhat in the direction of the Rugby game. But for all that, a marked, and essential difference between the two games still exists. While in the rugby game the great aim is to pick up the ball while bounding along the ground and to run off with it, and in the Association game it is positively forbidden as a rule to even touch the ball with the hands, it is evident that it is the principle rather than a question of mere details that is the point of difference. Men accustomed to the fiercer fun of the Rugby game often deem the Association game insipid. On the other hand the Association players in general think, we believe, that the Rugby game is too rough and too dangerous to limb for adoption among grown-up men; and parents and guardians have a horror of it for the schoolboys they have to watch over.

But for all this the enthusiasm for the Rugby game among those who play it is something quite marvellous. So much so is this the case that it seems quite out of the question to expect that the game will be modified in any way affecting its cardinal feature. The two styles are really antagonistic. The Rugby game is mere handball, not football, say the adherents of the Association; 'dribbling' is the epithet of reproach levelled at the other side of the Rugbyites. The disagreement at present appears to be radical and irreconcilable. Possibly, if each party give in a little, a compromise may be arrived at and a really national game of football be firmly established.

The prominence of later attained by football, in consequence of the establishment of the contest between England and Scotland, and for the Association Cup, will not unlikely cause the question to be seriously mooted. And if it be at all feasible so to combine the rival styles into one universal set of rules, possibly the attempt will be made.

The love for and practice of football has so greatly increased of late years that already it may be looked on as one of the great national pastimes. Formerly the game was confined almost, if not quite, exclusively to schools and colleges. Now the game has spread so much that nearly every district town and village has its club or clubs. It is needless and beside the mark to moralise on this. It is a fact significant, according to the views of the onlooker. Athleticism is clearly in the ascendant. Never was there more excitement about the great boat races. Cricket is more than ever the rage, almost the madness, of the people in England. Athletic sports and school and university are established institutions. Football has grown from a mere school game into a general winter amusement. It would seem as if, while the wear and tear of brain augments, that, as a corrective, muscular exertion is felt insensibly to be almost a necessity. Be this as it may, however, the fact is undeniable; athletic exercises of various kinds gain ground in the country. The great race of next Saturday and the great football match of today will, by the crowds of excited spectators assembled to witness them, testify to this phase, this characteristic of the stirring times we live in.

Nevertheless, when the officer of the Royal Engineers referred to the 1875 FA Cup final in his report as 'the trial of superiority', he was touching on the truth. The competition has always been enigmatic, and unlike a round robin or league championship it is a must-win tournament. Teams don't get a second chance, and its fascination lies mainly in its uncertainty. Usually played in wintry conditions that test stamina and courage as much as skill and talent, no matter how star-studded a team may be, the lesser-known clubs have always put all they can muster into a clash with a favoured team, and shocks, known as 'giant killings', are frequent. It is probably the best chance a lower-league player will have to get noticed and make a name for himself.

At the time when the FA Cup began, football rules were rudimentary. The crossbar was usually a length of tape and there were no nets. The duration of the game was ninety minutes as it is today, but teams changed ends each time a goal was scored. Therefore, if a team was playing against a strong wind, apart from the obvious reason, it was advantageous to score so they could get the wind at their backs. The pitch could be as long as 200 yards, and the playing area was mostly unmarked. When the ball went outside the field of play at the side of the pitch the first team to touch it gained possession, hence the term 'touchline'. The throw was with one arm, so the ball, which was any size, could be hauled for a considerable distance. There are reports of players taking a 'kick-in' instead of a throw-in, so it was not much different to a free kick.

The rule that is probably most strange to the modern enthusiast concerns when the ball went out of play behind the goals. If the defending team put the ball behind but not over the goal tape they were awarded a corner kick; and if the attacking team did the same the defending team were also awarded a corner kick, from their own end of the pitch, so presumably all they did was boot the ball as far up the pitch as they could. If the ball was kicked over the tape by either team then a goal kick was awarded to the defending team.

A team formation usually consisted of one defender, two midfielders (sometimes referred to as cover-goal) and no fewer than seven forwards. There were two players on each of the wings, and the three in the middle were usually stocky men picked for their aggression. The referee made his decisions known by waving a handkerchief, and each team was allowed to nominate an umpire. Players' jerseys were not numbered, so individuals were usually recognised by the colour of their headgear – or socks! It is recorded that twelve- or thirteen-a-side matches were arranged, or even more, so it is difficult to imagine how referees or umpires could keep up with the personnel on each team.

Play was rough, and kicking a man's legs from under him and the shoulder charge were allowed 'and used vigorously' – although even then barging from behind was considered too dangerous. Barging the goalkeeper, even knocking him senseless, was considered fair play, and many goals were scored from a 'goal rush'. The emphasis was on attack and individual dribbling skills. However, as might be expected from a military unit, the Royal Engineers were the first to make teamwork an important part of the game: 'This being their advantage over their opponents, and set a standard to be emulated by other clubs.'

Chapter 2

The British Army

During the first decade of the competition three teams associated with the military were involved in seventy-three matches, although three never took place. They won more than half of them and scored 156 goals. The army also produced one of the most respected administrators in the history of football, in the form of Major Francis Marindin of the Royal Engineers. He was involved in the founding of the FA Cup, played in two finals and refereed a further nine. The military players also include an Olympian, a successful racehorse trainer and an uncle of Sir Laurence Olivier.

Military men and units provided a number of 'firsts' in the early years of football: the Royal Engineers played in the first-ever FA Cup final; Lieutenant James Prinsep of the Essex Regiment was the youngest footballer to appear in the final until 2004, although he remains the youngest to complete a full match; Lieutenant William Maynard of the 1st Surrey Rifles played for England in the first-ever official international match against Scotland, which resulted in a goalless draw; Captain William Kenyon-Slaney of the Grenadier Guards scored the first-ever goal in an official international match, while playing for England; and Lieutenant Henry Renny-Tailyour of the Royal Engineers scored the first-ever goal for Scotland in the same match.

Most of the men who played went on to become high-ranking officers with all the responsibilities that went with it, and as they moved into the 1880s their services were needed in campaigns in Zululand, the Sudan and Burma, and in the 1890s on the North-West Frontier of India, the Sudan and South Africa. Hence, the army clubs were less prominent in football as players became unavailable, although the Army Football Association was founded in 1888. The three main military units which helped to get Association football established in the early years were:

The Corps of Royal Engineers

The Corps of Royal Engineers has one battle honour – *Ubique* – meaning 'Everywhere', which sums up their role perfectly as they have served in every campaign in which the British Army has been involved.

Before 1855, as war raged in the Crimea, the technical elements of the British Army, such as artillery and engineering, were provided by the Board of Ordnance. Artillery and engineer officers formed part of the early 'artillery trains', and the ancestor of the Corps of Royal Engineers emerged from the Board in 1717. Before 1782 the officers of the Royal Engineers did not have a military title, but they were first granted commissions in that year. It was not until 1787 that the military officers of the engineer department were constituted the Corps of Royal Engineers; the men being regimented into the Corps of Royal Military Artificers.

When Napoleon invaded Egypt in 1798, a detachment was sent to Constantinople to train the Turkish army; other companies performing good service in Malta, Italy, Sicily and the West Indies. In 1813 the title Corps of Royal Sappers and Miners replaced that of the Military Artificers, and did effective work under the Duke of Wellington in the Peninsular and Waterloo campaigns.

The Crimean War was the scene of manifold activities by the engineers in the construction of trenches to get closer to the Sebastopol fortifications, during which time they gained the unit's first eight Victoria Crosses, and afterwards the officers and men were united to form one Corps under the title Royal Engineers. After the Indian Mutiny in 1857–58 the Bengal, Madras and Bombay Corps of Engineers were transferred to the Royal Engineers.

As the Corps developed in a progressive world it became responsible for such things as the construction and maintenance of fortifications, ports and airfields, and the operation of railway systems. When an army is advancing the Engineers are occupied in drawing maps, repairing bridges and roads blown up by the enemy; and when retreating they are responsible for the demolition of roads and bridges behind them to hinder the enemy.

The Royal Engineers are believed to have played football at the Chatham Lines since 1842, and the British Army certainly took part in football matches prior to the Royal Engineers FC being established by William Merriman at Chatham in 1867, because it is recorded that a game between the Wanderers and the Officers was played at Aldershot on 5 November 1864. Under the guidance of Major Francis Marindin, they joined the Football Association in 1869.

The Engineers played in blue and red thin hooped shirts and blue shorts. They soon established a formidable reputation in the football world, becoming the most successful military team in history. They were able to keep good players available for matches by having them posted to HMS *Hood* docked at Chatham for submarine mining duties. They played their home matches on open fields at Great Lines, later moving to an enclosed cricket ground. Reports on early games tell how haystacks were cleared or sheep driven away and their droppings picked up before a game could start. On one occasion they played a match with a tree growing in the middle of the pitch. They went on to reach the first-ever FA Cup final in 1872; won the trophy in 1875, and also reached the finals of 1874 and 1878.

Being a technical unit, their style of play focused on teamwork and passing the ball, as opposed to kicking the ball forward and making a rush towards the opposition's goal. They were 'first to show the advantages of combination over the old style of individualism' – or 'the showy practice of dribbling and not passing the ball', as Charles Alcock put it.

1st Surrey Rifles

The 1st Surrey Rifles were raised on 14 June 1859, when the Government had requested Volunteer Corps to defend the country from a suspected invasion by France. Captain John Boucher of the 5th Dragoon Guards was appointed the unit's commanding officer.

In 1860 they became the 1st (South London) Volunteer Corps, then the 1st Surrey (South London) Rifle Volunteer Corps, East Surrey Regiment, with eight companies based at Camberwell.

They originally had their drill ground at Hanover Park in Peckham, and their uniform was green with scarlet facings. In 1863 a new branch of the local railway system was routed through Hanover Park and, after having to overcome some difficulties, a site was acquired in Brunswick Road, later renamed Flodden Road, which opened on 1 July 1865. The buildings were designed by a serving officer, Ensign John Thomas Lepard, and are still standing to this day.

They formed a football team for recreational purposes, and they played their home matches at their Flodden Road Headquarters at Brunswick Road in Camberwell. Their colours were navy blue shirts and white shorts.

The unit sent three volunteer detachments to take part in the Boer War in 1899–1902, to serve alongside the 2nd Battalion, East Surrey Regiment. For their service they received their first battle honour of South Africa, 1900–02.

11

On 1 July 1916, at Montauban on the Somme during the Great War, the 8th Battalion, East Surrey Regiment, took part in a famous football kick-about that was named 'The Great European Cup Tie Final – East Surreys v Bavarians'. At the end of that day 20,000 British soldiers had been killed in action. Battle honours displayed on their colours are Festubert, 1915; Loos; Somme 1916–18; Messines 1917; Cambrai 1917; Bapaume 1918; and Albert 1918.

In the grounds of St Giles' Church in Camberwell there is a memorial cross dedicated to members of the regiment who gave their lives in the Second Boer War, 1899–1902; the First World War, 1914–18; and the Second World War, 1939–45.

105th Regiment of Foot (Madras Light Infantry)

The 105th Regiment can trace its history to 1776 with the formation of the 2nd Madras European Fusiliers in the East India Company's army. The unit disbanded in 1830 but was re-raised in 1839 as the 2nd Madras (European) Regiment, becoming Light Infantry in 1842. After the terrible rebellion in northern India in 1857–58, many of the East India Company's units transferred to the British Army, and it became the 2nd Madras Light Infantry in November 1859. It was then renumbered as the 105th Regiment of Foot (Madras Light Infantry) on 30 September 1862.

The 105th came back to England from Aden in 1874 and formed the football team on its return. Their colours were red and yellow ringed shirts, white shorts and red socks, and they usually played their home games at Aldershot. The unit entered the FA Cup from 1875 to 1878, and then it was sent to Guernsey in the Channel Islands. It entered the 1878–79 competition but had to withdraw because it was sent to Ireland. When the British Army reorganised from numbered regiments on 1 July 1881 to take on county names, the 105th amalgamated with the 51st (2nd Yorkshire West Riding) Regiment to become the King's Own Yorkshire Light Infantry. After 1881 its garrison headquarters was at Pontefract.

A summary of British Army statistics in the early years of the FA Cup

Team	Played	Won	Drew	Lost	For	Against
Royal Engineers	58	34	7	17	149	72
1st Surrey Rifles	10	2	1	7	3	39
105th Regiment	5	1	1	3	4	11
Total	73	37	9	27	156	122

A chronological roll of the military operations of the time and the former army footballers who took part in them:

Crimean War in Russia, 1854–55 – *Francis Marindin*

Jowaki Expedition on the North-West Frontier of India, 1877–78 – *Chandos Hoskyns*

Perak War in Malaysia, 1875–76 – *Henry Rich*

Third Ashanti War in West Africa, 1873–74 – *Edmond Cotter*

Zulu War in South Africa, 1879 – *Henry Rich, Charles Haynes* and *Francis Bond*

Second Afghan War, 1878–80 – *Chandos Hoskyns, Gerald Onslow, Henry Olivier, Thomas Digby, George Sim, George Jones, William Stafford, Alexander Mein, Charles Mayne* and *Horace Barnet*

Transvaal (First Boer War) in South Africa, 1880–81 – *William Merriman, Morgan Lindsay* and *Oliver Ruck*

Mahsud Waziri Expedition on the North-West Frontier of India, 1881 – *William Stafford* and *John Tanner*

Egyptian War, 1882 – *Henry Rich, George Barker, William Kenyon-Slaney, John Blackburn, Francis Bond, Frederick Heath* and *Charles Learoyd*

Zhob Valley Expedition to Balochistan on the North-West Frontier of India, 1884–85 – *Edmond Cotter, Chandos Hoskyns* and *Riccardo Petrie*

Saukin Expedition in the Sudan, 1884 – *Morgan Lindsay* and *Charles Learoyd*

Nile Expedition in the Sudan, 1884–85 – *Edmond Cotter, Pelham von Donop, Charles Wood, Percy Rivett-Carnac, John Blackburn, George Sim, Frederick Heath, Morgan Lindsay, James Prinsep, William Kincaid, John Tanner, Edwin Newman* and *Charles Godby*

Battle of Tofrek in the Sudan, 22 March 1885 – *Morgan Lindsay, George Sim, Frederick Heath, Edwin Newman, Charles Godby, Charles Learoyd and John Tanner*

Bechuanaland Expedition in South Africa, 1884–85 – *Charles Haynes*

Third Burma War, 1885–89 – *Edmond Cotter, Gerald Onslow, Charles Learoyd, Teddy Wynyard* and *Riccardo Petrie*

Chin-Lushai Expedition in Burma, 1889–90 – *Henry Renny-Tailyour* and *Riccardo Petrie*

Hanzara Expedition on the North-West Frontier of India, 1991 – *Francis Bond*

Dongola Expedition in the Sudan, 1896 – *Cecil Keith-Falconer* and *William Kincaid*

Mashonaland Expedition in South Africa, 1897 – *Percy Rivett-Carnac*

Tochi Expedition to Waziristan, 1897 – *Thomas Digby*

Tirah Campaign on the North-West Frontier of India, 1897–98 – *Francis Bond*

Battle of Omdurman in the Sudan, 1898 – *Cecil Keith-Falconer, Lovick Friend* and *William Kincaid*

China (Boxer Rebellion), 1900 – *Riccardo Petrie*

Second Boer War in South Africa, 1899–1902 – *Chandos Hoskyns, Charles Wood, Herbert Rawson, George Sims, Percy Rivett-Carnac, William Stafford, Francis Bond, James Cowan, William Morris, Frederick Heath, Morgan Lindsay, Hugh Massy, William Kincaid and Cecil Keith-Falconer*

Easter Rising in Ireland, 1916 – *Edmond Cotter* and *Lovick Friend*

Great War in Europe, 1914–18 – *John Blackburn, Cecil Wingfield-Stratford, William Stafford, Richard Ruck, George Sim, Horace Barnet, Morgan Lindsay, Frederick Heath, James Cowan, Lovick Friend, Francis Bond, Charles Haynes, John Tanner, Teddy Wynyard, William Kincaid, Charles Godby, Riccardo Petrie* and *Bruce Russell*

Chapter 3

The 1871–72 Season

Fifteen clubs entered the first FA Cup competition, and fifteen ties were played in all. As previously stated, the first matches were scheduled to be played on 11 November 1871, but only three of the fifteen entrants for the first round were actually eliminated on the football pitch.

Upton Park and Clapham Rovers were drawn against each other at West Ham Park, and the first goal in FA Cup history is believed to have been scored by Jarvis Kenrick of Clapham Rovers to set them up for a 3-0 victory.

The Royal Engineers should have played Reigate Priory but Reigate withdrew; and the Wanderers should have played Harrow Chequers but Harrow withdrew. The fact that the two teams Charles Alcock was eligible to play for were brought together suggests that the draw was certainly not biased, and as several Harrow players could play for Wanderers it is likely that the school withdrew because the Wanderers had a wider scope of players to choose from.

What is not usually recorded is the fact that, as they had nothing better to do that day, and according to the Royal Engineers' club book, the Engineers and the Wanderers decided to play each other in a friendly match at The Oval. They drew 1-1, in what turned out to be a rehearsal of the final. On the same day six different players representing the Wanderers beat 1st Surrey Rifles in another friendly match at Camberwell by the only goal of the game.

Reigate Priory was formed in 1870. The club was one of the ten clubs present at the meeting in Guildford when the Surrey Football Association was founded, and when it decided to become affiliated to the FA on 16 March 1882. They were the first winners of the Surrey County Senior Cup in 1883, and they won the trophy six times in their nine final appearances up to 1897. In 1910 they won the International Cup Du Nord, beating Cercle Athletique of Paris 3-0 in the final.

The Civil Service Club turned up at Barnes with only eight men, and Barnes won with goals by A.R. Dunnage and T. Weston. Crystal Palace and Hitchin fought out a goalless draw at the Hitchin Cricket Ground. The rules at the time stated that when matches were drawn both teams went into the draw for the next round, so they both progressed.

Formed in 1861, Hitchin entered the competition until 1876, and again in 1887–88. They became Hitchin Town in 1906, but in 1911 the club folded because of financial problems and a fire at their ground. They re-formed, again as Hitchin Town, in 1928.

Queen's Park of Glasgow was drawn to play Donnington Grammar School from Spalding in Lincolnshire, and these were the two most northerly clubs in the competition. However, the distances caused complications and they could not agree on a date when the match could be played. Queen's Park had made a donation towards the cost of the Little Tin Idol, which probably prompted the Football Association to allow both clubs to advance into the second round.

Donnington School had been formed in 1870, and they did not enter the competition again. However, to celebrate the match that never took place, a team from the modern Donnington School went up to Hampden Park in 1971 to play Queen's Park, which the Glaswegians won.

Having been the first football club in Scotland (instituted on 9 July 1867), Queen's Park dominated Scottish football in its early years. They did not lose a match in the first seven years of their existence, and they provided all the Scottish team that played in the first official international match against England in 1872. They went on to win the Scottish FA Cup ten times between 1874 and 1883, and having reached the English FA Cup finals of 1884 and 1885, they were the last amateur club to do so.

Maidenhead defeated Great Marlow 2-0 at their York Road Ground, to begin a great rivalry between the clubs that exists to this day. Maidenhead had been formed by J.H. Clark in October 1870. They reached the quarter-finals in 1872–73, 1873–74 and 1874–75. The club is believed to have entered every FA Cup competition except for 1876–77.

Great Marlow FC had also been formed in 1870, after a meeting on the banks of the River Thames at the Compleat Angler Hotel on 22 November of that year. They reached the FA Cup semi-finals in 1881–82. One of their members was S.H. Wright, who refereed the 1877 cup final, and another was Cuthbert Ottaway, who played for Oxford University and Old Etonians in the three consecutive FA Cup finals of 1873, 1874 and 1875, and captained England in 1873 and 1874. Marlow are believed to have applied for entry into every FA Cup since its inception, except for the

1910–11 competition when they resigned from their league, and therefore also from the Football Association.

Hampstead Heathens received a bye into the second round. In the second round, with Captain William Merriman in goal, Captain Francis Marindin in defence, and their danger man, the Scottish international player Lieutenant Henry Renny-Tailyour, up front, the Royal Engineers trounced Hitchin 5-0, although, fortunately for Hitchin, they only played for fifty-five minutes due to bad light. Crystal Palace defeated Maidenhead 3-0; Wanderers beat Clapham Rovers on Clapham Common by the only goal of the game; and after Barnes and Hampstead Heathens drew 1-1, they played the first-ever replay in the history of the FA Cup, when the Heathens came out 1-0 winners.

In the third round, the Royal Engineers became the only club to actually win their place in the semi-finals when they beat Hampstead Heathens 3-0 at The Oval. On Clapham Common a week earlier Crystal Palace played their second goalless draw and advanced with their opponents, the Wanderers, while Queen's Park received another bye, and thus found themselves in the last four without kicking a ball!

All the semi-final matches were played at Kennington Oval; the home of the Surrey County Cricket Club and the Wembley Stadium of its day. The Royal Engineers drew 0-0 with Crystal Palace, the third goalless match for Palace, before returning to win 3-0, with two goals from Lieutenant Henry Renny-Tailyour and another by Lieutenant Hugh Mitchell. Wanderers and Queen's Park produced yet another goalless draw. However, the Scots could not afford the travelling expenses to return for the replay and were forced to withdraw; having not lost a game or had a goal scored against them.

The first FA Cup final would be between the Wanderers and the Royal Engineers. They had first played each other at Chatham on 18 January 1868, when the Wanderers won 2-0, but in a return game at the same venue on the following 25 February, the Engineers reversed the score. Since then they had met five more times, winning one game each and drawing three, so the results were even. However, during the 1868–69 season the Royal Military Academy had beaten Wanderers on two occasions.

The first half of the *Morning Post* leading article published on 16 March 1872, referred to earlier, stated:

A great event in the football world will come off today at Kennington Oval. The Association cup is to be contested for. This may now, perhaps, be considered as the Blue Riband of Football. The Cup was only established this year, and during the whole of the present season the various clubs belonging to the Association have been playing against each other, until now there are only three clubs left in that have not been beaten. These clubs are the celebrated Wanderers, the Royal Engineers, and the Queen's Park Club, Glasgow. The Scotsmen not long ago played the Wanderers, but the game was drawn; and as this Northern club could not arrange to come so far south again, they have retired from the contest; and thus have left the final tie between the Wanderers and the Royal Engineers.

The Wanderers club comprises nearly all the best football talent in the country. The great players, who have represented the universities and public schools, are mostly to be found enrolled in this, the leading club of the Association. The Wanderers, in fact, are the *crème de la crème* of the Association players. At any time, as has been proved, the Wanderers would be most difficult to beat, but on this occasion they will, no doubt, be especially formidable, for now they will be able to muster in their greatest strength. In their other ties they have been liable to lose for the occasion the services of some of their best men, whose first allegiance may have been to their local club; whereas now all but the Royal Engineers have been disposed of, they will all be free to play as required.

It will be seen therefore, that the scientific soldiers will have a task before them that might well cause them to feel doubtful of success. The habit of working together and understand each other's play will materially help the Engineers.

The Wanderers will probably bring into the field more players of admitted excellence than will their opponents, with their much more limited area of choice. The leading club will doubtless show more exceptionally brilliant individual form than the Engineers can be expected to show. But, if we mistake not, there will be an amount of cohesion, co-operation, and almost of discipline of the soldiers that will at all events go far to place them on a par with their so to speak more loosely organised but highly-skilled rivals. Anyhow, the game cannot be unusually exciting. Greek is about to meet Greek, and the tug of the mimic war must be severe. The victors will until next year claim to be at the head of the Association clubs. But the vanquished will still be able to say that they have proved themselves superior to all others save the winners today.

Wanderers 1 Royal Engineers 0

The clubs left to contest the inaugural FA Cup final were described as 'the two most powerful organisations supporting Association rules'. The Royal Engineers had put together the best sequence of results in the competition so far, scoring eight goals without reply. They had never been beaten, and were considered to have 'better organisation and combination'.

Their opponents for the final were the Wanderers, who selected their players from old boys of public schools, and membership of this great club was the desire of all the best players. Some of the Sappers were eligible to play for them but they all stayed loyal to the regiment. However, a walkover, two goalless draws and only one win had got them to the final, and the Royal Engineers were 7–4 favourites. But Wanderers were able to field their strongest squad for the first time in the competition, and the Football Association Challenge Cup proved to be unpredictable right from the start. The Wanderers team was English-born except for Edward Bowen, who was Irish; and the Engineers' team included four men with Scottish connections. At the age of 18 years 195 days, West Countryman Robert Walpole Sealy-Vidal, the original 'Prince of dribblers', was the youngest player on the winning team, and he would remain the youngest to win the FA Cup until 1881.

Two-thousand, 'very fashionable people' paid the then considerable sum of one shilling to get into The Oval to watch the match; many from the comfort of the carriages they had arrived in. Charles Alcock was the Wanderers captain, who won the toss and elected to play, 'with a wind, and a very powerful sun at their backs'. At just after three o'clock Captain Marindin became the first man ever to kick off in the final of a competitive football competition. The referee was Albert Stair of Upton Park, and the umpires were both from the Civil Service FC, they being John Kirkpatrick for the Wanderers, and John Hardinge Giffard for the Royal Engineers. The Wanderers had five Harrovians in their squad of ten English-born players and an Irishman.

According to the *Sporting Life*, it was, 'a most pleasant contest', and the Wanderers put the Sappers under pressure right from the start. It was reported that they 'displayed more co-operation than is their custom' and it seems they had decided to play the Engineers at their own game. After about ten minutes Lieutenant Herbert Cresswell of the Engineers was shoulder-charged so severely that he fell awkwardly and broke his collarbone. He 'stayed at his post' but made little contribution for the rest of the game. Play was concentrated in the middle of the field for about five minutes, until Bob Vidal – the Prince of Dribblers – got the ball out of a scrimmage, made a long solo run and passed it to A.H. Chequer, who scored with a well-directed shot. This was in fact, Morton Peto Betts of Harrow playing under an assumed name. He had been so disappointed that his school had withdrawn from the game against the Wanderers in the first round that he chose to represent them as 'A Harrow Chequer'.

Teams changed ends to give the army the advantage of the wind, and although the Sappers had a chance cleared off the line, the Wanderers stayed in control. Alcock got the ball over the line again, but it was disallowed for handball. Another Wanderers shot hit the post, and only the goalkeeping skills of Captain Merriman kept the score at 1-0 when time was called. The rule had only been established in 1871 that allowed goalkeepers to handle the ball. A contemporary report stated: 'It was generally admitted that the play all round was superior to anything that has been seen at The Oval.' It was the only match the Royal Engineers lost that season.

The Royal Engineers' secretary provided a good, unbiased report on the match, without a mention of the fact that they virtually played with only ten men for most of the game:

> The play shown throughout this match was the best ever seen in an Association game. Odds of 7 to 4 were wagered on the Royal Engineers at the outset, but the fine backing-up and general excellence of individual play on the part of the Wanderers enabled them to press the Engineers closely during the whole game, lasting over one hour and a half, the goal of the Wanderers being only twice in any danger. Time after time the Wanderers appeared likely to add to the goal won early in the match, but the wonderful goalkeeping of Captain Merriman prevented any further success. R W S Vidal and T C Hooman played well up for Wanderers, and A C Thompson and E Lubbock, back, were only passed once during the game.

The *Morning Post* of 18 March 1872 reported:

> THE CHAMPION CUP AT FOOTBALL – The officers of the Royal Engineers and the celebrated Wanderers played their final contest for the Association Challenge Cup at the Surrey Cricket Club ground on Saturday afternoon. There was a vast

number of spectators, including many ladies in the tent, and there were several open landaus on the ground.

The ball was kicked-off at three o'clock, and after a scrimmage the Wanderers got the ball down towards the Engineers, who had a downfall of their lines by a well-directed kick by E Chequers. Many battles were fought with no other result, the Wanderers having it all to their own way from the commencement to the end. The Engineers worked hard, but could not alter the state of affairs. It was a perfectly one-sided match, the Wanderers taking it comparatively easy, only defending their goal, having obtained their object by coming into possession of the trophy. The Engineers could never get within many yards of their opponents' quarters. It would be needless to state any other particulars.

It is but fair to state that Alcock, Crawford, Hooman, Lubbock, RW Vidal, and C Wollaston played in the first rate style of excellence for the Wanderers; and Captain Marindin, Lieutenant Renny-Tailyour, and others, played well but without success.

The report gave a list of the teams, with an interesting name of G. Barker included in the Engineers' twelve-man line-up. The Cup final was the Royal Engineers' only defeat of the season. In their other matches they won sixteen and drew four, scoring fifty-nine goals against three. The Wanderers had won the trophy by scoring only two goals. The recorded teams were:

Wanderers:
Goalkeeper – Reginald Courtenay Welch (Harrow); *Full-back* – Edgar Lubbock (Eton); *Half-back* – Albert Childers Meysey-Thompson (Eton); *Forwards*: *Left* – Charles William Alcock (captain) (Harrow); Edward Ernest Bowen (Harrow); *Centre* – Alexander George Bonsor (Eton); Morton Peto Betts (Harrow); William Parry Crake (Harrow); Thomas Charles Hooman (Charterhouse); *Right* – Robert Walpole Sealy-Vidal (Westminster); Charles Henry Reynolds Wollaston (Lancing).

Royal Engineers:
Goalkeeper – Captain William Merriman; *Full-backs* – Captain Francis Arthur Marindin (captain); Lieutenant George William Addison; *Half-back* – Lieutenant Alfred George Goodwyn; *Forwards*: *Right* – Lieutenant Hugh Mitchell; Lieutenant Edmund William Cresswell; *Centre* – Lieutenant

Henry Waugh Renny-Tailyour; Lieutenant Henry Bayard Rich; Lieutenant Herbert Hugh Muirhead; *Left* – Lieutenant Edmond William Cotter; Lieutenant Adam Bogle.

It seems the squad also included Lieutenants George Barker, William St George Ord and Chandos Hoskyns. Indeed, as stated, the *Morning Post* reported that the Royal Engineers were a twelve-man squad, with the addition of Lieutenant G. Barker; which suggests that he took part in the game. All three men appear in the photograph of the team, which looks like it was taken on the day of the defeat owing to the fact that the final was the only game the Engineers lost that season and the players look dejected. They are all wearing their football kits, and if George Barker was used as has been suggested, it is possible that the other two also took part in the game at some point.

At the Wanderers' annual dinner held at the Pall Mall Restaurant in Charing Cross, London, on 11 April 1872, Ebenezer Cobb Morley of Barnes FC, as the president of the Football Association, became the first person to present the FA Cup to the winners.

Royal Engineers Matches

1st Round	11 November 1871	Reigate Priory	withdrew
2nd Round	10 January 1872	Hitchin	won 5-0 The Oval
3rd Round	27 January 1872	Hampstead Heathens	won 3-0 The Oval
Semi-final	17 February 1872	Crystal Palace	drew 0-0 The Oval
Replay	9 March 1872	Crystal Palace	won 3-0 The Oval
Final	16 March 1872	Wanderers	lost 0–1 The Oval

Royal Engineers Players

Francis Arthur Marindin

Francis Marindin was one of the most respected administrators in the history of English football, being chairman of the Football Association for sixteen years. He was involved in the founding of the Football Association Challenge Cup, played in two finals and refereed a further nine. Known as the 'Major' because of his distinguished service in the Royal Engineers, he became an inspector at the Board of Trade, originating several important railway reforms and developing London's lighting system. He was knighted for his service to society and the Crown.

Marindin was born of Huguenot descent at Melcombe Regis near Weymouth in Dorset, on 1 May 1838, the second son in the large family of the Reverend Samuel Marindin (born in 1808), who came from Chesterton in Shropshire and served as a captain with the 2nd Life Guards from 1831 to 1834. He was rector of St John the Baptist Church at Buckhorn Weston near Gillingham in Dorset from 1834 to 1841, at the time when Francis was born, and at St Michael's Church in Penselwood near Wincanton in Somerset, from 1841 until his death on 3 January 1852. Francis's mother, Isabella (born at Langley Farm in Beckenham, Kent, on 24 April 1812 – died at Chesterton in Shropshire on 4 August 1896), was the daughter of Andrew Wedderburn Colville, who owned the estate of Ochiltree in Craigflower, Torryburn near Dunfermline, Fife.

Francis was educated at Eton College from 1851 to 1853, and entered the Royal Military Academy, from where he passed out top of his batch and was commissioned into the Corps of Royal Engineers as a second lieutenant on 28 December 1854.

Most of the Royal Engineers entered the Royal Military Academy at Woolwich, unless they wanted to be trained specifically for service with the army of the East India Company, in which case they attended the Addiscombe Military Seminar near Croydon. The course at Woolwich lasted two-and-a-half years and was designed to produce competent technicians rather than leaders of troops. The main subjects they would have studied were Artillery (practical and theoretical), Fortification and Bridging, Mathematics, Natural and Experimental Philosophy, Landscape Drawing, Mechanics and French and Hindustani (of which German was an alternative). He was also able to attend lectures in astronomy, mineralogy, geology and metallurgy. A course on Military History and the Art of War was started in 1855.

Crimean War, 1854–56

Marindin was appointed lieutenant on 13 January 1855, and after a course of instruction at Chatham he was sent for active service in the Crimean War. He remained on duty in the hospital at Scutari, where Florence Nightingale was dealing with the mass of casualties suffered as British troops twice stormed the barricades of the Great Redan at Sebastopol. Fighting was so fierce that thirty-one men were awarded the Victoria Cross for their actions during the engagements. Twenty were given for the failed assault on 18 June 1855, and eleven for the successful attack on 8 September 1855; five being awarded to members of the Royal Engineers. Lieutenant Marindin returned to England in August 1856, and for his service in the campaign he received the Crimea Medal with Sebastopol clasp.

Following nearly two years of home service, Marindin sailed to the sugar island of Mauritius on 10 June 1858, becoming aide-de-camp (ADC) and private secretary to William Stevenson, the governor of the island. He became acquainted with the governor's daughter, Kathleen May (born in Jamaica on 12 December 1840), and they married at Port Louis in Mauritius, on 13 July 1860. He did special service at Madagascar in 1861, being promoted second captain on 18 October 1861. The couple returned to Farnborough in Hampshire, on 2 May 1864. Their only child, Kathleen Mary Isabel, was born there on 1 May 1865.

Captain Marindin was selected to take over the command of 'A' Pontoon Troop at Aldershot, at the time when it was being converted into a bridging unit of the military train. He was involved with preparation for the new equipment, including the phasing out of the old cylindrical metal pontoons. He was appointed adjutant at the School of Military Engineering at Chatham in February 1866, being promoted captain while at Devonport on 22 January 1868. On 29 August 1869, he was appointed brigade major at Chatham, also finding time to serve as honorary secretary on the Royal Engineers Committee for a short while in 1869–70.

Marindin's five years as brigade major coincided with an era when many new sports were being established in England, and sport within the Royal Engineers flourished under his zealous guidance. He was on the organising committee when racquets, billiards and cricket matches were started, playing many times himself, and he was president of the boat club, organising yachting regattas and rowing races; all against the Royal Artillery. He was in the winning squad at the 1870 regatta. However, his main energies were concentrated on football.

He joined the FA Committee in 1871 and was appointed president in 1874. Described as 'a tall, well-built, broad-shouldered back' who was 'clever and shrewd', he played for the Royal Engineers in the 1872 and 1874 FA Cup finals, but he had been posted to Hawick so he was unavailable to play at the time of the 1875 final. He remained at Hawick until June 1877. After two gruelling FA Cup final defeats in 1875 and 1876, which both went to replays, the Old Etonians had withdrawn from the Cup in 1876–77 and had not even entered for the 1877–78 tournament; the major was instrumental in reviving them in October 1878. In their next FA Cup match for the 1878–79 season they defeated Wanderers, who had won the previous three competitions, and then had a gruelling three-match epic against Darwen FC. However, he missed out for a fourth time when he received an injury and missed the semi-final and final, which Old Etonians won.

On 29 October 1879 Marindin retired from the Royal Engineers and devoted more time to administration. He was a founder of the Royal Engineers Sports Club, a member of the MCC, and of the Scottish Conservatives. He was considered 'one of the outstanding referees who really know the rules'. He took charge of the 1880 final, and those from 1884 to 1890, including a replay at Derby in 1886. The 1881, 1882 and 1883 finals involved the Old Etonians so he did not officiate. During his last final in charge, the crowd invaded the pitch and soldiers had to clear the field. During his term of office the advent of professionalism caused great upheaval within the sport, and it was eventually legalised in 1885. His disenchantment with this, and the pressure of work, prompted him to stand down as FA president in 1890.

In 1877 he had become Inspecting Officer at the Board of Trade. From 1893 to 1890 he was one of the inspectors for the Board of Trade during the construction of the Forth Bridge. In May 1889 he produced a report on the development of London's new lighting system, giving advice on how the power could be distributed fairly. He originated several important railway reforms, and in 1899 he reported on accidents to workers, on which a new Act of Parliament concerning safety on the rail network was based. He became Senior Inspector of Railways in 1895, and was appointed to the Railway Council two years later. He received the special thanks of the Board of Trade for his outstanding work. For his valuable service to society and the Crown he was created Knight's Commander of St Michael and St George (KCMG) on 22 June 1897; the year of Queen Victoria's Diamond Jubilee celebrations.

Overtaxed by work and suffering from influenza, Sir Francis Marindin fell into a weakened state and contracted pneumonia. He died at his home, 3 Hans Crescent, Knightsbridge, London, on 21 April 1900, aged 61. He was buried at Crombie Old Parish Churchyard on the Craigflower Estate in Torryburn near Dunfermline; which is now in ruins. At the time of his funeral, a memorial service was held at the Holy Trinity Church in Sloane Square, London, which was attended by his old colleague and adversary, Charles Alcock. When his wife Katherine died at Westgate-on-Sea near Margate in Kent, on 16 February 1939, she was in her one-hundredth year. She was buried with Sir Francis at Old Crombie churchyard; as was their daughter, who died on 23 February 1945. Unfortunately the grave is badly damaged. At the time of publication I am making efforts to have the gravesite renovated.

William Merriman

William Merriman was the goalkeeper and the oldest member of the Royal Engineers' 1872 finalists, having been born the month before Francis Marindin. The oldest player in the final was Edward Ernest Bowen of The Wanderers, who was born in 1836.

Merriman was born at 13 Young Street, off Kensington High Street in London, on 2 April 1838. The house later became the home of the novelist William Makepeace Thackeray. He was the eighth of nine children to Dr John Merriman (1800–81), and his wife, Caroline (formerly Jones, 1800–70). Several of his family had acted as physicians to Queen Victoria. He was baptised at St Mary Abbots Church in Kensington on 25 May 1838.

William was educated at Kensington School before attending the Addiscombe Military Seminar near Croydon in 1856, where officers were trained for service with the army of the East India Company. He was commissioned as ensign in the East India Company's Royal Engineers on 12 December 1856. He became lieutenant on 27 August 1858, serving in India from 1858 to 1866, where he was adjutant at Poona, after which he returned to England and was employed as a fieldwork instructor at Chatham. He was promoted captain on 31 December 1868.

Merriman married Emily Jane Anna Elizabeth Somerset (1851–1923) at St Stephen's Church in South Kensington, on 13 February 1872, just four days before the Royal Engineers played in their semi-final match. She was the daughter of Colonel Fitzroy Somerset of the Royal Engineers. They had two sons and three daughters born between 1873 and 1880, but their second son, William Somerset, died at Gillingham in Kent in 1874, having survived for only three days.

Although Merriman was on the losing team in the 1872 final, his goalkeeping was described as 'perfect', and in general he was considered to be 'one of the very best goalkeepers of the day, plucky, cool, and difficult to pass'. He was a member of the Royal Engineers squad that toured the north in 1873. Only he and Henry Renny-Tailyour played in all three of the 1872, 1874 and 1875 finals. He was on the FA Committee from 1874 to 1877, being described as 'the most popular of all football chiefs'.

A memoir in *The Sapper* in 1896 stated:

Who does not remember the Major Merriman of twenty years ago who was never more delighted than when organising sport – football, cricket, and other matches – for the sapper's pleasure? I can see him now, in winter time, coming out on the Barrack

Square with a football under his arm and giving a mighty kick, shouting out for the men to come and join him, and in less time than I can write it the Barracks would be swarming, and there would be rare fun.

Transvaal (First Boer War) in South Africa, 1880–81

Merriman was promoted major on 13 March 1874, becoming district officer at Colchester from 1875 to 1881. He was then posted for active service in the Transvaal, or First Boer War. Ever since Britain had annexed the bankrupt province of Transvaal on 12 April 1877, the Boer farmers had remained discontented, and on 16 December 1880 rose up in rebellion and claimed the Transvaal as a republic on 30 December.

A British column of 1,000 men and 6 field pieces, under Major General George Colley, advanced into Transvaal from Natal, but the Boers dug in at a hill called Laing's Nek and their snipers waited. On 28 January 1881, in the last engagement in which the British took their colours into action, as they advanced up the slopes, the Boers opened up a withering fusillade. Facing such devastating fire, nearly all the British officers leading their men fell at once. Apparently, one of them shouted 'Floreat Etona' – 'Long Live Eton' – as he fell. Of the 480 men engaged, 150 did not return.

In a similar engagement at the 600ft-high Majuba Hill, which began at dawn on 27 February 1881, some 1,000 Boers opened a heavy fire on the British troops, mainly Highlanders, as they struggled to get to them at the top of the steep hill. The British attack faltered and as they retreated they left nearly 100 dead on the slopes, including General Colley, and 133 wounded. To the British commander-in-chief: 'Majuba was almost unparalleled in the long annals of our Army.'

The History of the Corps stated:

> Fresh troops including the 7th Field Company of Royal Engineers under Major Merryman, was hurried out to Natal, and pushed forward in the vicinity of Laing's Nek; but before any further action could be taken peace was made by a complete surrender of all our claims on the Transvaal, and the Company returned to England at the end of the year.

The defeat led to the signing of a peace treaty in Pretoria between the British and the reinstated South African Republic. Several Victoria Crosses were awarded, but the British Government was so humiliated that they did not issue a campaign medal. The British lion had been wounded, Queen Victoria stated: 'I do not like peace before we have retrieved our honour,' and some day the war against the Boers would have to be fought again.

From 1882 Merriman was employed in the coast defences of Western India, and he was promoted colonel on 1 July 1885. In 1892 he became chief engineer on the staff of Sir George Greaves, the Commander-in-Chief at Bombay. He was also a Fellow of the University of Bombay, vice-commodore at the exclusive Royal Bombay Yacht Club at Wellington Pier (now Colaba in Mumbai), and steward at the equally exclusive Bombay Turf Club (now the Royal Western India Turf Club). He retired from military service in 1893. On 1 January 1890, he was appointed a Commander of the Indian Empire (CIE) for his services involving the coast defences in India and Aden.

He died at the family home of Creffield House on Gray Road in Colchester, on 11 March 1917, aged 78. His son, Arthur Drummond Nairne (1876–1966), served as a major in the Royal Irish Rifles in the Great War, being awarded a Distinguished Service Order for his gallantry; and he served in the Taunton Home Guard during the Second World War.

Edmond William Cotter

Edmond Cotter was in the forward line as the youngest member of the Royal Engineers team to play in the first FA Cup final, and only Robert Sealy-Vidal of Wanderers was younger (born in 1853). William Crake of Wanderers was one day older than Edmond. Cotter saw active service in the Ashanti War, 1873–74; the Zhob Valley Expedition, 1884–85; the Nile Expedition, Sudan, 1885; and in Burma, 1887–88.

He was born on 13 February 1852, at Valletta in Malta, the second of three children to John Cotter (1823–82), and his wife, Jane Maria (formerly Hickey, 1830–57). His father had enlisted into the 3rd Regiment (The Buffs) in 1840, and was posted for active service in the Crimean War the year after Edmond was born. He returned from the campaign as a lieutenant and rose to the rank of captain.

Edmond was on the school list at the Roman Catholic St Munchin's College at Crescent House in Limerick, Ireland, in 1863 (renamed the Sacred Heart College). He was a cadet at the Royal Military Academy, from where he was commissioned as lieutenant in the Royal Engineers on 2 August 1871, and fellow graduates on the same day were Alfred Goodwyn and Herbert Muirhead, who also played in the 1872 final, and Richard Ruck, who played in the 1875 final.

Third Ashanti War in West Africa, 1873–74

As his teammates in the Royal Engineers were playing their way to the 1874 FA Cup final, Cotter was on active service in the fever-ridden jungle of Ashanti in West Africa. The Ashanti were a fierce race, and their fearsome leader Kofi Karikari, who came to be known as King Koffee, had gained a reputation for committing dreadful savagery. The experienced British commander General Garnet Wolseley was appointed to lead an expedition on 13 August 1873, having been instructed to deal with the situation and to try to achieve a swift victory before the March rains made the terrain impassable.

A team of Royal Engineers landed on 27 September 1873, and their job was to help to clear and expand a 160-mile (260km) road through dense jungle, so thick that it was almost impossible for the troops to provide adequate protection from attack as they engaged in the task, and they were continually held up by tropical storms. Consequently, they were made to do what no other European party was ever required to do in warfare, namely to work under fire in the face of the enemy without a covering party. Bridges were built across streams using trees, bamboo and creepers for ropes. Eventually they came upon the 63yd (58m) expanse of the River Prah.

The serious obstacle could not be overcome using local materials, so the situation was reported back to the depot. Lieutenant Cotter landed at Cape Coast Castle with the 28th Company, Royal Engineers, on 10 December 1874, with pre-designed and manufactured iron pieces brought from Chatham. Dosed with quinine, he and his men played a leading part in preparing the rest of the way for the regular troops to arrive. They established fortified supply bases about 10 miles apart all along the road, which included the construction of 237 bridges. There was no question of failing because the assault troops were on their way.

The first major engagement with the enemy came at Abagoo, on 17 January 1874, and during the battle of Amoaful on the last day of the month, Lieutenant Cotter was left at an outpost called Quarman in charge of only ten sappers, with orders to place the post in a state of defence. The post came under fierce attack by the Ashanti but they managed to hold out until being relieved by the Rifle Brigade.

After another fearsome battle at Becquah, the final engagement with the enemy took place at Ordahsu on 4 February 1874, an action for which Lieutenant Mark Sever Bell of the Royal Engineers received the Victoria Cross. Lieutenant Cotter was with the triumphant troops as they swept into Kumasi on the following day. The capital is said to have stank with blood, and the soldiers were appalled to find the remains of thousands of sacrificial victims, the sight of which made Wolseley physically sick.

Having become short on supplies and fearing disease and the oncoming March rains, Wolseley ordered Kumasi to be burnt to the ground and rushed his men back to the coast. He later described the campaign as: '... the most horrible war I ever took part in'. Lieutenant Cotter was with the last detachment of troops to leave on 4 March 1874, just ten days before his colleagues lost in the Cup final to Oxford. On their return to England the troops were feted with invitations to balls and banquets to celebrate the victory. For his service Lieutenant Cotter received the Ashanti Medal with Coomassie clasp.

Cotter married Jessie Tyeth Frost on 8 October 1876, at St Stephens-by-Saltash Church in Cornwall, which was just over the River Tamar from Plymouth, and in 1881 they lived at The Laburnums at Portsea in Hampshire. They had five children, born between 1877 and 1884.

Zhob Valley Expedition to Balochistan, 1884–85

Cotter was promoted captain on 2 August 1883, and in November 1884 he was with an expedition that marched into the Zhob (long) Valley in Balochistan, on the North-West Frontier of India (now Pakistan), which was organised to track down and punish the Kakar Pathans for their raids into British territory. Edmond was employed on the construction of roads through the mountainous region, and to prepare maps of the area, which was practically unknown to Europeans before the expedition. The valley is about 100 miles long and 20 miles wide. The region was opened up to Europeans after the expedition, and in 1889 the Zhob Valley and Gomal Pass were taken under the control of the British Government. In December 1889 the town of Zhob, then known as Appozai, was occupied by the British and named Fort Sandeman.

Nile Expedition in the Sudan, 1884–85

Cotter's next posting on active duty was to take part in the Nile Expedition. When news was received in Britain that General Gordon was besieged by Mahdist forces in Khartoum, General Wolseley was ordered to organise a force to attempt to rescue him. Wolseley had decided to use the River Nile route to Khartoum, and the force set off south in specially constructed boats on the Nile; but progress was slow.

On 17 January 1885, they reached Abu Klea, an oasis for caravans consisting of a number of wells, where they came upon 10,000 Dervishes. The British formed into a square and waited for the attack. Armed with rifles, spears, swords and axes, and dressed in rough light-coloured jibbahs sewn with patches, a symbol of righteous poverty, the frenzied Dervish warriors beat their drums and sang religious chants as they moved in a determined rush across the desert sand. Heavy guns and rifles poured shells and bullets into their dense masses and mowed them down in their hundreds. In spite of this, the Dervishes came on with their banners waving and their war chants getting louder; and they were getting dangerously close. Many men in the British ranks particularly remembered the thunder of their feet as they raced forward.

The Royal Navy had recently adopted the Gardner machine gun because of its reputation for reliability, and a unit of sailors from HMS *Alexandra* had one in the square. The Heavy Camel Corps moved aside at the rear-left of the square to allow the Gardner to come into action, but after firing seventy rounds the gun jammed, the Dervishes took advantage, and by weight of numbers drove in the weakened ranks. They were left perilously exposed and the Dervishes swarmed all over the machine-gun team, and in a five-minute bloody free-for-all of hacking, slashing and shooting the enemy inflicted serious casualties.

Fortunately the embattled British force recovered their nerve and forced the Dervishes back out of the square, reformed the line and saved the day. In what Winston Churchill described as 'a most savage and bloody action', which lasted about fifteen minutes, the defeated Mahdists left 2,000 warriors dead on the battlefield.

Third Burma War, 1885–89

In 1885 Cotter received orders for active service in the east, in what became known as the Third Burma War. The region was extremely hostile, costing the British Army more casualties from disease and sickness than from the enemy, and they were relieved to get back to India.

Thibaw, the king of the Burmese, had been expressing much anti-British sentiments for many years. In 1885 a British force had advanced up the Irrawaddy River and occupied Mandalay in a swift, almost bloodless campaign. Upper Burma was annexed to the British Crown, to be administered as a province of India. However, the Burmese army refused to surrender and took refuge in the vast, thick jungle, from where they launched a campaign of guerrilla warfare. Their scattered units became known as Decoit bands, which spent their time marauding across the region to disrupt the everyday life of the British. They twice raided Mandalay, setting fire to much of it, and British troops were faced with the massive task of pacification, while protecting British interests.

To give an idea of the type of terrain and enemy Cotter had to deal with, the following is an extract from a first-hand account by Colour Sergeant Edward J. Owen of the Hampshire Regiment:

> We had conquered Mandalay and taken it, but we had not quelled the Burmese, who set to work to worry us, and succeeded amazingly well.
>
> Gangs of Decoits broke into the city, in spite of all our precautions, and killed people, and set fire to places, and scurried off before even their presence was known. The buildings were mostly made of wood and bamboo, and burnt fiercely when they were once alight, especially as there were practically no fire appliances. Sometimes several acres were destroyed before the flames were conquered.
>
> The Decoits used to slip in and out at night, seldom trying their luck in the daytime, for they had a holy dread of British rifles. They were positively merciless, and for some time after the occupation of the city it was unsafe to move about singly. No men were allowed to go outside the walls unless properly armed, and in parties of at least three.
>
> Mandalay was very unhealthy, and I was glad when I was ordered away to chase Decoits, though I should have thought better of it if I had known what the work really meant. For eighteen months I was away from civilisation, marching through a country where no proper roads existed, and thinking that I had done well if an average of ten miles a day had been covered.
>
> Decoit hunting in a hot, dangerous climate was hard work, with very little glory in it. We seldom got the enemy to close quarters, as he was so nimble, and the country so jungly. The robber-murderers had runs like rabbits, and it was almost impossible to follow them. It was woe indeed for the soldier who fell into their clutches.

For his service Cotter was awarded the Indian General Service Medal, 1854, with Burma 1885–87 and Burma 1887–89 clasps.

Cotter was serving with the Madras Sappers and Miners in the Indian Army in 1889, and on being promoted major on 18 January 1890, he was posted to Egypt. He was back in India the following year, being stationed at Allahabad. He was promoted to lieutenant colonel on 1 October 1897, and he was appointed commanding Royal Engineer for the Cork District in Ireland, and he was promoted to full colonel on 24 December 1901. Cotter retired from the army as colonel on 12 October 1904, at the relatively young age of 52.

In 1891 Cotter and his wife lived at 5 Windsor Terrace in Saltash, with their three daughters. Their sons, Edmond Brian and John Luis, were living as boarders at the home of their Aunt Phoebe at 10 Windsor Terrace. After his retirement Cotter is known to have lived in Yeovil, but by 1911 he had settled in Bournemouth, where he lived at Fairview on Castlemaine Avenue. His son, Edmond, was awarded the Distinguished Service Order for service with the Royal Garrison Artillery during the Great War, and he rose to the rank of lieutenant colonel.

Easter Rising in Ireland, 1916

According to Cotter's family, during his service in Ireland 'he became keenly and publicly interested in the United Irish Movement'. He got into trouble with the authorities because of his Irish republican sympathies, and apparently when he visited members of his family who were serving with the British forces aboard Royal Navy ships he would cause a scene and embarrass them. In 1915 he used his British Army pension to travel to Dublin to work for the Irish Volunteers, where he was appointed chief of staff and attempted to organise them on military lines. However, he returned to England after three months because he ran out of funds to support himself.

On Easter Monday, 25 April 1916, members of the Irish Volunteers and the Irish Citizen Army marched through Bank Holiday crowds in Dublin and seized several major buildings without firing a shot, at the start of what became known as the Easter Rising. It was the most determined attempt to set up an independent Irish Republic since the insurrection of 1798. However, the leadership was bungled, and only one in five of the rebels reported for duty. One troop commandeered a tram and actually paid their fares of 58 tuppenies. Once the British brought in troops and deployed their artillery the rising collapsed after five days. As a military operation it was a farce, but as a symbolic act it had significant effect and fifteen rebel leaders were executed.

Cotter was a tough character, and it is believed that he was known as 'Terror Cotter' because he had a violent temper. It was also stated that 'he had a weak heart and was somewhat impulsive and excitable'. He died at 97 Cranleigh Road in Bournemouth, on 23 August 1934, aged 82.

Henry Bayard Rich

In his short life, Henry Rich played on the forward line for the Royal Engineers in the first FA Cup final of 1872. He later saw active service in Perak, Zululand and in Egypt.

Henry was born on 14 June 1849, at Berbice in British Guiana (now Guyana), the son of Colonel Frederick Henry Rich (1824–1904) of the Royal Engineers, and his wife Elizabeth (formerly Bayard, 1826–85), who was the daughter of a US senator in Delaware.

Henry was educated at Marlborough College in Wiltshire, from April 1864 until Christmas 1866, where he began his football career. He then attended the Royal Military Academy from 1867 to 1870, where he played for the college football team. During his cadetship he was reputed to be 'one of the fastest runners on the athletics track', and he was considered to be one of the best horse riders in the Royal Engineers. He entered the Royal Engineers as lieutenant on 8 January 1870, along with Hugh Mitchell and Edmund Cresswell.

Rich spent his first years as an Engineer either at Chatham, Aldershot, or on leave, and before the end of the year he won the Cup with the Royal Engineers he was posted to the Hong Kong station.

Perak War in Malaysia, 1875–76

On 2 November 1875, the governor of Perak in Malaysia was murdered, and Lieutenant Rich was with thousands of British soldiers sent from India to capture the culprits in 'a highly effective display of British determination'. For his service he was mentioned in despatches, and was awarded the Indian General Service Medal with Perak clasp. His War Office Papers state: 'Mentioned very favourably in the confidential report of Colonel Maggridge in connection with the affair in Malay on 29 February 1876.' He returned to Hong Kong on 26 March 1876, and then back to the Aldershot depot in August 1876.

Zulu War in South Africa, 1879

Rich's next posting was to South Africa for active service in the re-invasion of Zululand. For most of the nineteenth century South Africa was disturbed by continuous friction between its mixed peoples, and there were many disputes over land boundaries between Cape Colonists, Boer farmers and African Bantu tribes, which kept the British Army on constant alert.

However, the main threat to stability in the region came from the highly disciplined army of fearless Zulu warriors. General Garnet

Wolseley stated: 'These Zulus are a great danger to our Colony.' The British Government knew that they had to be subdued before there could be any progress towards a united nation under one flag, which would be easier for administration and the hard-pressed British Army. In order to deal with the Zulu threat, the British issued a deliberately unworkable ultimatum to the Zulu king, Cetshwayo, and British forces began to build up at strategic places along the border with Zululand. No response to the ultimatum was received and the invasion of Zululand began on 11 January 1879.

The 3rd or Central Column, which invaded Zululand at a place called Rorke's Drift, was made up mainly of troops of the 24th (2nd Warwickshire) Regiment, and they made camp at a place called Isandlwana. On 22 January 1879, a Zulu army of about 20,000 warriors swept down on them in a devastating surprise attack. The British fought gallantly until they were overpowered and cut to pieces – literally. Only about 100 white men survived the carnage, in what was the most devastating single defeat inflicted on the British Army in the Victorian era. The Zulus too had suffered fearful losses, with about 2,000 warriors killed and wounded.

Some pride was restored later that day when a small garrison of British soldiers of the 24th Regiment, under the command of Lieutenants John Chard of the Royal Engineers and Gonville Bromhead of the 24th Regiment, which was guarding the field hospital and storehouse at Rorke's Drift, was attacked by about 3,000 warriors. The British had managed to construct a makeshift barricade, and despite repeated attacks by the Zulus they held out until a relief column arrived the following morning. For their valour fifteen gallantry medals were awarded to the defenders.

A re-invasion had to be planned and reinforcements were requested out from Britain. The tide of the war turned when the British defeated an army of Zulu warriors at Khambula on 29 March 1879. After forming a Flying Column and a 1st Division of troops, the British advanced on the Zulu capital at Ulundi, and on 4 July 1879 they inflicted a final crushing defeat on Cetshwayo's warriors.

Lieutenant Rich was ordered for active service in South Africa in April 1879, where he served with the Telegraph troop in charge of the signallers with the 1st Division. His War Office Papers state: 'Served in the Zulu War from May to November 1879, with Telegraph Troop; employed in charge of signalling with 1st Division.' For his service he was awarded the South Africa Medal with 1879 clasp.

Egyptian War of 1882

Having been promoted to captain on 8 January 1882, Rich's next tour of active service was in the British conquest of Egypt, also known as the Egyptian War. In 1881 an Egyptian Army officer named Ahmed Bey Urabi mutinied and initiated a revolt against Tewfik Pasha, the Khedive of Egypt and Sudan. To show that Britain intended to protect its interests in Egypt, including the Suez Canal, a fleet of British warships made their presence known off the coast of Alexandria, and when they realised that the action had no effect on the Egyptians, they bombarded their defensive forts and occupied the town with Marines.

The large British force that invaded Egypt had a military train that included Royal Engineers bridging, telegraph and railway troops; and the 8th, 17th and 18th Field Companies. Captain Rich was employed with the troop. After several confrontations with the Egyptian Army, particularly at Kafr El Dawwar on 5 August 1882, and Kassassin Lock on 28 August 1882, the decisive battle of the campaign was fought at Tel-el-Kebir on 13 September 1882. The British made a dawn attack on Egyptian defensive positions, which was so devastating that the Egyptians did not have time to fire a single shell from their big guns before they were overwhelmed. It was a decisive victory; the British entered Cairo and the Khedive was restored to power. For his service Lieutenant Rich was awarded the Egypt Medal with Tel-el-Kebir clasp, and the Khedive's Bronze Star.

Rich married Ada Melvill Simons at Sydenham Hill on 3 May 1881. They had no children. After returning to Aldershot from Egypt on 20 October 1882, he was posted to Bengal in India on 7 September 1883. On 17 November 1884, while playing polo at Rawalpindi in Bengal, he collided with another officer and was thrown violently to the ground. He suffered a fractured skull and died from his injuries. He was aged 35. He was buried in Rawalpindi, and the inscription on his grave reads: 'In loving memory of Henry Bayard Rich, captain Royal Engineers, who died from the effects of an accident at Polo, 17 November 1884.'

Henry Waugh Renny-Tailyour

Only Henry Renny-Tailyour and William Merriman played for the Royal Engineers in the 1872, 1874 and 1875 FA Cup finals; scoring five of the six semi-final goals in the three competitions. Renny-Tailyour was the first man to score a goal for Scotland in an official international match. In his prime he was considered to be the best cricketer in the

British Army, and one of the best all-round sportsmen who ever joined the Royal Engineers. He saw active service during the Chin-Lushai Expedition in Burma.

Henry was born at Mussoorie, a British Army hill station in the north-west provinces of India, on 9 October 1849. His father, Thomas (1812–85), was serving as a colonel in the Bengal Engineers, while his mother was Isabella Elizabeth Cook (formerly Atkinson, 1820–96). He had a sister named Elizabeth Lauderdale (1852–1917) and they grew up at Newmanswalls in Montrose.

Henry was educated at Cheltenham College from August 1859 to December 1867, and then at the Royal Military Academy from January 1868, until he was commissioned as lieutenant in the Royal Engineers on 23 August 1870.

He was a member of the Marylebone Cricket Club (MCC), and from 1870 to 1888 he had over 300 innings for the Royal Engineers, scoring over 12,000 runs, including 52 centuries. In 1880 he scored 331 not out in a match against the Civil Service.

One of Renny-Tailyour's obituaries stated:

> While he was at the 'Shop' he was in the cricket team, becoming captain in 1870. He scored 106 not out for the RMA against the Corps at Chatham Lines. He was in the football 'fifteen' in 1868 and 1869, and in 1870 he won several middle distance races. It was recorded 'Everyone will admit that to him was mainly due the raising of Royal Engineers cricket to a position which it had never occupied previously and which has been so well maintained since. It was not merely by his own contributions to the score sheets, large as they were, but his keenness in the field was infectious, and made everyone play the game to the best of their ability. He filled the position of captain of the Eleven, with a few brief intervals, over a period of 17 or 18 years. In the years 1871–75 inclusive, his average each season was never less than 40, and in 1875 he had an average of 50; there were at that time no boundaries, practically speaking, on the Lines, and every hit had to be run out. In 1873, he was at the head of the batting averages, 46 for 31 innings, and he took 62 wickets with an average of less than 13 runs per wicket. He played for the Gentlemen against the Players in 1873, and for Kent occasionally between 1873 and 1883, but he never accepted an invitation to play in outside matches if his presence was necessary in the Royal Engineers team.

Sir Richard Ruck said of him:

> Renny-Tailyour almost, if not quite, as good at football as he was at cricket, was frequently mentioned for his fine work as a centre-forward, and possessed the happy knack of scoring goals when they were most wanted. He held the unique distinction of representing Scotland v England in both Rugby and Association games.

Having played for the Royal Military Academy rugby XV in 1869 and 1870, on 5 February 1872 Renny-Tailyour played for Scotland against England at Rugby in front of 4,000 spectators at The Oval. Such was the scoring system at the time that, although England scored three tries, only the goals counted, and England won 2-1. Two other military men were on the Scottish team in the form of R.P. Maitland of the Royal Artillery and F.T. Maxwell of the Royal Engineers. The England squad included Francis D'Aguilar (1849–96) of the Royal Engineers, who scored the first try, and Charles William Sherrard (1849–1938) also of the Royal Engineers, who later served in the Zulu War of 1879.

On 17 November 1871 Renny-Tailyour played for Scotland against England in an unofficial international football match at The Oval. On 8 March 1873, he was selected to play in the first official international match between England and Scotland at The Oval. The Scots could only afford to send seven players and an umpire to London, so they had to recruit locally, and two of the players chosen were Henry Renny-Tailyour and John Edward Blackburn of the Royal Engineers, who happened to be at Chatham. The English team included Alfred George Goodwyn and Pelham von Donop of the Royal Engineers; and William Slaney Kenyon-Slaney of the Household Brigade. Three-thousand spectators watched England win 4-2, with two goals by Kenyon-Slaney, although Henry Renny-Tailyour became the first man to score for Scotland in an official international match.

He scored two goals against Crystal Palace in 1872, which got the Royal Engineers into the final; and two against Swifts in 1874, which got them into their second final. In 1875 he scored all three goals in the final and replay, which won the trophy for the Engineers. Renny, as he was known, was described as 'one of the very best forwards of the day ...'.

On 9 September 1875, Renny-Tailyour married Emily Rose (1855–1904), the younger sister of Cecil Wingfield-Stratford, one of his teammates in the 1875 FA Cup-winning team. By her he had a family of four sons and six daughters. One son died in Africa and his youngest son, in the Sappers, was killed in action near Ypres in 1914; his eldest son commanded a battery of Horse Artillery in Mesopotamia, and was several times mentioned in dispatches.

Renny-Tailyour was posted to Portsmouth until May 1873, when he joined the 4th Company of Submarine Miners on board HMS *Hood*, which was moored at Gillingham Pier on the Medway. In February 1876 he was posted to Ireland as extra aide-de-camp to the Lord Lieutenant, and the following January he was ordered to Gibraltar for a year. He spent three years at Chatham as assistant-instructor in telegraphy from May 1878 to February 1881, and from April 1881 to August 1884, he held the appointment of instructor in fortifications at the Royal Military Academy; during which time he was promoted captain on 23 July 1882. Renny-Tailyour returned to Chatham as assistant instructor in field fortifications, an appointment he held for nearly four years from 1884 to 1888.

Chin-Lushai Expedition in Burma, 1889–90

On being promoted to major on 1 December 1888, Renny-Tailyour went on his only tour of active duty in Burma, where he took part in the Chin-Lushai Expedition of 1889–90. Three columns of troops, named the Chittagong Field Force, entered the Chin Hills to punish the various tribesmen known as the Tashons, who had been marauding into British Indian territory attacking military outposts and killing and looting whenever they could. The whole area was eventually brought under British control, although as usual the region remained hostile.

The *London Gazette* of 12 September 1890, stated: 'The Governor-General notices with satisfaction the excellent reports and the good work done ... by the Signalling service with the various columns, and by the survey parties under Lieutenants Bythell and Renny-Tailyour RE [he was actually a major]'.

On Renny-Tailyour's return he became the president of his local football club in Montrose, and then he spent three years in a colonial appointment in Sydney, Australia, as Chief Royal Engineer of the New South Wales defences. He left Australia on 31 August 1894, and he returned to Chatham, where he commanded the Training Battalion from 12 August 1895, being promoted lieutenant colonel on that date. He was promoted colonel on 12 August 1899, and he retired from military service in October 1899.

With the new century Renny-Tailyour took up the appointment of assistant managing director at the Guinness Brewery in Dublin.

He became managing director in 1913. On leaving Dublin, he went to live at Newmanswalls in Montrose, a property that, with Borrowfield, had belonged to the family for several hundred years. There he spent his time fishing and shooting, and playing golf; and he had a keen interest in gardening.

Henry was 'quite unexpectedly taken ill' and he passed away after a week's illness at Newmanswalls on 15 June 1920, aged 70. He was buried in the family grave at the New Cemetery in Rosehill, Montrose.

George William Addison

George Addison played as full-back for the Royal Engineers in the 1872 and 1874 FA Cup finals, and went on to a career of high administration.

Addison was born at Chestnut Cottage in Manningham, Bradford, on 18 September 1849, the first son of a worsted spinner named George Addison (1816–74), and his wife Jane (formerly Orr, 1824–1916). He was baptised at the Cathedral Church of St Peter in Bradford on 15 December 1849. George was educated at Cheltenham College from January 1863 to December 1866, and at the Royal Military Academy from 1867 until being commissioned as lieutenant in the Royal Engineers on 7 July 1869; along with Lieutenants Chandos Hoskyns and William St George Ord.

On 30 June 1875, he married Caroline Augusta Stevenson (1850–1938) at St Stephen's Church in South Kensington, London, and they had two boys and four girls between 1876 and 1885, who all lived well past their 80th birthdays. Two of his daughters, Muriel and Violet, became centenarians. George Henry (1876–1964) entered the Royal Engineers and reached the rank of lieutenant colonel, having been awarded the CB CMG DSO for service in the Great War. On 3 June 1947, his son, William Henry, married Mrs Winifred Legard, the widowed daughter of Colonel William George Morris, who played for the Royal Engineers in the 1878 FA Cup final. Arthur Mervyn (1879–1962) served as a major in the Royal Artillery during the Great War. His son, and George's grandson, was John Mervyn Addison (1920–98), who was a composer usually remembered for his film scores.

Addison was based at Chatham until January 1882, before spending a year in Brighton, where he was engaged in the construction of the Grand Magazines at Newhaven Fort. He returned to Chatham in April 1873. He was employed in the torpedo service in Malta from November 1875 until August 1877, commanding the 3rd Section of the 33rd Company of Royal Engineers. He was ADC at the War Office firstly to Major General Thomas Gallway, the Inspector General of Fortifications, from August 1880, and then to Major General Sir Andrew Clarke, until December 1882; during which time he was promoted captain on 7 July 1881. He was secretary to the Royal Engineers Committee from December 1882 to July 1885, and from August 1885 to February 1886 he was assistant private secretary at the War Office to the Right Hon. William Henry Smith, the Conservative Secretary of State for War, who was the son in the newsagents of W.H. Smith and Son. Between 1886 and 1894 he worked with the Royal Engineers on telegraphs, joining the 2nd Telegraph Battalion in September 1889. He was promoted lieutenant colonel on 29 March 1895. He retired from the army on 4 October 1899.

Having been promoted major on 1 April 1888, Addison was assigned to the Board of Trade for telegraphic and general electrical development in July 1894. While in this employ it was his responsibility to investigate railway accidents, particularly if they were caused by signal failure or another type of electrical fault. He reported on accidents at New Station in Leeds, on 23 March 1895; on the Eastbourne to Tunbridge Wells line on 1 September 1897; and a Belfast to Larne train on 13 July 1898. He attributed most of the blame to human error.

Addison joined the Guinness brewing company as the 1st Earl of Iveagh's personal assistant in England. He was appointed a trustee of the Guinness Trust, and in 1903 to its successor, the Iveagh Trust, which provided affordable housing for the people of London and Dublin. He retired from the post in 1927. Colonel Addison represented the Royal Engineers at the funerals of Pelham von Donop in 1921 and George Barker in 1930.

Addison died at 16 Ashburn Place in Kensington, on 8 November 1937. He was the oldest surviving member of the Royal Engineers 1872 finalists, only being survived by two Wanderers players: Reginald Welch (died in 1939) and Thomas Hooman (died in 1938).

Alfred George Goodwyn

Alfred Goodwyn played as half-back for the Royal Engineers in the 1872 FA Cup final and in the first few rounds of the 1872–73 competition. He was capped for England in 1873.

Goodwyn was born at Roorhir (now Ruhea) in Bengal, northern India (now Bangladesh), on 13 March 1850. He entered the Royal Military Academy at Woolwich in 1869, and he was commissioned as lieutenant in the Royal Engineers on 2 August 1871. Fellow graduates on the same day were Edmond Cotter and Herbert Muirhead, who also played in the 1872 final, and Richard Ruck, who played in the 1875 final.

Goodwyn was selected to play for England in the second official international match against Scotland, played at Kennington Oval on 8 March 1873, which England won 4-2. His Royal Engineers colleague Pelham von Donop, played alongside him in the defence, while John Edward Blackburn and Henry Waugh Renny-Tailyour played for Scotland. It was reported: 'The back play of A G Goodwyn … was faultless'. William Slaney Kenyon-Slaney of the Grenadier Guards scored twice for England.

Goodwyn was posted to India, and on 12 March 1874, the day before his 24th birthday, he was riding his horse at Roorkee when he fell from his mount and suffered injuries from which he died two days later. He was the first-ever England international player to die, which ironically was on the same day as the Royal Engineers lost 2-0 to Oxford University in the Cup final.

Hugh Mitchell

Hugh Mitchell played on the forward line in the 1872 FA Cup final, scoring one of the goals that got the Royal Engineers there, and he was a Scottish international. He later worked as a lawyer.

Mitchell was born on 3 December 1849, at 29 Cavendish Road West in Marylebone, London, the son of Lieutenant Colonel Hugh Mitchell of the Madras Army, and his wife Jessie (formerly McGaskill).

He was educated at Harrow School from 1864 to 1867 and at the Royal Military Academy until he entered the Royal Engineers as lieutenant on 8 January 1870, along with Edmund Cresswell and Henry Rich.

He sailed to Bermuda in October 1870, being employed in the building of fortifications at the Hamilton Dockyard. The British Government had begun to view Bermuda more as a base than a colony, and in 1869 work began on a floating dry dock. It is likely that Lieutenant Mitchell was employed with this project.

He and Edmund Cresswell had graduated from the Royal Military Academy together, and he met one of Lieutenant Cresswell's sisters, Mary Catherine, whom he married in 1878.

His son, Sir Philip Euen Mitchell (1890–1964), served as governor of Uganda, Fiji and Kenya, being appointed GCMG for his services, and was awarded a Military Cross for gallantry during the Great War.

Hugh became a student of the Inner Temple on 21 January 1881, at the comparatively late age of 31, and he was called to the Bar on 7 May

1884. He lived at 44 Hogarth Road in West London, before he moved to Wales, where he operated on the South Wales and Chester circuits, and the Glamorgan sessions. He practised in Gibraltar and Tangier from 1896.

Hugh retired in 1926, and died at Brakpan in South Africa on 16 August 1937, aged 87. He was the second-to-last member of the Royal Engineers 1872 finalists to pass away, being survived by George Addison by fewer than three months.

Edmund William Cresswell

Edmund Cresswell played on the forward line in the 1872 FA Cup final, where he sustained a serious injury but remained on the pitch.

Cresswell was born in Gibraltar on 7 November 1849, the eldest of two sons in the family of four children to Edmund Cresswell (1800–77), who was the chief postmaster on the Rock, and his wife Mary (formerly Fraser, 1826–92). He was educated at Bruce Castle School in Tottenham and at the Royal Military Academy, from where he entered the Royal Engineers as lieutenant on 8 January 1870, along with Hugh Mitchell and Henry Rich.

On 30 January 1875, at Byculla in South Bombay (now Mumbai), he married Emma Mary Carver (1853–99). They had nine children, including a son named Edmund Fraser (1876–1941). Edmund junior became a colonel in the Royal Artillery, and was awarded the Distinguished Service Order (DSO) during the Great War.

Cresswell will forever be remembered for the 1872 FA Cup final, when he broke his collarbone but remained on the pitch. *The Sportsman* reported: 'Too much praise cannot be accorded to him for the pluck he showed in maintaining his post, although completely disabled and in severe pain, until the finish.' He played cricket for the Royal Engineers and other clubs, including the Gentlemen of Hampshire from 1868 to 1886.

Cresswell was involved mainly in administrative and staff work. Until August 1872 he was based at Chatham, before being posted to India on 23 October 1872 as assistant engineer; returning to Chatham in February 1880. From 1 April 1881 and 31 March 1888 he was employed working on ordnance survey, during which time he was promoted captain on 8 January 1882. Having been promoted major on 1 August 1888, he was posted to South Africa from 19 April 1888 to 18 November 1892. He was based at Liverpool until 3 June 1894, when he was transferred to Shoeburyness in Essex. He was employed with the military works department in India from 12 January 1897 until his retirement. He was promoted lieutenant colonel on 12 August 1895 and colonel 12 August 1899. He retired from military service on 12 August 1900.

Emma died on 11 May 1899 and on 19 October 1907 he married a Parisian girl named Isabel Agnes Vulliamy (1869–1956) in St Marylebone, London. They had a son named Michael Justin (1909–86), who became the UK ambassador to Finland, Yugoslavia and Argentina between 1954 and 1969, and his son and Edmund's grandson, Alexander, is a renowned architectural artist.

Cresswell died at Copse Hill in Ewhurst near Guildford, Surrey, on 1 May 1931, aged 81. Copse Hill features in the paintings *The Letter* and *The White Drawing Room* by Leonard Campbell Taylor.

Herbert Hugh Muirhead

Herbert Muirhead played on the forward line for the Royal Engineers in the first FA Cup final in 1872 and he became an expert in the building of fortifications.

Muirhead was born at 3 Oriental Place in Brighton, on 10 December 1850, the third son of four in the family of six children born between 1845 and 1854 to James Patrick Muirhead (1813–98), and his wife, Katherine Elizabeth (1816–90), the second daughter of Matthew Robinson Boulton, an engineer and partner of James Watt, the inventor of the steam engine. They had married on 27 January 1844. His father was a well-known Scottish advocate and author, who wrote a biography of James Watt. His oldest brother, Lionel, composed hymns, and his oldest sister, Marion, wrote their father's biography. In 1853 the artist, Julian E. Drummond painted a picture of Francis, Beatrix and Herbert, when he was aged 3.

Muirhead was educated at Eton College from 1864 to 1867, Wellington College, and at the Royal Military Academy, before being commissioned as lieutenant in the Royal Engineers on 2 August 1871. Fellow graduates on the same day were Edmond Cotter and Alfred Goodwyn, who also played in the 1872 final, and Richard Ruck, who played in the 1875 final.

He played on the forward line in the 1872 FA Cup final, and during the match 'a fine run by Lieutenant Muirhead brought the ball within a few yards of the centre of the posts'. He was generally notied for his 'excellent and fine runs'.

Muirhead's military career mainly involved the building of fortifications. He was based at Chatham from October 1871 to September

1873, and then he spent two years in Ireland. He was posted to Bermuda from January 1876 until November 1878, then transferred to Gibraltar before returning to Aldershot in May 1881. He remained there until November 1881, when he was posted to the Curragh Camp in Ireland. He was promoted captain on 31 July 1883, and returned to Chatham the following December. Muirhead was employed at the Royal Arsenal, where he served until July 1893; during which time he was promoted major on 17 December 1889. From August 1893 to September 1898 he was employed in building and maintaining the west coast defences at the Esquimalt Royal Naval Dockyard on Canada's Pacific coast, during which time he was promoted to lieutenant colonel on 4 April 1897. He spent the last five years of his military service at Pembroke Dock in South Wales, before he retired from army service on 4 April 1902.

Colonel Muirhead died of pleura-pneumonia at 34 Seymour Street in Marylebone, London, on 4 March 1904, aged 53.

Adam Bogle

Adam Bogle played on the forward line for the Royal Engineers in the first FA Cup final. He was a career soldier, mainly being posted to home stations, or employed overseas in the building of fortifications.

Bogle was born in Glasgow on 21 June 1848, the son of a colonial merchant named John Bogle (1808–79) and his wife, Jane Sarah (1818–85), the daughter of Benjamin Duterrau, a well-known artist. His parents married in Hobart in Tasmania in 1838. They eventually returned to live at Woodside near Torquay.

He was educated at Harrow School from 1862 to 1865, where he represented the school at football, and then the Royal Military Academy, from where he was commissioned as lieutenant on 15 July 1868; along with John Rouse Merriott Chard, who would later be awarded the Victoria Cross as the hero of Rorke's Drift during the Zulu War.

Bogle was based at Chatham until 1870, and then he spent a year in Ireland. Between August 1871 and March 1874 he was based at the Royal Arsenal in Woolwich, during which time he played in the 1872 FA Cup final. His first overseas duty was at Bermuda in October 1876, and then he transferred to Gibraltar until March 1879. From April 1879 to May 1880 he was based at the Curragh Camp in Ireland, before returning to Chatham. He was promoted captain on 10 December 1880. In February 1881 he was posted to Aldershot, where he was instructor of fortifications from February 1882 until 1889. He was promoted major on

17 December 1889. His last tour of duty was in Jamaica, 1889–90, and he was based in Dover until his retirement on 25 May 1892.

Adam married Ethel (1857–1945), the daughter of Colonel John James Glossop of the Royal Fusiliers, at St Matthias Church in Torquay, on 20 July 1882. It seems that they travelled a lot and the couple had no children. They were listed as living at Steephurst House in 1898 (where Bedales School now stands), and at the turn of the century they had moved to a rented home named Collyers near Steep in Hampshire. When Bogle was at home he was known to have supported the Steep cricket club, and acted as its vice-president in 1898–99. He died at home on 3 March 1915, aged 66, and he was buried at All Saints' Church in Steep.

George Barker

George Barker appears in the 1872 picture of the Royal Engineers' Cup final team, and may well have played at some time during the game. Indeed, the *Morning Post* published a twelve-man team for the Royal Engineers, which included Lieutenant G. Barker.

Barker was born at Bengal in India on 17 December 1850, the only child of Colonel George Barker, who was in the service of the Honourable East India Company; and his wife, Mary Katherine, daughter of Lieutenant General Edward Vaughan Worsley of the Royal Artillery. He was baptised on 15 November 1875, at Ferozepore in Bengal, India, when he was aged 26.

He attended the Royal Military Academy, from where he passed out as lieutenant in the Royal Engineers on 13 January 1869.

In his account of Royal Engineers football, Sir Richard Ruck, who played in the 1875 final, while describing the dribbling ability of Pelham von Donop, pointed out that he did many moves with other wing men such as George Barker. In the old Club Book it was recorded how in 1873 the Engineers were displeased with the rough play of an opponent:

> Our fellows being by this time fairly well disgusted began to peg into them pretty sharp, and 'little George' (now Major General Sir George Barker ...) very soon sent a man to grass with a very sweet but fair hack, which was heard all over the ground; the individual was afterwards seen standing in goal on one leg like a stork.

Barker saw active service in the Egyptian Campaign of 1882, as captain and adjutant to Colonel John Drake, the commanding Royal Engineer of

46

the 1st Division. He received the Egypt Medal, 1882–89, the Khedive's Bronze Star and the Order of the Medjidie, 4th class.

On 4 September 1888, at St Paul's Church in Adlington, Buckinghamshire, Barker married the Honourable Clemency (1856–1940), daughter of John Gellibrand Hubbard, 1st Baron Adlington, and the Honourable Maria Margaret Napier. They had a daughter named Dorothea, who was born at Westminster in 1891, and a son named Evelyn Hugh, known as 'Bubbles' who was born at Southsea on 22 May 1894. Evelyn went on to serve the British Army with great distinction in several theatres of war, including the two world wars, and he attained the rank of general.

Colonel Barker was appointed Companion of the Order of the Bath (CB) on 30 June 1905, for his work as Inspector of Royal Engineers, and as a major general he was appointed Knight Commander, Order of the Bath (KCB). On his retirement Major General Barker lived at Salthill House in Chichester, West Sussex. There is a fine art painting of Salthill House depicting it as it looked in 1882.

Barker died in the Stockbridge Nursing Home on 5 March 1930, aged 80. The *Portsmouth Evening News* for 10 March 1930 reported:

Military Funeral – Tributes to Major-General, Sir George Barker, KCB, at East Lavant. The funeral of Major-General, Sir George Barker, KCB, who died in the Stockbridge Nursing Home in his 80th year, took place at St Mary's, East Lavant, Chichester, on Saturday afternoon. There was a large gathering at the graveside and also in the church, among whom were many residents and officers of the late officer's old regiment, including Colonel George Addison, who played in the 1872 final.

The remains were conveyed from the residence of the deceased, Salt Hill House, on a gun-carriage, the team, officers and men being supplied from the RA camp at Bordon. The coffin was covered with the Union Jack, and was carried from the main road to St Mary's Church, by non-commissioned officers of the Royal Engineers. On the coffin were the General's swords and medals, etc.

The cortege was met by Bishop Southwell and the Reverend S L Buchell, Rector of Lavant. The service in the church was fully choral, and as the cortege left the church Mr J Harmsworth played Chopin's 'Funeral March'. The last rites in the churchyard adjoining were performed by Bishop Southwell and the remains were buried by the side of those of the general's father, the late Colonel G Barker. The 'Last Post' and 'Reveille' were sounded by buglers from the mounted RE Depot at Aldershot.

Chandos Hoskyns

Chandos Hoskyns appears in the 1872 picture of the Royal Engineers' Cup final team wearing his kit, and may well have played at some time during the game. He saw active service in the Jowaki Expedition, the Second Afghan War, the Zhob Valley Expedition and in the Second Anglo-Boer War.

Hoskyns was born on 28 April 1848 in the village of Aston Tirrold near Didcot in Berkshire. He was the second son of six in the family of nine children to the Reverend Sir John Leigh (1817–1911), 9th Baron Hoskyns of Harewood, County Hereford, and his wife Phyllis Emma (formerly Peyton). The Baronetcy had been granted on 18 December 1676. Chandos was one of twins and his elder twin, John, became a lieutenant in the 24th (2nd Warwickshire) Regiment, and died while serving in Burma on 13 March 1887 aged 35; another brother was Benedict George (1856–1935), who became an eminent Anglican priest.

Hoskyns' father was the rector of St Michael and All Angels parish church in Aston Tirrold from 1845 until his death. He was also canon of Christ Church, Oxford, 1880, and a Justice of the Peace for Berkshire. Chandos was educated at the Royal Military Academy, from where he was commissioned as lieutenant in the Royal Engineers on 7 July 1869, along with Lieutenants William Addison and William St George Ord.

Jowaki Expedition on the North-West Frontier of India, 1877–78

Hoskyns' military career was mainly on the North-West Frontier of India, where his first active service took him on the Jowaki Expedition of 1877–78. In 1877 the British Government in India proposed to reduce the payments given to the Jowaki Afridi tribe of Pathans for guarding the strategic Kohat Pass. The Jowaki resented it and retaliated by making hostile raids into British territory. A force of 1,500 British troops penetrated the region to punish the Jowaki, and Lieutenant Hoskyns was with two companies of Sappers and Miners in the 1st Brigade that supported the 51st (2nd Yorkshire) Regiment, which three years later amalgamated with the 105th Regiment.

Second Afghanistan War, 1878–80

Hoskyns' next tour of active service took him to the Second Afghan War of 1878–80. With Afghanistan considered to be 'the door into India', the British set out to close it on the ever-expanding Russian Empire, which came to be known as 'The Great Game'. Russian envoys entered Kabul on 22 July 1878, and Britain responded by sending an army of 50,000 troops into Afghanistan. After British victories over the Afghan army at Ali Masjid on 21 November 1878 and at Peiwar Kotal on 28–29 November 1878, the first phase of the war was ended by the signing of the Treaty of Gandamak on 26 May 1879. However, an uprising in Kabul on 3 September 1879, led to the murder the following day of the British representative, Sir Louis Cavagnari, along with his staff and guards, which provoked the second phase of the war.

Within a month of the murders a British force under the popular general Sir Frederick 'Bobs' Roberts was occupying the Bala Hissar citadel in Kabul, and British authority in Afghanistan seemed to have been restored. Then a whole British brigade was practically wiped out at the battle of Maiwand on 27 July 1880. The Afghan forces were led by Ayub Khan, a claimant for the vacant Afghan throne, and the British in Kandahar came under siege.

On 11 August 1880, General Roberts set out from Kabul to relieve Kandahar and smash the rebels. His force of 10,000 troops, 8,000 followers, 8,250 pack animals and 18 guns struggled on an epic march of more than 300 miles. They hauled their way over mountains under appalling conditions. At night it was freezing cold and during the day temperatures soared to 110 degrees, dust storms raged and delays forced them to cut their rations.

When the troops reached Kandahar, Roberts and about 1,000 of his men were weakened by the effects of fever, but his troops had such faith in him that their spirits remained high. Ayub Khan cautiously withdrew his army a mile or two away from the city, but the very next day, 1 September 1880, Roberts smashed his enemy by skilful deployment of his cavalry and artillery. The brilliant victory and the epic march became linked as another great Imperial legend, and 'Bobs' was raised to the Peerage as Lord Roberts of Kandahar.

Hoskyns served as captain and orderly officer to Brigadier General C.H. Pallister in the Peshawar Field Force, being mentioned in despatches. He gave a lecture on the Peshawar Field Force to the Royal United Services Institute.

On 22 July 1886 he married Jean Bannatyne, the daughter of David MacDuff Latham, and they had three daughters: Euphemia, Muriel and Elizabeth Mary.

Hoskyns' tour of duty in Afghanistan was followed by his taking part in the Zhob Valley Expedition of 1884; and his fourth and last tour of active service was in the Second Boer War in South Africa.

Second Boer War in South Africa, 1899–1902

Tension between the two independent Boer republics of Transvaal and the Orange Free State and British interests in South Africa had been building up for years, until diplomacy finally broke down. In early October 1899, 10,000 men from the Indian and Mediterranean garrisons began to arrive in Natal, and the 1st Army Corps mobilised in England. On 11 October 1899, Boer commando units invaded British territory, laying siege to the garrison towns of Kimberley and Mafeking in Cape Colony, and Ladysmith in Natal.

Fighting on home soil in mounted commando units, in some cases containing three generations of the same family, the Boers were a formidable enemy. With superior firearms and smokeless ammunition, and camouflaged in the drab colours of their ordinary farming clothes, skilled Boer marksmen knew how to conceal themselves in the rocky terrain and snipe from long range, as the British advanced in parade-ground fashion across the open veldt. Then, with excellent horsemanship, the Boers would leave the scene before the British could react effectively.

British relief forces made a two-pronged advance, during which they suffered three serious reverses in mid-December, at Magersfontein and Stromberg in the Cape, and at Colenso in Natal, which came to be known as 'Black Week'. As the Natal Field Force struggled northwards, they suffered their worst defeat of the campaign at the notorious battle of Spion Kop on 24 January 1900, before reaching Ladysmith four days later. Kimberley, under Cecil Rhodes, was retaken at about the same time, and the relief of Mafeking on 17 May 1900, which had been under the leadership of Robert Baden-Powell, caused a frenzy of Imperial hysteria in Britain.

Eventually, General 'Bobs' Roberts, whose son had been killed in action while gaining a posthumous Victoria Cross at Colenso, took over command. His experience turned the tide and British forces entered the Boer capital of Pretoria on 5 June 1900. The British then launched a campaign, mainly in the eastern Transvaal, to track down the Boer commanders, while the Boers took to guerrilla tactics, attacking isolated outposts, supply convoys and patrols.

In October 1900, General Herbert Kitchener took command, and countered Boer strategy by dividing the country into fenced sections, guarded by blockhouses. With his 'Scorched Earth' policy, the farms of hostile Boers were burned to diminish their chances of refuge. Their families were put in secure compounds, which came to be known notoriously as concentration camps. Not surprisingly, the Boers began to lose heart, but sporadic fighting by the 'bitter-enders' continued to keep British troops on alert. Hostilities finally ended officially when a peace treaty was signed on Lord Kitchener's dining table at Vereeniging on 31 May 1902.

Hoskyns was made a colonel in 1902 and served at some time as staff colonel of the Royal Engineers. He retired from the army in 1905. He was knighted for his services, and succeeded as the 10th Baron Hoskyns of Harewood, County Hereford, on the death of his father on 7 December 1911. His mother died on 7 May 1914, and he died at Nairn in northern Scotland on 22 July, aged 66. James Prinsep had died in the town in 1895.

The *Aberdeen Press and Journal* for 23 July 1914 reported:

> The death took place yesterday, with startling suddenness, of Colonel Sir Chandos Hoskyns, Bt, at the age of 66. Last night Sir Chandos seemed to be in his usual health, but he took suddenly ill yesterday morning, and passed away in the forenoon. Sir Chandos, who succeeded to the baronetcy about two years ago, was a constant visitor to Nairn, and only a week ago took possession of a fine mansion house at Delnies near Nairn.

William St George Ord

William St George Ord appears in the 1872 picture of the Royal Engineers' Cup final team wearing his football kit, and he may have played at some time during the game.

Ord was born at Chatham in 1849, being baptised on 13 March 1849. He was the middle son of three to Major General Sir Harry St George Ord (1819–85), who served with the Royal Engineers from 1837 to 1856. He was a veteran of the Crimean War, and a colonial administrator. His mother was Julia Graham, the daughter of Admiral James Carpenter of Exmouth. William and Julia had married at Westminster in London on 28 June 1846. William's older brother, Harry St George, went to live in Australia while his father was governor there from 1878 to 1880; and his younger brother, St John St George, became a major in the Royal Artillery. His great-grandfather was the antiquarian Craven Ord (1756–1832).

Ord attended the Royal Military Academy, from where he passed out and was commissioned as lieutenant in the Royal Engineers on 7 July 1869; along with lieutenants William Addison and Chandos Hoskyns.

The family lived at Fornham House in Fornham St Martin near Bury St Edmunds in Suffolk, and were influential in the area. Ord paid for the local village school to be enlarged in 1872, the year of the first FA Cup final.

Captain Ord died at Buttermere in Cumberland (now Cumbria) on 13 March 1909, in his fifty-ninth year. There are a number of memorials dedicated to the Ord family in the church and there is an Ord Road in the village, and the village institute in Fornham was built in his father's name, with funds donated by the Maharajah of Johore.

Duke of Wellington's (West Riding) Regiment

Percy Temple Rivett-Carnac

Percy Temple Rivett-Carnac played seven times for the Wanderers during their first Cup-winning season, and later saw active service during the Nile Expedition, the Mashonaland Expedition and during the Second Boer War.

Rivett-Carnac was born at Rawalpindi in India, on 12 January 1852, the fourth son of six in the family of seven children, born between 1846 and 1864, to William John Rivett-Carnac of the East India Company, and his wife, Mary Anstruther, the daughter of the Reverend Percy Spearman Wilkinson. The Rivett-Carnac family had prospered in India for generations, and Rudyard Kipling had known members of the 'ubiquitous' Rivett-Carnacs. Two members of the family disappeared in mysterious circumstances. Claud James went missing in 1908 and was never found, and Colonel Percy Harrison Fawcett disappeared without trace in the Amazon jungle in 1925.

Rivett-Carnac was appointed sub lieutenant in the 43rd (Oxfordshire) Light Infantry on 3 July 1873. He was also paymaster for the 1st Battalion, West Riding Regiment, and the 61st (South Gloucestershire) Regiment. Having been promoted captain on 19 December 1883, in the 2nd Battalion, Duke of Wellington's Regiment, he served with the Nile Expedition of 1884–85, for which he received the Queen's Sudan Medal and the Khedive's Bronze Star. Having been promoted to major on 6 October 1892, he took part in the Mashonaland Expedition of 1897, where he served with G Company of Mounted Infantry with the 2nd Battalion, Duke of Wellington's Regiment. He took part in several engagements in the Matobo Districts, during which he was wounded.

On 1 January 1898 Rivett-Carnac married Alice Mary Granville, daughter of Major Sydney Herbert. They had two children: Alice Mary in 1899 and Percival Sydney in 1904.

He saw active service in the Boer War of 1899 to 1902. He gained the rank of lieutenant colonel in the 1st Battalion, Duke of Wellington's West Riding Regiment. He later served as aide-de-camp to King George V.

Rivett-Carnac died in Canada on 5 November 1932, aged 80, and he was buried at the St Michael and All Angels Cemetery at Chemainus on Vancouver Island, British Columbia.

There is a W. Rivett-Carnac recorded as playing twice for the Wanderers in 1869, and L.W.G. Rivett-Carnac (1854–1904) played for Wanderers against Harrow School in 1876 and later became the administrator general of Bombay. Another family sportsman was Charles James Rivett-Carnac (1853–1935), who won a gold medal for the 7m class of sailing at the 1908 London Olympic Games. His great-granddaughter, Cleone Patricia 'Cleo' Rivett-Carnac, won a javelin bronze medal for New Zealand at the 1950 British Empire (now Commonwealth) Games held in Auckland.

Chapter 4

The 1872–73 Season

For the second FA Cup competition the Royal Engineers were joined by the 1st Surrey Rifles based at Camberwell. There were sixteen entrants in all, and fourteen ties were played; one fewer than the previous year, and including one match that was eventually void. All the cards were stacked in favour of the Wanderers, as the rules allowed for the holders of the Cup to be exempt from playing any matches until the final, and the other fifteen clubs had to play for the right to challenge them at a venue chosen by them. Two other clubs new to the competition were South Norwood and Oxford University, who were destined to reach the final at their first attempt.

In the first round the Royal Engineers defeated Civil Service 3-0 at Chatham, and the 1st Surrey Rifles made a successful debut in the competition by beating Upton Park 2-0 at Camberwell, with goals by Allport and Hastie. In the other matches, Maidenhead knocked out Great Marlow by one goal to nil. Oxford University appeared for the first time when they defeated Crystal Palace by the odd goal in five. Reigate Priory actually took part in the competition on this occasion, but they lost to Windsor Home Park, who were spearheaded by Ernest, the oldest of the five Bambridge brothers.

The Royal Engineers received a bye in the second round, while 1st Surrey Rifles travelled to the York Road Ground in Maidenhead, where they were defeated 3-0. Oxford University travelled to Clapham Common to beat Rovers 3-0, while South Norwood beat Windsor Home Park 1-0 at Portland Road. However, the match was said to have ended before ninety minutes and the FA ordered a replay to take place at Home Park in Windsor. Windsor won and one of their three goals was scored by Frank Heron, who made a name for himself while playing for Wanderers.

In the third round the Engineers travelled to the Parks at Oxford University, where they lost by the only goal of the match, in what was their only defeat of the season. They won all the other nineteen matches they played, scoring seventy-four goals and conceding only two. Maidenhead won 1-0 at Home Park.

There was only one quarter-final match, in which Oxford University beat Maidenhead 4-0, and they should have played Queen's Park in the semi-final for the right to challenge the Wanderers for the trophy, but the Scots could not make the journey to London due to the various business commitments of their players.

Wanderers 2 Oxford University 0

In their half-blue and half-white jerseys, Oxford University faced the Wanderers on 29 March 1873. It was the first of his nine record appearances in the final for Arthur, Lord Kinnaird. Sporting a bushy red beard, he was a robust character who did not mind rough play and would never wear shin pads. Captain Marindin was a close friend of the family, and on one visit Lady Kinnaird expressed to him her worry that: 'Arthur would one day come home with a broken leg.' 'Don't be alarmed,' Marindin replied with a smile, 'for if he does it will not be his own.' He himself considered football to be: 'The best of games for developing manliness of character.'

The champions had chosen the ground of the Amateur Athletic Club at Lillie Bridge in West Brompton, London, as the venue. Three-thousand spectators watched the game, with Alfred Stair in charge again. As one of the final teams was Oxford University, the game kicked off at 11.30 in the morning, a time that would allow the participants and spectators to watch the Boat Race between Oxford and Cambridge later in the day. Oxford lost that too! Although Oxford seemed to have had the best of the play in the early part of the game, with five Etonians in the team, including Charles Meysey-Thompson, the brother of Albert, Wanderers retained the trophy with a goal in each half of the match, the second being blamed on the fact that the Oxford goalkeeper had started to play in the forward line. The Oxford team was composed entirely of Englishmen, but the mixed Wanderers squad included Julian Sturgis (1848–1904) of Boston, Massachusetts, who became the first non-Briton to be a member of an FA Cup-winning team.

From 1883 to 1895 the Wanderers goalkeeper, Reginald Welch, was an army tutor at the Army College in Heath End, Farnham. The teams were:

Wanderers: *Goalkeeper* – Reginald Courtenay Welch (Harrow); *Full-back* – Leonard Sedgwick Howell (Westminster); *Half-back* – Edward Ernest Bowen (Harrow); *Forwards: Right* – Charles Henry Reynolds Wollaston

(Lancing), Robert Kennett Kingsford (Marlborough); *Centre* – Alexander George Bonsor (Eton), Captain William Slaney Kenyon-Slaney (Eton), Charles Maud Meysey-Thompson (Eton), Julian Russell Sturgis (Eton); *Left* – Arthur Fitzgerald Kinnaird (captain) (Eton), Reverend Henry Holmes Stewart (Repton).

Oxford University: *Goalkeeper* – Andrew John Leach (St John's College); *Full-back* – Charles Colleridge Mackarness (Exeter); *Half-back* – Francis Hornby Birley (University College); *Forwards: Right* – Charles James Longman (University College), Arnold Kirke-Smith (captain) (University College); *Centre* – Robert Walpole Sealy-Vidal (Christ Church), Frederick Brunning Maddison (Brasenose), Cuthbert John Ottaway (Christ Church), Harold Baily Dixon (Christ Church); *Left* – Walter Boldero Paton (University College), John Robert Edwards Sumner (Christ Church).

Royal Engineers Matches

1st Round	26 October 1872	Civil Service	won 3-0 at Chatham
2nd Round	Bye		
3rd Round	9 December 1872	Oxford University	lost 0-1 at the Parks, Oxford

1st Surrey Rifles Matches

1st Round	26 October 1872	Upton Park	won 2-0 at Camberwell
2nd Round	23 November 1872	Maidenhead	lost 3-0 at Maidenhead

1st Surrey Rifles

William John Maynard

William Maynard was a prominent player for the 1st Surrey Rifles during the early years of the FA Cup, and he played for England in the first-ever official international match against Scotland.

Maynard was born on 18 March 1853, at Albany Road in Walworth, Surrey (now in the London borough of Southwark), and he was baptised at St George's Church in Camberwell in the following month. At the time of the 1861 census he was the oldest of three sons living with a solicitor's clerk named William Connolly and his wife, Elizabeth (formerly Stent), at 4 Camden Place in Camberwell; and they employed a servant. A decade later he was employed as a clerk in the county court, and was living with his mother and two younger brothers at Rectory Villas on the Crystal Palace Road in St Giles, London, where they retained a servant.

He was the only military man to play for England against Scotland in the first-ever official international football match, which took place on 30 November 1872, before a crowd of 4,000 people at the West of Scotland Cricket Ground at Hamilton Crescent in Partick. At 19 years and 257 days, he was the youngest player on the pitch. Maynard represented England as a winger for a second time on 4 March 1876, as the only military man, when England lost 3-0 to Scotland in Partick. He also played for Wanderers for a season. He was the youngest man to keep goal for England for sixteen years, and one of only four teenagers to play in that position. He represented Surrey in 1877.

By 1881 Maynard was still a court clerk, living with his father at Euston Lodge in Croxteth Road, Camberwell, where they employed a second servant.

He married Annie, the daughter of Samuel Smith the local vicar, in the church where he had been christened, on 2 August 1883. They had two daughters, both born in Sevenoaks. A decade later they had five children and the family home was at 9 Laurel Grove in Croydon, Surrey.

Maynard's son, Alfred Frederick, who was born at Anerly in Kent on 23 March 1894, represented England at rugby union, winning three caps as a hooker during the 1914 Five Nations Championship. As Lieutenant Maynard of the Royal Naval Division he was killed in action at Beaumont Hamel on 13 November 1916 during the Great War.

By 1911 William and his family lived at 33 South Street in Crossgate, Durham. He served as a district probate registrar from 1903 until his death on 2 September 1921, aged 68. It seems that he lived in the Rose and Crown Hotel in Durham, and had been in failing health when he died at the Roker Hotel in Sunderland. His effects went to his wife, Annie. He also left two sons and a daughter.

Grenadier Guards

William Slaney Kenyon-Slaney

William Kenyon-Slaney played for Wanderers in the 1873 Cup-winning team, and for Old Etonians in the 1975 and 1876 Cup finals. He scored the first-ever goal in an official international match, while playing for England. He later went on active service in the conquest of Egypt in 1882.

Kenyon-Slaney was born at Rajkot in Gujarat, India, on 24 August 1847, the second oldest of six sons in the family of ten children to Captain William Kenyon (1815–84) of the 2nd Bombay Light Cavalry, which saw service during the Indian Mutiny of 1857–58, and later became the 32nd Lancers, and Frances Catharine (1823–96), the daughter and co-heiress of Robert Aglionby Slaney, of Hatton Grange at Shifnal in Shropshire. On her father's death in 1862 the family assumed by Royal Licence the additional surname of Slaney, and the estate at Hatton Grange. Lloyd, 1st Lord Kenyon, was his great-grandfather. The 1851 census records that the family home was at the medieval mansion of Hengwrt near Dolgellau in north-west Wales, where they employed nine servants.

Two of Kenyon-Slaney's younger brothers also joined the army. Major General Walter Kenyon-Slaney CB (1851–1936) saw active service with the Rifle Brigade in the Second Anglo-Boer War and in the Great War, while Colonel Frances Kenyon-Slaney CBE (1858–1938) saw active service with the Durham Light Infantry in the Great War. William is sometimes stated to be the oldest sibling, but some sources record that he had an older brother named Charles, who was born at Habberley near Shrewsbury in 1845.

Kenyon-Slaney was described as a 'fair' scholar and a good all-round sportsman. He began his education at Eton in September 1860, where he was a member of the William Evans House, for whom he played football and cricket. At the time of the 1861 census they lived at Walford Hall in Baschurch near Shrewsbury in Shropshire, where they employed a governess and seven servants for the ever-growing family. From 1862 they lived at Hatton Grange, which is a large Georgian house with its own cricket pavilion. William left Eton in December 1865, having already matriculated for Christ Church, Oxford University, two months earlier and where he only resided in 1866–67.

He was a keen cricketer, playing for Shropshire County from 1865 to 1879, and he also played for the Household Brigade and one match for the I Zingari club in 1880. He played as a right-hand batsman in eleven matches for the Marylebone Cricket Club (MCC) between 1869 and 1880, scoring 145 runs, with a top innings score of 34. As a fielder he took two catches.

Kenyon-Slaney was eligible to play Association football for Old Etonians, Oxford University and Wanderers. He played for Oxford University in the 1873 Cup-winning team, and for Old Etonians in the

1975 and 1876 Cup finals. He was selected to play for England against Scotland in the second official international played at The Oval on 8 March 1873. He scored in the first minute of the game, the first goal ever scored in an international match, and he scored again on the hour. He was noted for his 'dashing and effective play', and in 1874 he was acknowledged as 'being the most successful forward of the year'. He was elected president of the Shropshire Football Association, but when the organisation re-formed in the following year he declined to continue because he disagreed with proposed changes.

Kenyon-Slaney was gazetted for the 3rd Battalion, Grenadier Guards, on 20 November 1867, at Dublin, and he became lieutenant without purchase on 8 September 1878. In 1882 his battalion formed part of the Brigade of Guards, and he was posted for active service during the Egyptian Campaign. He took part in the action at Mahuta and in the decisive battle of Tel-el-Kebir on 13 September 1882. For his service he received the Egypt Medal, 1882–89, with the Tel-el-Kebir clasp and the Khedive's bronze star. He was promoted major on 21 July 1883 and colonel on 23 November 1887, when he was placed on half-pay, and having become involved in politics, he retired from the army in 1892.

At St Andrew's Church in Weston, Shifnal, on 22 February 1887, Kenyon-Slaney married Lady Mabel Selina Bridgeman, eldest daughter of the 3rd Earl of Bradford. Kenyon-Slaney was president of the Shifnal football club, and at the wedding celebrations Aston Villa, who would win their first FA Cup a couple of months later, played an exhibition match against them. They had two children, Sybil Agnes in 1888 and Robert Orlando Rodolph in 1892. Rodolph was High Sheriff of Shropshire in 1935.

Having unsuccessfully contested the Parliamentary Division of Wellington in Shropshire in 1885, Kenyon-Slaney was elected Conservative Member of Parliament for the Newport Division of Shropshire during the General Election on 1 July 1886. He was re-elected in 1892, 1895, 1900 and 1904. William was president of the Shropshire Naval and Military Veterans' Association, and often spoke out in Parliament for the cause of old soldiers.

When on parliamentary duties Kenyon-Slaney lived at 36 Lowndes Street in Chelsea. The 1891 census makes for interesting reading. William and Mabel, along with their daughter, were visiting her parents at Weston Park, Weston-under-Lizard, in Shifnal. Also there that day were all Mabel's brothers and sisters and their children, and six other visitors; all attended by no fewer than thirty-six servants.

Kenyon-Slaney was president of the Shropshire Chess Association, and in 1908 he was appointed president of the Severnside Bowling Club in Shrewsbury, but he died soon afterwards. As a mark of respect, the position remained vacant for the remainder of the season. He declined the offer of a Baronetcy in 1902, but he became a Privy Councillor in 1904. He owned about 4,000 acres of land, and he was described as 'a model landlord', making sure that every cottage on his estate had at least three bedrooms, good drainage and adequate water supply.

After a severe attack of gout, Kenyon-Slaney died at Hatton Grange, on 24 April 1908, aged 60. Local newspapers reported:

> On Tuesday afternoon a large concourse of spectators took their last farewell of all that was mortal in the late Colonel Kenyon-Slaney, and the scene in the pretty parish church of Ryton [St Andrew's], four miles from Shifnal, and at the graveside was very impressive ... Lady Mabel Kenyon-Slaney, the Countess of Harewood, Miss Kenyon-Slaney (daughter), and Mrs F Kenyon-Slaney ... were escorted into the church by two soldier brothers of the late Colonel Slaney [Walter and Francis] ... Each side of the pathway leading from the road to the church were drawn up as a guard of honour 25 old soldiers, who have fought in the Crimean War, the Indian Mutiny, Afghanistan, New Zealand and Zulu War, and the Egyptian campaign, each wearing medals for active service.

Almost everyone who was anyone in the county of Shropshire attended the funeral, and a memorial service was held at Shrewsbury.

At the mayor's banquet in Shrewsbury in the year before Kenyon-Slaney died he stated: 'Of all the pride of which my nature is capable, the proudest pride I have ever possessed is the pride of being a Salopian.' At the time of his death, his constituents were having portraits of himself and his wife prepared in celebration of his twenty-one years' service in the House of Commons.

Chapter 5

The 1873–74 Season

Twenty-eight teams entered the third competition, and two teams from the north of England took part for the first time – Sheffield FC and Shropshire Wanderers. The system of regionalising cup matches to help keep down travelling expenses meant that they were drawn to play against each other, and after two games in which nobody scored, Shropshire Wanderers became the only team ever to be eliminated by the toss of a coin.

The round was spoiled by five matches not taking place because of withdrawals. The Royal Engineers defeated Brondesbury of London 5-0 at Chatham, with Lieutenant George Addison being recorded as scoring at least one goal. The 1st Surrey Rifles drew 0-0 with Barnes at Camberwell, before losing the replay at Barnes Green by the only goal of the game. Cambridge University appeared in the Cup for the first time and made it through to the second round; and the name of Old Etonians appeared in the draw for the first time but they withdrew before their match with High Wycombe. Reigate Priory lost to Woodford Wells by the odd goal in five. The Gitanos club from Battersea appeared in the Cup for the first time, but they lost at Uxbridge, and Oxford University defeated Upton Park 4-0.

The Engineers played their second round match at Chatham, when they defeated Uxbridge by the odd goal in three. There were other wins for Oxford University, Maidenhead and Sheffield FC, but the most notable tie was between Clapham Rovers and Cambridge University. After two drawn games, Clapham won the third 4-1; the first second replay in the FA Cup.

In the third round the Royal Engineers entertained Maidenhead and scored seven goals without reply. This was Lieutenant Alfred Goodwyn's last match in the Cup for the Engineers, although he went on the tour of the north, after which he was posted to India; he never returned. In the following January, the Oxford University team entertained Wanderers at The Parks Ground in a replay and inflicted the first-ever defeat on the holders in the competition, which deprived them of winning the

Little Tin Idol outright. In the other match, Clapham Rovers defeated Sheffield FC at Peterborough.

Both semi-finals were played at Kennington Oval. The Royal Engineers were drawn to play Swifts of Slough. They would be formidable opponents as the squad included the three Bambridge brothers from Windsor, whose father was a teacher at Eton College. Edward Charles 'Charlie' (1858–1935) was capped eighteen times for England from 1879 to 1887, scoring eleven goals. He was his country's top scorer in 1879, 1881, 1884 and 1885. Arthur Leopold (1861–1923) played three times for England in 1881, 1883 and 1884. Ernest Henry (1848–1917) played for England in 1876, and he acted as umpire for England against Scotland in 1881. Nevertheless, the Royal Engineers earned their place in the final with two goals from Lieutenant Henry Renny-Tailyour.

They had to wait a month to find out their final opponents when Oxford University beat Clapham Rovers by the only goal of the game. They spent the run-up to the final in special training for the match. The secretary of the Engineers reported:

> The betting was very nearly even – determined to leave no stone unturned in order to secure the victory, and if possible bring back the cup in triumph, for the past fortnight before the match we had gone into a regular course of training, at least as far as was sufficient to get us into thorough good condition ...

Oxford University 2 Royal Engineers 0

Two-thousand spectators turned up at The Oval on 14 March 1874. Alfred Stair took charge for a third time, and the umpire for the Engineers was Alexander Morten of the Crystal Palace club.

Both teams played with two half-backs for the first time. The corner kick had been introduced in the previous year, and the first one to be given in an FA Cup final went to Oxford University after only ten minutes. From the kick, the ball got caught up in a loose 'scrimmage', right in front of the Engineers' goal. It came to the foot of Charles Mackarness, who kicked it over the heads of the players who had crowded the goal area, and it went between the posts before Captain Merriman saw it. Mackarness was the only full-back to score in an FA Cup final for many years.

Spurred on by the need for an equaliser, the Engineers went on the attack, and Lieutenant Renny-Tailyour hit a post. However, after twenty more minutes three Oxford players gained possession of the ball and broke away with it. Captain Merriman ran out to meet them, but they passed it to Fred Patton, one of the centres, who scored what the ever-unbiased Royal Engineers' secretary reported as '… a really fine goal, and Oxford deserved it'.

It was reported that a free kick from the corner post went across the Engineers' goal line but no claim was made and there was no appeal, so play was allowed to go on. However, this may have been the reporters mistaking a corner kick for a free kick because a goal direct from a corner kick was not allowed until the rules were changed in 1927.

The Royal Engineers continued to press hard, but the Oxford goalkeeper, Charles Nepean, a founder member of Oxford University FC, was in fine form, and the score had not changed when time was called. It was the third season in a row that Royal Engineers lost only one match. They won twenty-two and drew two, scoring seventy goals against eight conceded.

Several newspapers reported on the match, with one stating:

> Favoured with fine weather and with the prospect of a grand contest, upwards of 2,000 people visited the Surrey cricket ground on Saturday afternoon last, in order to witness the last tie for the possession (annually) of the Association Cup. In 1872 and 1873 the Cup was held by the Wanderers, and would have become their absolute property had they succeeded in winning it again this year. Unfortunately for them they had to meet the dark blues on their own ground at Oxford, and took down such a miserably weak team that they were forced to submit to a most decisive defeat, only, however, as it transpires, at the hands of the new holders of the Cup, as in the match on Saturday the University, after a magnificent contest, were declared the victors by two goals to love.
>
> The Engineers began badly by losing the toss and were compelled to kick off from the Gasometer end against a somewhat strong wind. Both teams soon gave evidence of their excellence, and the ball vacillated between the goals, being first at one and then at the other. Von Donop distinguished himself greatly by means of a very fine piece of dribbling play, but was eventually stopped by Ottaway, who forced the ball well back into the opposition territory again. Shortly after this a claim of 'hands' was allowed against the Sappers, and almost immediately afterwards the Engineers sent the ball behind their

own line, and as a consequence a corner kick was allowed to the Oxonians, which resulted in a loose scrimmage directly in the jaws of the RE fortress, and it was not long before the ball was well kicked through the posts by Mackarness, who thus was credited with the first goal for his University.

Ends were changed, and the game became more than ever spirited, the Engineers seemingly aroused to fresh efforts, strongly attacked the Oxford goal, and almost overthrowing the same. The Varsity men, however, were much elated with their primary success, and determined not to let slip a chance, they – chiefly by the aid of Ottaway, Maddison and Vidal – again overcame all opposition and rapidly carried the ball back into the Engineers quarters, and finally Patton shot it between the posts, and thus obtained the second goal for the University.

The all-round play which followed was very brilliant, and although both goals were imminently threatened on more than one occasion, no further advantage accrued to either side previous to the call of 'no side' by the referee. When we remember how well all played, it seems almost invidious to make special mention of individual play, but, nevertheless, we cannot close without a word of extra praise for Ottaway, Birley, Rawson, Patton, and Vidal for the University; and Renny-Tailyour, Digby, and Von Donop for the Engineers.

The teams were:

Oxford University: *Goalkeeper* – Charles Edward Burroughs Nepean (University College); *Full-back* – Charles Coleridge Mackarness (Exeter); *Half-backs* – Francis Hornby Birley (University College), Frederick Thomas Green (New College); *Forwards: Right* – Cuthbert John Ottaway (captain) (Christ Church), Robert Walpole Sealy-Vidal (Christ Church); *Centre* – William Stepney Rawson (Christ Church), Robert Henry 'Robin' Benson (Balliol), Frederick Joseph Patton (Balliol); *Left* – Frederick Brunning Maddison (Brasenose), Arthur Henry Johnson (All Souls).

Royal Engineers: *Goalkeeper* – Captain William Merriman; *Full-back* – Major Francis Arthur Marindin (captain); *Half-backs* – Lieutenant George William Addison, Lieutenant Gerald Charles Penrice Onslow; *Forwards: Right* – Lieutenant Pelham George von Donop, Lieutenant John Edward

Blackburn; *Centre* – Lieutenant Herbert Edward Rawson, Lieutenant Henry Waugh Renny-Tailyour, Lieutenant Henry Dacres Olivier; *Left* – Lieutenant Charles Knight Wood, Lieutenant Thomas Digby.

Royal Engineers Matches

1st Round	11 October 1872	Brondesbury	won 5-0 at Chatham
2nd Round	26 November 1873	Uxbridge	won 2-1 at Chatham
3rd Round	10 December 1873	Maidenhead	won 7-0 at Chatham
Semi-final	28 January 1874	Swifts	won 2-0
Final	14 March 1874	Oxford University	lost 0-2 at The Oval

1st Surrey Rifles Matches

1st Round	25 October 1873	Barnes	drew 0-0 at Camberwell
Replay	8 November 1873	Barnes	lost 0-1 away

Royal Engineers Players

Gerald Charles Penrice Onslow

Gerald Onslow played at half-back for the Royal Engineers in the 1874 and 1875 FA Cup finals, and saw active service in Afghanistan and in Burma.

Onslow was born on 7 February 1853, at Deyrah in India. He was the second son of three in the family of six children to Lieutenant Colonel Arthur Walton Onslow (1818–95) of the Bengal Army, and his wife, Isabella (formerly Penrice). His older brother, Herbert Arthur Walton Onslow (1851–1906), became a rear admiral in the Royal Navy, and his younger brother, Richard Cranley Onslow (1857–1934), gained the rank of colonel in the Indian Army.

Onslow was educated at Cheltenham College, and at the Royal Military Academy, from where he was commissioned as lieutenant in the Royal Engineers on 29 April 1873.

He played for the Royal Engineers in 1874 and 1875, and he was considered to be 'one of the most brilliant half-backs of his day'.

Onslow saw two tours of active service. The first was in the Second Afghan War in 1878–80, where he was present in the action at Charasiab near Kabul on 6 October 1879, under General 'Bobs' Roberts, and he was involved in the operations around Kabul in December 1879. For his service he received the Afghanistan Medal with two clasps.

In Cheltenham on 16 November 1880, Onslow married Flora Frances Mary, the only daughter of William Donald of Lisle House in Cheltenham. They had four sons and three daughters.

Onslow was promoted captain on 8 January 1885, the rank he held during his active service in the Third Burma War, for which he received the Indian General Service Medal, 1854, with 1885–87 clasp.

Onslow died at a house named Camperdown on Goldsmith's Avenue in Crowborough, East Sussex, on 16 April 1909, aged 56.

It is difficult to imagine how Onslow's wife felt after losing her husband, and then all her four sons went off to fight in the Great War. Three were killed in action, and another was taken prisoner. Arthur Gerald (1885–1916), became a lieutenant commander in the Royal Navy in 1900, and took part in the Somaliland Expedition of 1904. During the Great War he was awarded the Distinguished Service Cross (DSC) for gallantry on several occasions. He was killed in action while in command of HMS *Onslaught* during the battle of Jutland on 1 June 1916 and was buried in Scotland. Milo Richard Beaumont (1888–1917) became a major in the 21st Prince Albert Victor's Own Cavalry (Daly's Horse), Indian Army. He took part in the Mohmand Expedition in 1908. During the Great War he was twice wounded, and died of his wounds on 5 November 1917. He was buried in Baghdad. Brian Walton Onslow (1892–1915) was a lieutenant in the 11th (King Edward's Own) Bengal Lancers (Probyn's Horse), and he was ADC to General, Sir William Birdwood. He was killed in action at Gallipoli on 28 July 1915 and buried there. Eric Montague Onslow (born in 1890) was a major in the Royal Warwickshire Regiment. He was mentioned in despatches and became a prisoner of war. All the sons are commemorated on the Crowborough War Memorial. Flora lived until 2 May 1951.

Pelham George von Donop

Pelham von Donop played in the 1874 and 1875 FA Cup finals, and was the only Royal Engineer to be twice capped for England. He saw active service in the Nile Expedition, and later became chief inspecting officer of railways.

Von Donop was born on 28 April 1851 at Sydney Lodge, 8 Elm Grove in Southsea, Hampshire, although the family home was in Bath. He was the second eldest child, and oldest of four sons in the family of seven children of Commander (later Vice Admiral) Edward

Pelham Brenton von Donop of the Royal Navy and his wife, Louisa Mary Diana Brenton, of Felcham in Surrey. Pelham's grandfather was the German statesman and historian Baron Georg von Donop (1767–1845), and one of his younger brothers, Stanley Brenton (1860–41), rose to the rank of major general with the Royal Artillery. He served in the Second Boer War and in the Great War, and was knighted for his services. Pelham was a godfather to the writer Pelham Grenville (P.G.) Wodehouse, when he was christened in Guildford in 1881; the writer being given the name Pelham in his honour.

Von Donop was educated at the Royal Somersetshire College in Bath, and attended the Royal Military Academy from 1869 to 1871, from where he was commissioned as lieutenant in the Royal Engineers on 15 December 1871.

He was a prominent batsman both for the Royal Military Academy and for the Royal Engineers. His most noted achievement for the Engineers was a century against I Zingari at Chatham in 1875, in a total of 726 for 8 wickets. Von Donop became a member of the Marylebone Cricket Club (MCC) in 1886, and he was also a member of the Free Foresters.

Noted for his speed at football, he was considered to be 'the best right-winger of his day'. He played in England's 4-2 victory against Scotland on 8 March 1873 at The Oval, and again against Scotland on 6 March 1875 at The Oval in a 2-2 draw. He was on the losing side in the 1874 FA Cup final, before winning the trophy in 1875.

Sir Richard Ruck said of him:

> Von Donop was, in my opinion, in a class quite by himself as a wing forward, the 'Prince of Dribblers' as one of the sporting papers called him. He was constantly being mentioned in the accounts of the matches either for brilliant runs on his own, or perhaps more frequently, for a combined movement with another wing player such as G Barker, J Blackburn or CK Wood. I shall never forget the extraordinary manner in which he seemed to pivot round the opposing players one after another and then finish off with a most accurate shot to the centre.

Von Donop was posted to Bermuda in 1879, along with Lieutenant Charles Wood, and while they were there they won the men's doubles title at the Bermuda Open Tennis Championships. He competed in the All England Lawn Tennis Championships at Wimbledon in 1882, and won the West of England Championships at Bath in 1884. He was also a keen golfer, and was known to try to find the nearest course wherever he was to play a round, even after a hard day's work.

While in charge of the Postal Telegraph Service from 1880 to 1884, von Donop was promoted captain on 15 December 1883. He was posted for active service in the Nile Expedition in the Sudan in 1884, where he was employed as traffic manager of the railway supplying the field forces. From 1889 to 1894 he worked on submarine defences in India, during which time his father died in Bath on 27 January 1890, and he was promoted to major on 6 May 1890.

He married on 10 May 1890, and *John Bull* magazine of 10 May 1890 reported:

> At St Thomas's Cathedral, Bombay, was celebrated recently a remarkably bright and pretty wedding. The bride was Miss Ethel Orr, eldest daughter of Mr J W Orr, Prothonotary, High Court of Bombay. The bridegroom was Major von Donop, RE, eldest son of the late Admiral von Donop. All branches of the legal and military professions were all represented, and added much to the splendour of the scene. The bride wore a dress of white brocade; white satin petticoat, veiled with lisse and Irish point lace, and trimmed with orange blossoms, white heather, and myrtle; her tulle veil was fastened by a diamond ornament; and her necklace and brooch of pearls and moonstones and her splendid bouquet were the gifts of the bridegroom. The bridesmaids were Miss Latham and Miss West, and the groomsmen were Mr Tudor Jones, RE, and Major Lugard, RA. The service was performed by the Ven. Archdeacon Lewis, assisted by the Rev. W W Scott, of Byculla Church.

From 1894 to 1898 Von Donop was employed with the Telegraph Battalion in the 2nd Division, where he supervised the whole of the postal telegraphs south of the River Thames. He was promoted to lieutenant colonel on 23 November 1897, and he was commanding Royal Engineer at Dover, 1888–90. He retired in 1899.

From 1899 to 1913 he was inspecting officer at the Board of Trade, and chief inspecting officer of railways until 1916, when he retired.

Von Donop lived mainly at Camberley, where he enjoyed playing golf and looking after his garden. He died at 11 Montpelier Square in South Kensington, London, on 7 November 1921, aged 70, and he was buried at Mortlake. Among the mourners at his funeral were William Addison, John Blackburn and Henry Olivier.

Charles Knight Wood

Charles Wood played for Royal Engineers in the 1874 and 1875 FA Cup finals, and later saw active service in the Nile Expedition and in the Second Boer War.

Wood was born at Ledbury in Herefordshire, on 1 July 1851, the youngest child in the family of four boys and three girls, born between 1840 and 1851 to Dr Miles Astman Wood (1806–98), and his wife, Annie (formerly Webb, 1810–72), who was the daughter of a Ledbury banker and Justice of the Peace. The family home was at Orchardleigh in Ledbury.

Charles was educated at Cheltenham College from 1868 to December 1869, and at the Royal Military Academy, from where he was commissioned as lieutenant in the Royal Engineers on 6 January 1872.

He played at inside-right for the Royal Engineers in the 1874 and 1875 FA Cup finals; although he did not appear in the photograph of the team. He and Pelham von Donop were said to have formed the most redoubtable right-wing partnership of the day. He was a good all-round sportsman, a fast runner and a 21ft 7in long-jumper. He played cricket for the Royal Engineers, was a good equestrian and an expert canoeist. Wood was posted to Bermuda in 1879, along with Lieutenant Pelham von Donop, and while they were there they won the men's doubles title at the Bermuda Open Tennis Championships.

Having been promoted to captain on 6 January 1884, Wood was posted for active service in the Nile Expedition of 1884–85, where he was employed with the Telegraph Department, in charge of about 1,200 miles of telegraph lines. He led a mounted section of the Telegraph Battalion during the building of the railway from Saukin to Tofrek.

Wood was adjutant of the Royal Engineers Volunteers from 15 May 1889 to 16 September 1894, during which time he was promoted major on 6 May 1891. He was promoted to lieutenant colonel on 1 September 1898.

Wood was posted for active service during the Second Boer War in South Africa, as Commanding Royal Engineer of Colonel Redvers Buller's Natal Field Force from 23 November 1899 to April 1900 during its advance to Ladysmith. Wood took part in the battles of Colenso on 15 December 1899; Spion Kop on 23 to 24 January 1900; Vaal Kranz on 5 to 7 February 1900; Tugela Heights from 14 February to 27 February 1900; and Pieter's Hill on 27 February 1900. The garrison at Ladysmith was finally relieved on 1 March 1900.

In subsequent operations, Wood was present during the engagement at Laing's Nek on 2 to 9 June 1900; Belfast on 21 to 27 August 1900, and Lydenberg on 6 September 1900. For his service he was mentioned in despatches (*London Gazette* on 8 February 1901), and received the Queen's South Africa Medal with Cape Colony, Tugela Heights, Orange Free State, Relief of Ladysmith, Laing's Nek and Belfast clasps.

From 26 April 1900 to 9 January 1901 he was chief engineer on the Staff in Natal. His brother, Elliot, was also a Royal Engineer, who saw active service in Egypt and the Sudan, and was present at the siege of Ladysmith. He became major general and was appointed KCB.

On 30 September 1900, the new Ledbury church clock was completed, the chimes of which were placed in the tower by the Wood family as a memorial to their late father and mother. Colonel Wood returned from South Africa to Ledbury on 22 November that year, where a band and procession escorted him to Orchardleigh, the town being decorated and illuminated. At the market place he was presented with a commemorative illuminated address.

Wood retired in December 1904, and became secretary of the Herefordshire Territorial Institution from its establishment until he was aged over 70. He remained fit, and it is reported that at the age of 52 he cycled 162 miles on a route he had never travelled before. He also enjoyed the arts, and acted in a charity performance at the Kemble Theatre in Hereford shortly before he died.

His son, Lieutenant Charles Knight Wood, was killed in action on 3 August 1918, while serving with the Army Service Corps during the Great War.

General Wood died of bronchial pneumonia at The Moor in Bodenham near Hereford on 12 February 1923, aged 72 – just two months before the first Wembley FA Cup final – and he was buried at St Mary the Virgin Church in Humber near Hereford.

John Edward Blackburn

John Blackburn played for the Royal Engineers in the 1874 FA Cup final, and he was selected to play for Scotland in the second official international in 1873.

Blackburn was born in the parish of St Cuthbert in Edinburgh on 30 April 1851, the oldest son of four in the family of nine children, all born in Edinburgh between 1848 and 1867 to Robert Bogle Blackburn (1821–75) and his wife, Rebecca Leslie (formerly Gilles, 1788–1864). His father was a member of the Scottish Bar, an Advocate Deputy and Sheriff of Stirling and Linlithgow; and his uncle, Lord Blackburn, was a Lord of Appeal in Ordinary, 'one of the greatest names in the history of

English law'. At the time of the 1861 census the family address was at Edinburgh St Cuthbert.

Blackburn was educated at Trinity College in Glenalmond, at Eton College and at Wimbledon College. He entered the Royal Military Academy at Woolwich in 1869, and was commissioned as lieutenant in the Royal Engineers on 15 December 1871.

Noted for his accurate ball distribution from the right wing, Blackburn was selected to play for Scotland in their first trip to The Oval on 8 March 1873, where they lost 4-2. Scotland could only afford to send seven players and an official to London, so John and Henry Renny-Tailyour were selected to make up the team because they were posted in Chatham at the time. He played for the Royal Engineers in the 1874 final.

Blackburn saw active service in the Egypt Campaign in 1882, for which he received the Egypt Medal with Tel-el-Kebir clasp and the Khedive's Bronze Star. On being promoted to captain on 15 December 1883, he served in the Nile Expedition of 1884–85, for which he received the Sudan Medal, and he remained in the Sudan for another year. He was appointed major on 2 July 1890, lieutenant colonel on 16 April 1898 and colonel in 1902. He retired from military service in 1908.

He was recalled for active service in the Great War, 1915–1916, for which he was appointed Companion of the Bath (CB) in the 1917 New Year Honours' List.

Colonel Blackburn represented the Royal Engineers at the funeral of Pelham von Donop in 1921, and died at 183 Ashley Gardens in Victoria, London, on 29 September 1927, aged 77.

Herbert Edward Rawson

Herbert Rawson played for the Royal Engineers in the 1874 final, and he scored at least one goal to help his club on their way to winning the Cup in 1875; he scored six goals in the 1875–76 Cup, and at least two in the following year's competition. He played for England in 1875. He saw distinguished service in the South Africa (Boer) War of 1899–1902.

Rawson was born on 3 September 1852 at Port Louis in British Mauritius. He was the second son of Sir Rawson William Rawson, KCMG, CB, and his wife, Sofia Mary Anne, daughter of the Honourable Reverend H. Ward. His father was treasurer and paymaster general in Mauritius. Two of his younger brothers played in FA Cup finals. William Stepney was born in Cape Town in 1854 and played for Oxford University in the 1874 and 1876 finals, and Frederick Lawrence was born in Westminster in 1859 and played for Clapham Rovers in the 1879 final.

Herbert was educated at Westminster School, where he became the captain of the football team, and attended the Royal Military Academy at Woolwich. When his father was working overseas he stayed with his Uncle Frederick and Aunty Frances Jane Hewlett at St Augustine's Rectory at Ticehurst in East Sussex.

Rawson was a holder of the Royal Engineers Fowke Medal, which was established by the Institution of the Royal Engineers in 1865 as a memorial prize for young officers at the School of Military Engineering. The inscription on the medal reads: 'Memorial Medal Established by the Officers of the Royal Engineers as an Architectural Prize in the Corps'. Francis Fowke (1823–65) was an Irish engineer and architect, who designed the Royal Albert Hall and the Victoria & Albert Museum.

Rawson was commissioned as lieutenant in the Royal Engineers on 12 September 1872 and was involved in submarine mining activities in 1874.

As a member of the Marylebone Cricket Club (MCC), he kept wicket for Kent in September 1873, against W.G. Grace's Gravesend XI. He took four wickets but did not score any runs. He also played for the Free Foresters, and he was president of the Old Westminsters CC.

Rawson represented England in their fourth international match against Scotland on 6 March 1875 at The Oval, which ended in a 2-2 draw. His brother, William, was also selected, and it was the first occasion that two brothers played for England in the same match.

His older brother, William Stepney (1854–32), played for Oxford University, and at 19 years and 151 days he was the youngest player in the final. Another brother, Frederick Lawrence Rawson, played for Clapham Rovers in the 1879 final. Sir Richard Ruck said: 'Rawson, an Old Westminster boy, was a very expert dribbler and centre-forward.'

On 8 July 1875, he married Elizabeth Georgina Stuart Armstrong, daughter of Richard Owen, JP, of County Dublin, at Christ Church in Kingstown, Co. Dublin.

In 1877 Rawson was employed in the maintaining of fortifications at the Hamilton Dockyard in Bermuda. He was employed at the Treasury from 1880 to 1884, and then he was posted to Malta, where he was again employed in the maintaining of defences. A programme to improve Malta's defences was under way to protect the dockyard and harbour from attack. He was in Canada 1885 to 1889, where he raised a submarine mining militia. He was secretary of the Royal Engineers Committee and the War Office Committee from 1890 to 1894.

On 6 October 1899 Rawson was posted for active service during the Second Boer War in South Africa. He was commanding Royal Engineer on the lines of communication in Natal, and then CRE of the Natal District. He was present at the Relief of Ladysmith, including operations on Tugela Heights from 14 to 17 February 1900, and at the action on Pieter's Hill. He served in operations in the Transvaal in May and June 1900 and in the operations in Natal from March to June 1900, including the action at Laing's Nek. His last actions were on the frontier of Zululand and Natal in September and October 1901, where he took part in the battle of Itala in September 1901. He was mentioned in despatches eight times, and General Redvers Buller VC stated

> Lt-Colonel H Rawson, CRE, who has charge of the whole of Engineering works on the Lines of Communication, has been indefatigable; his technical knowledge, his vigour of mind and body, and his tact have overcome every difficulty; I can confidently recommend him for your most favourable recommendation.

For his service Rawson was awarded the Queen's South Africa Medal, 1899–1902 with Tugela Heights, Relief of Ladysmith, Transvaal and Laing's Nek clasps, and the King's South Africa Medal with South Africa, 1901, and South Africa, 1902 clasps. He was appointed Commander of the Bath, Military (CB) on 13 October 1902.

After the war Rawson was appointed as a member of the Natal Defences Commission in 1902 and, as the chief engineer and commanding Royal Engineer in South Africa from 1905 to 1907, he was on the Commission for Natal Native Affairs, 1906–07. He was chief engineer, Northern Command from 1907 until he retired in 1909.

A London Freemason, he was vice-president of the Royal Meteorological Society, a fellow of the Royal Geographical Society (FRGS), a Fellow of the Royal Horticultural Society (FRHS) and he was on the council of the African Aeronautical Society. He wrote many articles for the *Royal United Services Institute Journal*, and several other publications. He lived at Home Close in Heronsgate, Rickmansworth, where he was a Justice of the Peace for Hertfordshire, and he was one of the first people in the Rickmansworth area to have a telephone installed.

He died at 46 St George's Road in Westminster on 18 October 1924, aged 72. His medal set and miniatures were sold at auction in 2013.

Henry Dacres Olivier

Henry Olivier played for the Royal Engineers in the 1874 FA Cup final, and later had a distinguished military career in India.

Olivier was born at Court Hill in Potterne near Devizes, Wiltshire, on 22 October 1850, the oldest of four sons in the family of eight children of the Reverend Henry Arnold Olivier (1826–1912) and his wife, Anne Elizabeth, daughter of Joseph Arnould and Elizabeth Hardcastle. The Reverend Olivier was rector at St Peter's Church in Poulshot near Devizes, and he was High Sheriff of Wiltshire in 1843. Henry's brother, Sydney, was the first and last Baron Olivier, and the eminent English actor Sir Laurence Olivier was his nephew.

Henry was educated at Haileybury Imperial Services College near Hertford, where he was noted for his rugby abilities, and at the Royal Military Academy, from where he was commissioned as lieutenant in the Royal Engineers on 15 December 1871.

Described as 'a very useful centre-forward', Olivier was often mentioned in newspaper reports. He went on the Royal Engineers tour of the north in 1873, where he scored two goals in the first match. In the year after his Cup final appearance he qualified as an Associated Member of the Institute of Civil Engineers (AMICE) and he was posted to India. He was employed by the Bombay Public Works Department from 1 June 1875.

Olivier was posted for active service in the Second Afghan War of 1878–80. He was appointed executive engineer and consulting engineer for Bombay railways in March 1884, and then he joined the Sudan railways in 1885, to work on improving the railway system after the Nile Expedition. On returning to India, from 1889 to 1891 he was under-secretary to the Bombay Public Works Department; from August 1894 he was agent to the Bombay, Baroda, and Central India Railway Company; and from September 1900 he was superintendent engineer. He retired in August 1904.

Olivier represented the Royal Engineers at the funeral of Pelham von Donop in 1921, and he died at the family home of Shapley Hill in Winchfield near Basingstoke, Hampshire, on 30 March 1935, aged 84. He was buried at St Mary's Church in Winchfield.

Thomas Digby

Thomas Digby played in the 1874 FA Cup final, and saw two tours of active service on the North-West Frontier of India.

Digby was born on 20 October 1851, and was educated at the Royal Military Academy, from where he was commissioned as lieutenant in the Royal Engineers on 2 May 1872.

He made a good reputation for himself as a half-back, considering he had a relatively short football career. He was said to deserve 'extra praise' for his FA Cup final performance in 1874.

Digby was posted for active service in the Second Afghan War of 1878–80, including the action at Bhesud, where he was mentioned in despatches. He was promoted captain on 2 May 1884 and major on 13 August 1891.

Tochi Valley Expedition on the North-West Frontier of India, 1897

Digby was posted for active service during the severe unrest in that region, and was a member of the expedition into the Tochi Valley in Waziristan. The Madda Khel tribesmen of the Waziris had begun a rebellion in June 1897, and the British assembled the Tochi Field Force in response. The rebellion was put down by October 1897. Digby was promoted to lieutenant colonel on 8 March 1899, and he retired with the rank of colonel.

Digby was injured in a bicycle accident near Westward Ho! golf course on 29 May 1919, and died at his home, Woodlands, Orchard Hill, Northam, Bideford in Devon, on 10 June, aged 67. He was buried at Northam Church.

* * *

At the end of 1873 the Royal Engineers became the first team to embark on a tour, when they played games at Sheffield, Derby and Nottingham. It was stated that the Engineers wanted to introduce the combination game to a wider audience.

In his 1928 article, Richard Ruck stated:

> The chief feature of the 1873–74 season was perhaps the Northern tour of the RE, which was undertaken at the invitation of the Northern Clubs, the most important of which was Sheffield. This club, which possessed an unbeaten record in the North of England, wished to measure its strength against the best of the Southern Clubs, the arrangement being that the game was to be played half-time under each set of rules, the chief difference in the Sheffield Rules being the absence of

off-side. Matches were also arranged with South Derbyshire and Nottingham under the usual Association code; the whole tour to be completed in four days (including Sunday): pretty strenuous work.

These matches resulted in a victory for the RE in each case. Four goals to one against Sheffield [it was actually 4-0]; and two goals to one against both South Derbyshire and Nottingham; the RE suffering somewhat from staleness and injuries in the last two matches.

Very large crowds assembled to see these matches, and the RE were most hospitably entertained, not only by their adversaries, but also by a highly-distinguished officer of the RE, Sir William Abney FRS, who had a house in Derbyshire, where he put up a large portion of the RE team.

I have already given a description of the games played by the RE during this tour, extracted from the Sheffield local Press, who gave special praise to Von Donop, Wood, Rawson, Renny-Tailyour, Goodwyn and Olivier, but I expect that the merit might have been divided pretty equally among the whole team.

A very hearty appreciation from the Sheffield executive closes the account of this tour, which was, no doubt, very useful in furthering the interests of the Association game in the North. The RE enjoyed their outing, but vowed that never again would they attempt to play three matches in four days.

The players who embarked on the tour were: *Goalkeeper* – Captain William Merriman; *Half-backs* – Major Francis Arthur Marindin (captain), Lieutenant Alfred George Goodwyn; *Cover-goal* – Lieutenant Thomas Digby, Lieutenant George Hamilton Sim; *Forwards* – Lieutenant Pelham George von Donop, Lieutenant Henry Dacres Olivier, Lieutenant John Edward Blackburn, Lieutenant Charles Knight Wood, Lieutenant Henry Edward Rawson, Lieutenant Henry Waugh Renny-Tailyour, Lieutenant Charles Cunnyngham Ellis, Lieutenant George Turner Jones.

Although it has been noted how few defending players were used at that time, it is interesting to note how one of the Sheffield reporters described how the Engineers prevented a goal. 'Their defence of the Citadel was remarkable, and in one case of more than ordinary danger the whole eleven were discovered in the mouth of the goal, much to the amusement of the spectators. The ball was no sooner out of danger than out went the skirmishers to return again if need be.'

There are numerous reports of the day confirming that teams simply crowded their goal area to prevent a score.

Saturday, 20 December 1873: the Royal Engineers versus Sheffield Association at Bramall Lane. The Royal Engineers won 4-0 with goals by Herbert Rawson, Pelham von Donop and Henry Olivier (2). Henry Renny-Tailyour acted as umpire for the Royal Engineers.

A local newspaper report on the Sheffield game stated:

> Both the Sheffield Association and the Engineers were playing under considerable disadvantages, the Engineers losing the services of Mr Leach, one of their best players, who unfortunately got his wrist broken in their last match against the Old Wykehamists, and Mr Renny-Tailyour, who was also injured in the same match, was not sufficiently recovered to take part in the contest, but officiated as umpire for his side.

There was an interesting statement made by a Sheffield reporter concerning incidents when the ball went over the 'touch line' while they were playing under Association rules in the second half:

> At this part of the match the ball was frequently out, and much valuable time lost by throwing it, which is quite obviated by the Sheffield system, which awards a kick-in as a penalty for sending the ball out, a much more sensible arrangement than the throw-in, which is sometimes a penalty instead of an advantage to the side claiming the throw-in.

The report stated:

> The match was undoubtedly the best ever played at Bramall Lane. The Engineers are by far the best trained and most evenly-balanced team that have ever visited Sheffield, not having a weak player in the eleven. The spectators evinced the greatest interest throughout, and everyone spoke in the highest terms of the treat provided for them.

After the game the players and several friends sat down to a 'sumptuous repast' at the Adelphi Hotel. I noted the number of military references the writer made during his report – the goal was 'the fortress'; the Engineers were 'the enemy'; an attack was 'an onslaught'; and a shot at goal was referred to as 'bombarding it'.

* * *

Monday, 22 December 1873: the Royal Engineers versus South Derbyshire at the South Derbyshire Cricket Ground. The Royal Engineers won 2-1, with goals by Herbert Rawson and Pelham von Donop. Charles Wood acted as umpire for the Royal Engineers.

A local newspaper reported:

> This important match was played at the South Derbyshire Cricket Ground on Monday afternoon. There was a large attendance of spectators. After the Royal Engineers thrashing of Sheffield on Saturday last so easily, Derbyshire felt rather nervous, particularly on its being known that Mr Owen, the best man in the North of England, could not play for his county. Although the Chatham defenders won the toss, and the wind was in their favour, Derbyshire made a gallant fight, and only lost by one goal.
>
> The Derbyshire captain (Houseman) kicked-off at 2:15 pm, and after a quarter of an hour's lively play the Engineers secured a goal in a scrimmage; Lt H E Rawson being the kicker. The Derbyshire team had now the wind in their favour and they very quickly secured a goal, and that through the valuable assistance and playing of H F Gadsby. Up to half-time no further score was made by either side.
>
> The Engineers now began playing on their own rules, and still had the wind in their favour, and in ten minutes Lieutenant P G Von Donop secured, after a hard struggle a second goal. The Derbyshire team had now the wind in their favour, and up to time being called play was 'fast and furious,' but no score was made.
>
> The Derbyshire players throughout charged terrifically, which spoiled the grand dribbling exhibited by the Engineers at Sheffield. On the part of Derbyshire, Shuker, as half-back, kicked magnificently, and Gretton was a wonderful goalkeeper, his powers being very often put to the test. Gadsby, Abney and Tomlinson worked wonderfully well in the middle of the field. Generally, the Engineers had a little the best of the game. Von Donop and Tailyour being conspicuous as forwards, and Goodwyn, as usual, playing superbly as back.
>
> Before the game the players had a capital luncheon at Mr King's Bell Hotel, and after the play they enjoyed a splendid banquet at the same hotel.

* * *

Tuesday, 23 December 1873: the Royal Engineers versus Nottingham Forest at Trent Bridge. The Royal Engineers won 2-1, with goals by Pelham von Donop and C.F. Ellis.

The local report stated:

> A second match was played by the Engineers at Nottingham on the following day, when, by a strange coincidence they were again victorious by two goals to one. As at Derby, there was a grand number of spectators at the Trent Bridge ground, in spite of the wind being rather high at times.
>
> The Engineers started successfully by winning the toss, and elected to play with the wind, the ball being kicked-off at 12:40pm. They worked well together and the ball was soon placed to their credit by Von Donop. A second goal was quickly scored by the Engineers on the change of ends, but disallowed as the 'off-side' rule had been infringed. The resistance offered by the Engineers was of the most determined description; S W Widdowson being well to the fore.
>
> The Royal Engineers, however, more than once threatened the home party's fortress, the vigilance of Tomlinson and White turning the ball aside. A little before half-past-one, Spencer conducted the ball into the Engineers quarters, and being well backed-up by Widdowson, succeeded in sending it between the posts, thus bringing the score level. On ends being re-changed the Engineers again had the wind in their favour, and, by a capital rush, scored a second goal. Ellis giving the final kick.
>
> The game was shortly after brought to a conclusion and the Royal Engineers hailed the winners by two goals to one. We are glad to state that Lieutenant Renny-Tailyour was able to take part in both the above matches.

As a point of note, Lieutenant George Turner Jones, who had passed out of the Royal Military Academy on 9 January 1873, served in the Afghan War of 1878–80 with the Bombay Sappers and Miners in the Quetta Column. On 12 August a party had been sent out to demolish some walls that were being used as cover by the enemy. On this occasion it was recorded in the official account that Lieutenants Waller and Jones RE gallantly brought in a wounded man of the 19th Native Infantry under heavy fire. They were both recommended for the Victoria Cross by General Brooke, and would doubtless have received it had not that gallant officer, who was an eyewitness of the deed, been killed at Deh Khoja four days afterwards.

It is also interesting to note that Nottingham Forest, who won the FA Cup in 1898 and 1959, are the only club to have played FA Cup matches in all four home countries. In 1885 they travelled to Glasgow to play a replay against Queen's Park; in 1889 they travelled to Belfast to play Linfield Athletic for another replay, although Linfield withdrew and played a friendly match instead; and in 1922 they were drawn to play Cardiff City in the Welsh capital. They have, of course, played many FA Cup ties in England.

Chapter 6

The 1874–75 Season

Twenty-nine teams entered the fourth competition. It was to become the most successful season the Royal Engineers would ever enjoy, and they defeated three FA Cup-winning clubs to get to the final.

The Royal Engineers opened their account by defeating Great Marlow by three clear goals, Lieutenant Pelham von Donop being recorded as one of the scorers. Wanderers opened their account with a 16-0 thrashing of Farningham, a club that was established from the village cricket club near Sevenoaks in Kent. Bob Kingsford scored five of the goals, which was a record for the club for one match. There were straight wins for Oxford University, Woodford Wells, Clapham Rovers and Maidenhead, but Cambridge University beat Crystal Palace after a replay, and the tie between Old Etonians and their near neighbours Swifts went to a third game before the Etonians triumphed.

In the second round, the Royal Engineers entertained Cambridge University at Chatham. It was the first of three FA Cup matches they would contest with Cambridge, and on this occasion they won easily, 5-0, with goals from Lieutenants Henry Lyle Mulholland; Herbert Rawson and William Stafford. Wanderers put five past Barnes, and there were other wins for Shropshire Wanderers, Clapham Rovers, Maidenhead and Woodford Wells.

The Engineers won their third-round match at Chatham against Clapham Rovers by the odd goal in five, with at least two of the goals coming from Lieutenants Alexander Mein and William Stafford. Old Etonians beat Maidenhead, and Shropshire Wanderers defeated Woodford Wells after a replay. The surprise of the round happened when Oxford University defeated Wanderers for the second year running.

In the semi-finals, Old Etonians reached the final by beating Shropshire Wanderers 1-0, while the Engineers and Oxford University drew 1-1 after extra time. Captain Henry Renny-Tailyour had scored twice in the two previous semi-finals the Royal Engineers had appeared in, and he kept this up exceptional record by scoring the goal in the first meeting at the Parks in Oxford and the only goal of the match in the replay.

After the 1874 final the Engineers' secretary had recorded: 'There seems indeed a strange fatality about our winning the cup.' Sir Richard Ruck played in the final, and he stated:

> We looked upon the University as our most formidable competitor that year and as the accounts showed, it was anybody's game. A little luck would have turned the scales either way; perhaps we had it, but, as reported, the RE team combined together in their very best manner and just managed to pull through. The last match against Oxford, after a tie, was described by the press as one of the finest ever played in the competition for the cup ...

Royal Engineers 1 Old Etonians 1

(after extra time)

The final took place at The Oval on 13 March 1875, with Captain Merriman and Lieutenant Renny-Tailyour now having both played in all three FA Cup finals of 1872, 1874 and 1875. The referee was Charles Alcock, and John Hardinge Giffard was again the umpire for the Engineers. Although it was a very windy day, 2,000 spectators turned up.

Having won the toss, the Etonians chose to play with the wind behind them, but the Engineers managed to keep the Etonians at bay for thirty minutes, until they conceded a corner kick. Alex Bonsor took the kick, and according to *The Field* '... a gust catching the ball well-aimed by Bonsor carried it between the Engineers posts, just out of reach of the goalkeeper.' In fact, this goal should not have been given, because it was against the rules to score a goal direct from a corner kick until the rules were changed in 1927.

Nevertheless, the teams changed ends, and with the wind in their favour, after only five minutes of pressure from the Engineers' forwards, Lieutenant Pelham von Donop made a run down the right wing and centred the ball to Lieutenant Henry Renny-Tailyour, whereupon it glanced off his knee and went through the posts.

Lieutenant George Sim took everyone by surprise when he did the then-unusual move of heading the ball. Sir Richard Ruck stated:

'I believe, [Sim] was the first player who made a practice of heading the ball, a method now brought to such a pitch of perfection.' The Engineers had had to play against a strong wind for all but five minutes of normal time, and for half of the thirty minutes of extra time, after which the score remained a draw.

Sir Richard reported:

> The first match against the Etonians was spoilt by a very high wind in which we were placed at a curious disadvantage, as we had to play an hour and forty minutes against a strong wind, and only twenty minutes with it in our favour. But such is the luck of the game and we managed to make it a draw by one goal each.

The Field for 13 March 1875 reported on the game, a copy of the article being kept in the Royal Engineers' club book:

> After a competition extending over just five months, three clubs [it was, of course, only two] were left in to contend for the final tie of the cup, recently relinquished by Oxford University, and held by the Wanderers during the first two years of its institution. Saturday last was the day chosen for the meeting, and as the two clubs were in public formed evenly matched it was not surprising that the Surrey Cricket Ground at Kennington should have been visited by a very large number of spectators, in the anticipation of a stiff fight. Careful preparation had made the ground in fine condition; but the weather was not so favourable as it might have been, as a very strong breeze from the north-east blew straight down the ground and spoiled the play of the backs materially at times.
>
> The Engineers losing the toss, had therefore a serious drawback on the onset, and at half past three o'clock Onslow kicked-off on their behalf against the wind. At first their backs were altogether unable to make headway, and the Etonians, by vigorous forward play, kept the ball well up in their lines, R H Benson allowing a goal chance to escape. Not long after this a fine shot by A F Kinnaird almost eluded the vigilance of Major Merriman, and it was only owing to the vigorous rushes of Rawson, Von Donop, Renny-Tailyour and Stafford, that the ball was at last removed into the quarters of the Old Etonians. For half-an-hour the Engineers faced the wind without loss, but here a corner kick fell to the Etonians, and a

gust catching the ball well-aimed by Bonsor carried it between the Engineers' posts just out of reach of their goalkeeper.

Ends were changed, but the Etonians soon had their success neutralised, as within five minutes their backs were charged in the act of kicking by the Sapper forwards, and in the scrimmage the ball was taken safely into the Etonians goal.

With the second change of positions the Engineers had again to cope with the wind, but on the other hand the Etonians were severely handicapped owing to an accident to C J Ottaway, who had to retire with a sprained ankle. Fifty-five minutes remained, but still nothing more was achieved by either side, though Mein, Rawson, Von Donop, Wood and Stratford of the one side, and Kinnaird, Strong, Benson, Patton and Bonsor of the other, worked untiringly up.

With one goal to each club at the end of the regulation period of an hour and a half it was agreed to play on for an additional half hour in the hope of a settlement. This extra period produced some of the best individual play of the match, notably some good runs by Mein for the Engineers, and by Patton and Kinnaird for the Etonians, but, despite the most vigorous efforts of the forwards, the half hour expired with the game still undecided. The back play of Onslow for the Engineers was very neat and effective, and without doubt the feature of the match.

Royal Engineers 2 Old Etonians 0

A replay was arranged for three days later, and this time 3,000 spectators turned up to watch the game. The Old Etonians brought in Captain Henry Home Drummond-Moray of the Scots Guards in goal for the replay, to replace Charles Farmer – who moved up to play at centre-forward.

The toss was won by the Royal Engineers for the only time, and the Old Etonians kicked off. After fifteen minutes, Fred Patton, one of the Etonian forwards, handled the ball in front of his own goal. The Engineers took the free kick and rushed the ball through the goal. The Etonians had an appeal for offside allowed, so the ball was returned to the same place and the kick was taken again. The ball was rushed through the posts again and this time the goal was allowed; eventually being credited to Lieutenant Henry Renny-Tailyour.

After several minutes of good defensive play by both teams, a second Engineers goal was disallowed for offside, but after seventy-five minutes the Engineers began to dominate the game and Lieutenant Henry Renny-Tailyour scored his second goal.

The Field reported on the replay:

> On Tuesday last the tie was played off at the Oval, the Engineers being represented as before, while the Old Etonians had several changes that greatly crippled their team. Kenyon-Slaney, Ottaway and Benson of the forwards were unable to present, so that T Hammond, A Lubbock and C E Farmer, had to take their places, while F H Wilson was advanced to help Lubbock at half-back in the absence of A C Thompson, and M Farrer and Captain Drummond-Moray had to officiate as back and goalkeeper in lieu of F H Wilson and C E Farmer, promoted to the front.
>
> There was very little wind this time so that the choice of position was of little moment. In spite of their comparative weakness, the Old Etonians played up so pluckily that for a long time the Engineers were unable to make any decided advance. At last, an unfortunate piece of handling by T Hammond close to the Etonian posts gave a free kick to the Engineers, and, with a vigorous dash, they carried the ball between the Eton posts.
>
> The change of ends produced little change in the aspect of affairs, though the Etonians had one or two corner kicks, and once Farmer nearly secured the downfall of the military goal. Before long the ball once again found its way between the Eton posts; but an appeal for off-side was allowed, and the score disallowed.
>
> Without further event the game continued until within a quarter of an hour of time, when a general rush of the Engineers forwards enabled Renny-Tailyour to secure the second goal for his side. The Etonians worked hard until the end, but without effect, and time was called, leaving the Engineers winners of the cup by two goals to none. The game was very slow in comparison with that of the previous Saturday, the kicking generally being very erratic.

It was noted that the Royal Engineers had played against a strong wind for 100 minutes of the first match, and for the next season the rules were changed and the teams only changed ends at half-time. The teams were:

Royal Engineers: *Goalkeeper* – Major William Merriman (captain); *Full-back* – Lieutenant George Hamilton Sim; *Half-backs* – Lieutenant Gerald Charles Penrice Onslow, Lieutenant Richard Mathews Ruck; *Forwards*:

Right – Lieutenant Pelham George von Donop, Lieutenant Charles Knight Wood; *Centre* – Lieutenant Herbert Edward Rawson, Lieutenant William Francis Howard Stafford, Lieutenant Henry Waugh Renny-Tailyour: *Left* – Lieutenant Alexander Lechmere Mein, Lieutenant Cecil Vernon Wingfield-Stratford.

Old Etonians: *Goalkeeper* – Charles Edward Farmer; *Defence* – Francis Heathcote Wilson, Albert Childers Meysey-Thompson, Edgar Lubbock; Forwards: *Left* – Arthur Fitzgerald Kinnaird (captain), Robert Henry 'Robin' Benson; *Centre* – William Slaney Kenyon-Slaney, Frederick Joseph Patton, Alexander George Bonsor; *Left* – Cuthbert John Ottaway, James Henry Strong.

For the replay the Royal Engineers kept the same team. For Old Etonians Albert Thompson, Robin Benson, William Kenyon-Slaney and Cuthbert Ottaway were replaced by Henry Home Drummond-Moray, Matthew George Farrer, Thomas Hammond and Alfred Lubbock.

Royal Engineers Matches

1st Round	7 November 1874	Great Marlow	won 3-0 at Chatham
2nd Round	5 December 1874	Cambridge University	won 5-0 at Chatham
3rd Round	30 January 1875	Clapham Rovers	won 3-2 at Chatham
Semi-final	27 February 1875	Oxford University	drew 1-1 (aet)
Replay	5 March 1875	Oxford University	won 1-0 at Chatham
Final	13 March 1875	Old Etonians	drew 1-1 at The Oval
Replay	16 March 1875	Old Etonians	won 2-0 at The Oval

The Royal Engineers did not lose a game all season. They won seventeen and drew three, scoring forty-one goals and conceding eight.

Royal Engineers Players

George Hamilton Sim

George Sim played for the Royal Engineers in the 1875 Cup-winning team, and later saw active service in Afghanistan, the Sudan and during the Second Anglo-Boer War in South Arica.

The Royal Military Academy at Woolwich, which came to be known as 'The Shop', was established in 1741, for the training of commissioned officers in the Corps of Royal Engineers or the Royal Regiment of Artillery. It saw the beginning of the careers of many famous military figures, including Lieutenant John Rouse Merriott Chard, who was awarded the Victoria Cross for valour during the defence of Rorke's Drift in the Zulu War of 1879; and General Charles George 'Chinese' Gordon. Ironically, several Royal Engineers who had entered the Academy after him and played in FA Cup finals were on the Nile Expedition in 1885, which attempted to relieve him from the siege of Khartoum. The Academy ceased its activity just before the start of the Second World War in 1939.

The famous gas towers at Kennington Oval in the 1960s when not much had changed at the ground since the 1870s. It was the scene of numerous FA Cup matches from 1872 until 1892, when the committee at the Surrey County Cricket Club stopped the Football Association from using it because they were ruining the pitch.

A contemporary sketch of the first-ever official international match in the world, played between England and Scotland at the West of Scotland Cricket Ground in Partick on 30 November 1872. The match was goalless. William Maynard of the 1st Surrey Rifles played in the forward line in the first half and as goalkeeper in the second half.

The Scotland team that played England in the second official international match. It included two Chatham-based Royal Engineers officers, Lieutenant Henry Renny-Tailyour (standing, third from left) and Lieutenant John Blackburn (seated, second from left). 'Renny' scored the first-ever Scottish international goal during the match, but England won by four goals to two.

C. W. Greenwood.

A. Meysey-Thompson. W. H. Ady. W. S. Kenyon-Slaney. J. H. Ridley. R. Meysey-Thompson.

E. W. Hamilton. THE HOUSE C. H. H. Parry. M. Horner.

J. R. Sturgis. CHALLENGE CUP. T. Carr-Lloyd.

To face page 10.

It is not surprising that the [William] Evans House football team won the 1865 Eton House Challenge Cup, as four members went on to play in FA Cup finals, all four of them being on winning teams. They all played together in the 1876 Old Etonians team. William Kenyon-Slaney (in the middle of the back row) played for Wanderers in the 1873 final, and for Old Etonians in 1875 and 1876. Albert Meysey-Thompson (far right of middle row, wearing cap) played for Wanderers in the first-ever FA Cup final of 1872, and for Old Etonians in 1875 and 1876. His brother Charles (at the far right of back row, wearing cap) played for Wanderers in the 1873 final and for Old Etonians in the 1876 final. Julian Sturgis (reclining at front left) was an American born in Boston who played for Wanderers in the 1873 final, and for Old Etonians in 1876.

Some of the dejected Royal Engineers squad pictured after their defeat in the 1872 FA Cup final. *Back, left to right:* Captain William Merriman, Lieutenant William St George Ord, Captain Francis Arthur Marindin, Lieutenant George William Addison, Lieutenant Hugh Mitchell. *Front, left to right:* Lieutenant Chandos Hoskyns, Lieutenant Henry Renny-Tailyour, Lieutenant Edmund William Creswell, Lieutenant Alfred George Goodwyn, Lieutenant George Barker, Lieutenant Henry Bayard Rich.

Francis Marindin (1838–1900), known as 'The Major' because of his distinguished service in the Royal Engineers. He was chairman of the Football Association for sixteen years, during which time he was involved in the founding of the Football Association Challenge Cup, played in two finals and refereed a further nine. He became an inspector at the Board of Trade, originating several important railway reforms and developing London's lighting system. He was knighted for his service to society and the Crown. He was buried at Crombie Old Parish Churchyard on the Craigflower Estate in Torryburn near Dunfermline, which unfortunately has been allowed to fall into ruin.

Henry Renny-Tailyour is considered by many to be the finest all-round sportsman ever produced by a military unit. He played in the 1872 and 1874 FA Cup finals, finally winning the trophy in 1875, one of only two players to appear in all three finals. He scored Scotland's first-ever international goal.

Herbert Muirhead is seen here on the far right of the picture, with his sister, Beatrix Marion (far left), and his brother, Francis Montague, in the middle. The picture was painted by Julian E. Drummond in 1853, when Herbert was 3 years old.

The Royal Engineers squad that embarked on the tour of the north during the Christmas period in 1873 in an attempt to introduce their style of play. They took part in three matches in four days and won them all. *Far back, left to right:* Lieutenant Henry Dacres Olivier; *Back row, left to right:* Lieutenants George Turner Jones, Henry Waugh Renny-Tailyour, Major Francis Arthur Marindin (captain), Captain William Merriman, Lieutenant Charles Cunnyngham Ellis. *Seated, left to right:* Lieutenants John Edward Blackburn, Henry Edward Rawson, Thomas Digby, Charles Knight Wood; *Seated on the floor, left to right:* Lieutenants Pelham George von Donop, George Hamilton Sim, Alfred George Goodwyn.

An undated photograph of the Royal Engineers football team. Based on the dejected appearance of the players, it was probably taken after the 1874 FA Cup final, which was the only match they lost that season.

The Royal Engineers pictured in 1875, having become the first and only military team to win the FA Cup. *Standing on the back row, left to right:* Lieutenants Henry Lyle Mulholland, Gerald Charles Penrice Onslow, William Francis Howard Stafford, Herbert Edward Rawson, Alexander Lechmere Mein and Cecil Vernon Wingfield-Stratford; *Seated on chairs, left to right:* Lieutenant Richard Matthews Ruck, Captain William Merriman, Lieutenants Henry Waugh Renny-Tailyour, Pelham George von Donop; *Seated on the ground, left to right:* Lieutenants George Hamilton Sim, George Turner Jones. Lieutenant Charles Knight Wood played in the 1874 and 1875 finals but does not appear in the photograph. Lieutenants Stafford, Rawson, Ruck and Sim were still serving Engineers.

William Kenyon-Slaney of the Grenadier Guards, pictured in 1886. He played in three FA Cup finals, and scored the first-ever goal in an international match. He was present at the decisive battle at Tel-el-Kebir in Egypt in 1882, and was a Shropshire MP for twenty-one years.

Pelham von Donop played in the 1874 and 1875 FA Cup finals, and was the only British Army officer to be twice capped for England. He was a good all-round sportsman who competed at the Wimbledon Lawn Tennis Championships in 1882. He saw active service in the Nile Expedition of 1884–85, and became chief inspecting officer of railways.

Richard Ruck was one of three Welsh-born men who played for the Royal Engineers in FA Cup finals; one of the others being his younger brother, Oliver. At the outbreak of the Great War he was appointed General Officer Commanding the London Defences. He was created KCB, CB and CMG. He never saw active service, but his domestic life was one of drama.

Henry Drummond-Moray played in goal for Old Etonians in the replay of the 1875 FA Cup final. He served with the Scots Guards and was a Member of Parliament for Perthshire.

Francis George Bond played in the 1878 FA Cup final, after which he fought on various fronts in defence of the Empire. In the following year he served in the Zulu War, and in Egypt in 1882. During active service on the North-West Frontier of India he took part in the Hazara Expedition of 1891, and in the Tirah campaign of 1897–98. He served in the Boer War in 1899–1900, and in the Great War. He was knighted for his highly distinguished military service.

Charles Haynes played in the 1878 FA Cup final, and less than a year later he saw active service in the Zulu War. During the operations around Eshowe, he used his practical ingenuity to construct heliograph apparatus to reflect the sun's rays and keep contact with the troops cut off in the Eshowe garrison.

Frederick Crofton Heath-Caldwell was the son of an admiral. He played in the 1878 FA Cup final, and later saw active service in Egypt in 1882, the Sudan in 1885 and in the Second Boer War. In retirement he was a magistrate in Chester.

Even in such company as this book has displayed, Welshman Morgan Lindsay led a comparatively extremely interesting life. He was on the 1878 Royal Engineers FA Cup team. He saw active service in the two campaigns against the Boers, in the Sudan, and during the Great War, and rose to the rank of colonel. Three of his four sons were killed during the Great War. He became a National Hunt trainer with several 'National' wins to his credit, and he even had a cricket pitch and pavilion constructed at his home. Despite all this, he was heavily involved in local politics and civic duties around Glamorgan.

Edwin Montague Browne Newman joined the Royal Engineers in 1881 and he scored in the first round of the 1882–83 FA Cup. He was ordered for active service in the Sudan with the 24th Field Company, Queen's Own Sappers and Miners, and he was killed in action at the engagement at Tofrek on 22 March 1885, aged 23.

Teddy Wynyard of the King's (Liverpool) Regiment was a good football and an even better cricketer.

Edmond Cotter saw active service during the Ashanti War in West Africa in 1873–74. Dosed with quinine, he and his men prepared a road through thick, disease-ridden jungle, which included the construction of 237 bridges. There was no question of failing because the assault troops were following up behind them.

Zulu warriors presented a fearful sight as they were forming up for the attack. They used what became known as the horns of the buffalo tactic based on an old hunting technique. The centre, or loins, would attack the enemy face on, and then the horns came around on both sides to attack the flanks. It was a 'jolly deadly' manoeuvre. Lieutenant Haynes would have witnessed this when 20,000 Zulu warriors attacked the British square formation at the battle of Ulundi.

Commemorative silver, like this Royal Engineers' dish stand, was commissioned by many of the regiments that had fought in the Zulu War.

A unit of Afghan guerrillas prepare to ambush a British patrol from a cave high above the Khyber Pass in 1880. No fewer than ten former members of the Royal Engineers FC took part in this campaign, and Lieutenant George Turner Jones was recommended for the Victoria Cross, although he did not receive it.

A Night Scene before the attack at Tel-el-Kebir, 13 September 1882 is the title of this painting from the Anne S.K. Brown Collection in the Brown University Library. It shows the British front line waiting for the order to attack the Egyptian trenches. The attack was so devastating that all the Egyptian heavy guns were captured, and none of them had been fired. Seven former military footballers took part in the campaign.

The expedition that set out from Cairo in October 1884 might have got to Khartoum in time to save General Gordon, but for the River Nile. Here teams of soldiers, including Royal Engineers, haul on bow ropes, while others pole furiously from the stern, as boats are inched laboriously through the Nile's broiling cataracts and on towards Khartoum. No fewer than thirteen former military footballers took part in the Nile Expedition. This total was exceeded only by the eighteen who saw active service during the Great War.

A party of Boer commandos pictured during the siege of Ladysmith. Royal Engineer field units were prominent in building the town's defences and repairing them when they had been destroyed by the Boer heavy guns. Thirteen former military footballers took part in the war.

Much of the duties tasked to the Royal Engineers during the Boer War were to repair roads, bridges and railway lines, which were prime targets for Boer commando units wishing to disrupt the British advance. Here a party of Engineers are working to repair the railway tracks at Kroonstad.

Sim was born at Paddington in London on 19 November 1852, the second son of a timber broker named Alexander Sim (1820–85) and his wife, Agnes (1827–1909), who was a daughter of Dr Archibald Billing FRS, a writer on art. Two of George's uncles, Edward Coysgame and Charles Alexander, became major generals in the Royal Engineers.

George was educated at Rugby School and at the Royal Military Academy, from where he was commissioned as lieutenant in the Royal Engineers on 12 September 1872.

Considered to be a key defender in the Royal Engineers team, Sir Richard Ruck stated: 'Sim was another very useful back and was, I believe, the first player who made a practice of heading the ball, a method now brought to such a pitch of perfection.'

Sim saw his first tour of active duty in the Second Afghan War of 1878–80. After being promoted to captain on 12 September 1884, he was posted for active service with the Nile Expedition of 1884–85, where he was attached to the 10th Railway Company during the construction of the railway from Saukin to Berber. For his service he received the Sudan Medal with clasp, and the Khedive's Bronze Star.

Sim was promoted to major on 16 March 1892, and served on the staff at School of Military Engineering in Chatham from 1893 to 1898. After being promoted to lieutenant colonel on 1 October 1899, he received orders for his third tour of duty during the Second Boer War in South Africa. He was present with Colonel Buller's field force that marched to the relief of Ladysmith, including the disastrous engagement at Spion Kop on 23–24 January 1900. For his service he was twice mentioned in despatches, and he received the Queen's South Africa Medal with Cape Colony, Tugela Heights, Relief of Ladysmith, Transvaal and Laing's Nek clasps, and the King's South Africa Medal with 1901 and 1902 clasps. He was also appointed Commander of the Bath (CB).

Sim was officer in charge of records from 1905 to 1909 when he retired. However, he was recalled for service during the Great War, and on 30 June 1915 was appointed (CMG).

At the time of his death he was living at the Junior United Services Club in Charles Street, Haymarket, London, and he died at the Barracks in Pontefract, Yorkshire, on 27 December 1929, aged 76.

Richard Mathews Ruck

Richard Ruck played in the victorious Royal Engineers FA Cup-winning team of 1875, and went on to serve for twenty-four years in administration for the Submarine Mining section of the unit.

Ruck was born at Pantlludu in Machynlleth, Montgomeryshire (now Powys) in Wales, on 27 May 1851. He and Oliver Ruck, who played in the 1878 final, were the two youngest siblings. He was the second son of three in the family of five children of a gentleman farmer named Laurence Ruck (1820–92), and his mother was Mary Anne (formerly Mathews). His parents were of Welsh extraction, and could trace their ancestry to Owain Glyndŵr, the last King of Wales. Laurence had moved from Wales when he inherited his uncle's estate of Cranbrook Manor House at Newington in Kent. His older brother, Arthur Ashley (1847–1939), became lieutenant colonel in the King's (Liverpool) Regiment and later chief constable of Caernarvonshire. All his siblings prospered or married well in life.

Ruck was educated privately and at the Royal Military Academy, from where he was commissioned as lieutenant in the Royal Engineers on 2 August 1871. Fellow graduates on the same day were Alfred Goodwyn, Herbert Muirhead and Edmond Cotter, who all played in the 1872 final. While at Woolwich he gained a reputation as an all-round athlete, including rugby, gymnastics, cricket, billiards and golf. His memoir in the *Royal Engineers Journal* states: 'On joining the RE he showed some proficiency at the dribbling game, played for the Corps, and was a member of the team which won the Association Cup in 1875. Later, when golf developed in England in the "eighties", he took this up keenly and soon became a scratch player.'

He completed his course at the School of Military Engineering in 1873, and in September 1874 he joined the Submarine Mining Service at Chatham, thus beginning a continuous service of twenty-four years in that branch of the Royal Engineers. He was employed for some years in command of a section of the 28th Company at Cork Harbour, Pembroke Dock, and other stations until March 1881, when he was appointed assistant instructor at the School of Military Engineering in charge of the Submarine Mining School in Gillingham. He was promoted captain on 2 August 1883, and in May 1885 he was moved to the War Office. In January 1886 he was appointed assistant inspector of Submarine Defences, with the temporary rank of major, dated 17 December 1889. In July 1891 he succeeded to the appointment of inspector, which he held until being promoted lieutenant colonel on 31 December 1896.

On 8 October 1878, at the Roman Catholic Church of Our Lady of the Rosary in Marylebone, Ruck married a widow named Mary Constance Pedley, who was the daughter of John Gully (1783–1863), a prize fighter and Member of Parliament for Pontefract from 1832 to 1837. Mary was eighteen years his junior and had ten children from her previous marriage. One of her daughters, Eve, married Richard's brother, Oliver.

On leaving the War Office, Ruck was appointed Commanding Royal Engineer at Shoeburyness, but after a period on half-pay because of illness he was posted abroad for his first foreign service as Commanding Royal Engineer for the West Sub-District at Malta, where he became involved in the building of the new barracks at St Andrews. He was asked by Lord Grenfell, the Governor of Malta, to form a sports club on the Marsa for officers of both services. He personally laid out the golf course and designed the club house.

In June 1902 Ruck was recalled to the War Office to take up the appointment of deputy inspector general of fortifications, a position he held until 1 April 1904, when he became director of fortifications and works until 1908. From 1908 until 1912 he was major general in administration at the Eastern Command. He was created Commander of the Bath (CB) during the Coronation honours on 23 June 1911, and he retired on 1 October 1912. A fellow officer said of him: 'He had a very strong character and a quiet efficiency which was very comforting to his subordinates.'

In January 1905 a man threatened to expose an affair a French woman known as Lisette Ducros was having with a married man working at the War Office, and with whom she had had a child in 1903. The blackmailer was arrested and tried at the Central Criminal Court, where he was found guilty of demanding money with menaces. The man Lisette was having the relationship with was Ruck, and they had two more children in 1905 and 1908. Ruck's wife, Mary Constance, died on 13 October 1914, and although Lisette had married another man, Ruck adopted the three children he had with her.

On the outbreak of the Great War, Ruck volunteered his service on 22 October 1914, and he was Chief Engineer of the Central Force, with the responsibility for organising Territorial units in London and eastern England, covering the coast from The Wash in East Anglia to Portsmouth. He was also employed in preparing the defences of London. When this post was combined with the Eastern Command in November 1915, he was appointed major general in charge of administration for the Easter Command. He retired for a second time on 6 June 1916. For his service he was mentioned in despatches, and was appointed Companion of the Most Distinguished Order of St Michael and St George (CMG) in the New Year Honours' List for 1917.

At the time of his death the *Aeronautical Journal* stated: 'Major-General Ruck was keenly interested in Aviation and as early as 1905, when asked his opinion, made the remarkable forecast "… that he was confident that in the early future the question of military supremacy would be decided by fighting in the air."' Ruck was chairman of the council of the Royal Aeronautical Society of Great Britain from 1912 to 1919, becoming vice-president in 1920. He was vice-chairman of the Air Inventions Committee from 1917 to 1919; and a member of the Civil Aerial Transport Committee from 1917 to 18.

On 1 April 1920 Ruck was created Knight Commander of the Order of the British Empire (KBE) for his work in the field of aeronautics. He was a member of the Institute of Electrical Engineers, and chairman of the Royal Engineers Institute Committee. In 1928 he wrote a valuable football article in the *Royal Engineers Journal*, which appears in the bibliography of this work. He continued his great interest in golf, and in 1891 he was a founder and first vice-president of the Welsh Golfing Union, becoming president in 1933, and he was a member of the Aberdovey Golf Club (now in Gwynedd, north-west Wales), and at the Woking Golf Club.

After the death of his friend, the 6th Marquess Townshend in 1921, he became trustee of the Townshend family Estate at Raynham in Norfolk, to help the 7th Marquess, who was only 5 when his father died.

The first child Richard had with Lisette Ducros was named Alice Bertha, who married the vicar of St Peter-in-the-Forest Church at Woodford in Essex (now in Greater London), the Reverend Geoffrey Warwick, and Richard spent the last few years of his life with them. His home was at 11 Charles Street in St James's, Westminster, London. Ruck's younger brother, Oliver, had died in 1934, and Richard died in a nursing home at 47 St John's Wood Park in London on 17 March 1935, aged 84. His funeral service took place at Golders Green Crematorium.

William Francis Howard Stafford

William Stafford played for the Royal Engineers in their Cup-winning team of 1875, and later saw active service in three theatres of war.

Stafford was born at Hansi (now Haryana) in the Punjab, India, on 19 December 1854. His father was Major General William Joseph Fitzmaurice Stafford (c.1820–87) of the Bengal Staff Corps and his mother was Emily Mary (c.1832–1909), the daughter of Major Gavin Young, who was judge advocate general of the Honourable East India Company.

He was educated at Wellington College from 1867 to 1871, and at the Royal Military Academy from 1872 until being commissioned as lieutenant in the Royal Engineers on 29 April 1873. Two of Stafford's brothers also joined the Royal Engineers. Henry Laurence Caulfield Howard Stafford (1859–1948) rose to the rank of lieutenant colonel, and a younger brother, Edmund Hyde Boyle Whalley Howard Stafford (1868–1940), became a major.

After two years training at the Royal School of Military Engineering at Chatham, Stafford was posted to Roorkee in India in February 1876 to join the Bengal Sappers and Miners, from where he was posted for active service in the Second Afghan War in 1878. He took command of the 6th (Field Telegraph) Company, Bengal Sappers and Miners, attached to the 1st Division of the Peshawar Field Force, under Lieutenant General Sir Sam Browne (of Sam Browne belt fame). During the first phase of the war he accompanied the Maidanak Expedition and the Lughman Valley Expedition. His company was responsible for road making, laying field telegraphs and fortifying posts on the lines of communication. During the second campaign of the war he was assistant field engineer with the Khyber Line Force, taking part in the advance to Kata Sang in late 1879, and in December he was present during the disturbances at Pezwan. He then accompanied the expedition to the Hissarak Valley in April 1880. For his service Stafford was mentioned in despatches, and he was awarded the Afghanistan Medal.

Mahsud Waziri Expedition on the North-West Frontier of India, 1881

Stafford remained on the North-West Frontier of India and took part in the Mahsud Waziri Expedition in 1881 as part of the Second Column. After the Afghan War was over Waziri tribesmen had continued to attack the British settlement at Tank, which was precariously close to the Indian border with Afghanistan, and a British force was sent on this expedition to subdue them. No clasp for the Indian General Service Medal was awarded for this campaign, but for his service Lieutenant Stafford was again mentioned in despatches.

In March 1883, he took up the post of assistant instructor in survey at the School of Military Engineering in Chatham, and he was promoted captain on 8 January 1885. Stafford remained in Chatham until March 1888. During this time he returned to play football for the Royal Engineers, scoring a goal in the first round of the Cup and a hat-trick in the second. It was the last time the Engineers got as far as the quarter-finals in the competition.

While he was serving at Chatham, on 9 February 1884, at Holy Trinity Church in Brompton, West London, he married Edith Mary Culling, daughter of Francis Culling Carr-Gomm. They had three daughters and a son between 1885 and 1890. The youngest child, John Howard

(1890–1976), followed his father into the Royal Engineers. He rose to the rank of brigadier and was appointed OBE in 1945.

Stafford joined the Richmond Rugby Club and was selected to play for England against Scotland in the 1874 international, which England won by one goal kick to nil. He took his strong and robust style onto the football pitch, playing at centre-forward for the Royal Engineers during the 1874–75 competition. Stafford scored at least two goals in the earlier rounds, and was part of the FA Cup-winning squad. He also played cricket for the Royal Military Academy, the Royal Engineers and for Norfolk in 1889.

Stafford spent two years at Colchester until April 1890, when he was posted to Egypt. He was promoted to major in Egypt on 13 November 1892, and remained there until November 1894. He had a brief posting to Malta, before returning to Chatham in March 1895, and for the next four years he was stationed at various bases throughout the British Isles, including serving at the Curragh Camp in Ireland from October 1886 to January 1899.

On the outbreak of the Second Boer War in South Africa in October 1899, he was posted for active service in command of the 26th Company, RE, with the troops under Lord Roberts. After the relief of Kimberley on 15 February 1900, the British troops advanced on Bloemfontein, and Major Stafford was present at the engagements at Poplar Grove on 7 March 1900 and Karee Siding on 29 March 1900. He was promoted to lieutenant colonel on 14 April 1900, and remained on active service in the Transvaal until August 1902. For his service he was mentioned in despatches, and received the Queen's South Africa Medal with three clasps and the King's South Africa Medal with 1901 and 1902 clasps. He was appointed Commander of the Bath (CB) on 26 June 1902.

From October 1902 to January 1903, Stafford was in command of the Royal Engineers at Victoria Barracks in Cork, and from January 1903 to April 1905 he was commanding Royal Engineer for the North-Western Command at Chester. He was promoted to brevet colonel on 10 February 1904. On 8 August 1906, he was appointed chief engineer for the Southern Command based at Salisbury, gaining the temporary rank of brigadier general on 5 October 1907. He retired from military service on 19 December 1911, and was awarded the honorary rank of brigadier general on 5 October 1912.

Stafford was recalled to the army for the Great War, being appointed officer commanding, South Irish Coastal Defences, on 6 June 1915, based at Victoria Barracks in Cork. As the troubles of the Easter Rising in Ireland began in April 1916, Tomás Mac Curtain, the commander of the Irish Volunteers in Cork, occupied the volunteer hall with his men. It was surrounded by British troops, and Colonel Stafford appointed his ADC to negotiate terms with the Irish leader to temporarily surrender his weapons so that the hall could be vacated. The arms were not surrendered but the Irish leader was arrested and imprisoned. Stafford was then posted for active service in France, 1917–18, where he was mentioned in despatches. He retired from military service on 11 April 1918.

Edith died in 1931, and General Stafford died at his home of Thornbury in Crowthorne, Berkshire, on 8 August 1942, aged 87. He was buried at St John the Baptist Church in Crowthorne.

Alexander Lechmere Mein

Alexander Mein played on the Royal Engineers Cup-winning team, and later saw active service in Afghanistan.

Mein was born in York on 15 July 1854, where his father, Major George Mein (1817–96), was stationed with the 21st Light Dragoons. His mother was Marianne (1815–85), the daughter of a solicitor named Frederick Coore. His father had served in the First Afghan War from 1839 to 1842.

He was educated at Wellington College in Berkshire and at the Royal Military Academy, from where he was commissioned as lieutenant in the Royal Engineers on 29 April 1873.

Described as a brilliant inside-left, Mein played in both matches when the Royal Engineers were triumphant in the 1875 FA Cup final, and he also played rugby for the Richmond club in 1874.

He had spent the first three years of service at Chatham, before being posted to Bengal in India in September 1876. He was posted for active service in the Second Afghan War in 1878, as assistant field engineer with the 2nd Division of the Peshawar Field Force. He took part in the opening battle of the war at Ali Masjid on 28 November 1878. On the signing of the treaty of Gandamak, his unit was employed in building defence works along the line of communication. During the second phase of the war Mein was attached to the Khyber Line Force as assistant field engineer, and took part in the Wazir Khugianis Expedition, the Hisarak Expedition in April 1880 and the Lughman Valley Expedition in May 1880. For his service he was mentioned in despatches and received the Afghanistan Medal with Ali Masjid clasp.

On 1 June 1887, at St Paul's Church in Sarisbury near Titchfield in Hampshire, Mein married Alice Ellen (1861–1937), a daughter of Captain Robert Lambert Turner-Irton, formerly of the 87th Royal Irish Fusiliers. They had six children born between 1888 and 1901, although their first child, Evelyn May, died when she was six weeks old. Their son, Lieutenant Dudley Mein MC, was killed in action while serving with the 31st Duke of Connaught's Own Lancers at Aleppo in Mesopotamia (now Syria) on 26 October 1918.

Mein spent most of the remainder of his career in Bengal, where he was promoted captain on 8 January 1885, major on 1 October 1892, lieutenant colonel on 24 January 1900, and brevet colonel on 24 January 1904. He retired with an Indian pension on 15 July 1911.

Colonel Mein died at the family home of Gangbridge in St Mary Bourne, Andover, in Hampshire, on 30 November 1927, aged 73. His funeral took place at St Peter's Church at St Mary Bourne. Gangbridge House is now a Grade II listed building. Copies of papers related to his father's military service and some photographs Mein took are kept at the Indian Office section in the British Library.

Cecil Vernon Wingfield-Stratford

Cecil Wingfield-Stratford played at outside-left in the Royal Engineers FA Cup-winning team of 1875 and he was capped for England in 1877. He went on to a career in military administration.

Wingfield-Stratford was born at Addington Place in Addington near West Malling in Kent, on 7 October 1853, the third son and seventh of thirteen children to John Wingfield-Stratford (1810–81), a Justice of the Peace, and his wife, Jane Elizabeth (formerly Guise, 1825–97). They employed eighteen servants. Cecil was a great-grandson of the 3rd Lord Powerscourt of County Wexford, and a descendant of the House of Stratford.

He attended a school on South Lancaster Road in Norwood Park, Croydon, and he was educated at the Royal Military Academy, from where he was commissioned as a lieutenant in the Royal Engineers on 29 October 1873.

Wingfield-Stratford played for the victorious Royal Engineers in the 1875 FA Cup final, and on 3 March 1877 he played for England against Scotland at The Oval, when England lost 3-1. He also played for Kent FC. He was also a good cricketer and a member of the MCC, and he was a member and supporter of the Fartherwell Hall cricket team.

On 9 September 1875, Wingfield-Stratford's sister, Emily Rose, married his Cup final teammate Henry Renny-Tailyour. On 13 October 1881, at All Saints Church in Birling, West Malling, he married Roasalind Isobel, the only daughter of the Hon. and Reverend Edward Vesey and Lady Isobel Mary Frances Nevill Bligh, sister of the Marquess of Abergavenny. At the time of the 1881 census they lived with the parents of his future bride at Fartherwell Hall in Ryarsh, West Malling. They employed fourteen servants. In 1891 they had two children, and were living at The Cracknells in Norton Green, Freshwater, on the Isle of Wight, which is now a Grade II listed building. A decade later they lived at Stowford House in Hartford, Devon, with their two eldest children. They employed eight servants.

Wingfield-Stratford was adjutant to the Submarine Mining Battalion from 1884 to 1889, during which time he was promoted captain on 8 January 1885. He was promoted major on 1 April 1893, lieutenant colonel on 12 August 1900 and brevet colonel on 10 February 1904. On 1 January 1907, he was promoted colonel, and was given the position of chief engineer of the Irish Command in Dublin. He retired in 1910.

One of his sons, Esme Cecil (1882–1971), who also played for the Fartherwell Hall cricket team, was described as an English historian, writer, mind trainer, outdoorsman, ruralist and patriot, who wrote several books including *The History of British Patriotism* in 1913 – 'a theme to which he several times returned'.

Wingfield-Stratford was recalled for service during the Great War, being appointed to the command of the North Midland Territorial Division, Royal Engineers. He was given the temporary rank of brigadier general, and he served on the staff at the Royal Hibernian Military School in Phoenix Park, Dublin; a position from which he retired on 7 October 1915 to go on active service on the Western Front.

He took part in the battle of Loos from 25 September to 8 October 1915, the attack on the Gommecourt Salient on 1 July 1916, the tragic first day of the battle of the Somme, and he was commanding Royal Engineer of the 46th Division when it broke the Hindenburg Line in 1918 during the advance to victory.

For his service on the Gommecourt Salient he was mentioned in despatches four times, was appointed Companion of the Order of St Michael and St George (CMG), on 1 January 1916; and Companion of the Bath (CB), in 1918.

Brigadier General Wingfield-Stratford died at Fartherwell Hall on 5 February 1939, aged 85.

Henry Lyle Mulholland

Henry Mulholland played for the Royal Engineers during their Cup-winning season. He scored in the second round of the competition, and he appears in the photograph of the Royal Engineers' winning team.

Mulholland was born on 30 January 1854, at Craigavad in County Down, the second son of three in the family of six children to John Mulholland (1819–95), 1st Baron Dunleath, and his wife, Frances Louisa, the daughter of Hugh Lyle. His father was a businessman involved in the cotton and linen industry, and the Conservative Member of Parliament for Downpatrick from 1874 to 1885.

He was educated at Eton College, and attended the Royal Military Academy, from where he was commissioned as lieutenant in the Royal Engineers on 29 April 1873. However, after serving at the Curragh Camp in Ireland in 1877, he relinquished his commission that year. He graduated with a Bachelor of Arts from Balliol College, Oxford University.

On 28 July 1881, Mulholland married Nora Louisa Fanny, the only surviving daughter of the Honourable Somerset Ward, and the granddaughter of the 3rd Viscount Bangor. They had four sons and a daughter between 1882 and 1892. Their eldest son, Andrew Edward Somerset (1882–1914), became a lieutenant in the Irish Guards and was killed in action during the Great War. The second eldest, Charles Henry George (1886–1956), became a lieutenant in the 11th Hussars, the famous regiment that had taken part in the Charge of the Light Brigade, and succeeded his father as 3rd Baron Dunleath.

The family lived at Ballywalter Park in County Down, where Mulholland became a Justice of the Peace, and he was High Sheriff in 1884. He was the Conservative Member of Parliament for the new constituency of North Londonderry from 1885 to 1895

He succeeded his father as the 2nd Baron Dunleath on the death of his father on 11 December 1895, and entered the House of Lords. From 1890 to 1896 he served as a major in the 5th Battalion, Royal Irish Rifles.

Mulholland died on 22 March 1931, aged 77. In 1937 a memorial window was erected at Down Cathedral in County Down in memory of Baron Dunleath and Nora.

Chapter 7

The 1875–76 Season

Thirty-two teams entered the fifth campaign, and it turned out to be a very high-scoring competition. For the first time, three military squads took part. In the first round Royal Engineers inflicted a heavy defeat on the team from High Wycombe at Chatham, scoring fifteen goals without reply. Lieutenants John Crawford Middlemass and Herbert Rawson scored five each, and Lieutenants John Blackburn and Pelham von Donop scored two each. The 1st Surrey Rifles came back into the competition, only to have to travel to face the Wanderers, where they lost 5-0. The 105th Regiment managed a goalless draw at home against Crystal Palace in front of 500 spectators, but in the replay at The Oval two weeks later they lost 3-0. A crowd of 1,578 watched the game.

Illustrated Sporting and Dramatic News reported:

> It may be remembered that the first ties for the Association Challenge Cup of Football had been got through last week, with the exception of that between the Crystal Palace Club and the 105th Regiment, who had met at Aldershot on the 6th inst; without any definite result being arrived at. On Saturday last they met for a second time at Kennington Oval, and soon after the ball was started Neame scored the first goal for the Palace from a long but well-directed kick. Up to half-time no further score was obtained by either side. Aided now by the wind the Palace team had no difficulty in keeping the ball pretty well always in their opponents quarters, and the backs of the 105th not offering much resistance, the captain of the Palace secured another goal for his side, which was followed up by a third by P Barlow. The Palace thus won by three goals to none.
>
> On Saturday last Cambridge University played the Royal Engineers, on Parker's Place and, although both sides showed

great determination, when time was called no score had been obtained, and the game thus ended in a draw.

A weak team of the Wanderers on the same day tried conclusions at the Parks, Oxford, against the full strength of the University, and, as might be expected, the Wanderers had to put up with a defeat, the University scoring three goals to one. As both Oxford and Cambridge are particularly strong this year a most determined and close contest may be anticipated on Saturday, when the two Universities meet at Kennington Oval.

Several other matches of interest took place last Saturday, the results of which may be briefly recapitulated here – Woodford Wells beat the 1st Surrey Rifles at Camberley by five goals to two.

Owing to the flooded state of the Timbrells at Eton the match between the College and the Swifts was played at Slough. The Etonians had the game nearly all in their own hands and won by a goal to nothing.

The Royal Engineers should have played a second-round tie, but their would-be opponents Panthers withdrew from the competition. This team played some of their football at Sandhurst, and there is still a club of the same name playing in the area. Clapham Rovers put twelve past Leyton, Old Etonians shocked the Maidenhead team by putting eight past them, and Cambridge University beat Reigate Priory by the same high score. Swifts defeated South Norwood 5-0, and the Wanderers beat Crystal Palace 3-0.

In the third round the Engineers entertained Swifts, who had not conceded a goal in their two previous ties. Lieutenant Herbert Rawson did manage to put a goal past them, but they replied with three of their own and brought the military teams' campaigns to a close.

In the semi-finals, the Bostonian Julian Sturgis scored the only goal of the match for Old Etonians against Oxford University, and the Wanderers beat Swifts 2-1 a week later, the only goal they had conceded so far.

Wanderers 1 Old Etonians 1

The final between the Wanderers and Old Etonians took place at The Oval on 11 March 1876, a day on which the wind was blowing 'great Guns'. Walter Scott Buchanan (1855–1926) of Clapham Rovers, who played for England that year, refereed the game, and 3,000 spectators watched a 1-1 draw, during which Arthur Kinnaird and Charles Meysey-Thompson were injured during the later stages. There were three sets of brothers involved in both games, named Heron, Lyttelton and Meysey-Thompson. Alexander Bonsor was playing in a record fourth final.

Wanderers: *Goalkeeper* – William Dallas Ochterlony Greig (Brighton College); *Full-backs* – Alfred Hugh Stratford (Malvern), William Lindsay (Winchester); *Half-backs* – Frederick Brunning Maddison (Marlborough), Francis Hornby Birley (captain) (Winchester); *Forwards: Right* – Charles Henry Reynolds Wollaston (Lancing), George Hubert Hugh Heron (Mill Hill); *Centre* – Charles Francis William Heron (Mill Hill), John Hawley Edwards (Shifnal Grammar School); *Left* – Thomas Bridges Hughes (Winchester), Jarvis Kenrick (Lancing).

Old Etonians: *Goalkeeper* – Quintin Hogg; *Full-back* – James Edward Cowell Welldon; *Half-backs* – Albert Childers Meysey-Thompson, Hon. Edward Lyttelton; *Forwards: Right* – Herbert Percy Alleyne, Alexander Bonsor; *Centres* – Julian Russell Sturgis (Eton) , Hon. Alfred Lyttelton; *Left:* – Arthur Fitzgerald Kinnaird (captain), Charles Maude Meysey-Thompson.

Wanderers 3 Old Etonians 0

The weather on the following Saturday was bitterly cold and there had been a threat of snow, but 3,500 spectators watched the game. It was the second FA Cup final replay for Old Etonians. The injury to Charles Meysey-Thompson kept him out of the match, and both he and his brother had to be replaced; as did Quintin Hogg and James Welldon. Arthur Kinnaird had not fully recovered from his injury in the first match, but the team thought his presence would still be advantageous. The replacements were Matthew George Farrer, James Henry Stronge and Francis Heathcote Wilson. Their main full-back, Edgar Lubbock, had missed the first game because of injury and was still not match fit when he lined up for the replay, and therefore the Etonians went onto the pitch with a somewhat weakened team. Herbert Rawson's brother, William, of Oxford University, took charge of the replay. Alexander Bonsor was playing in his fourth final. The early play of the Etonians was 'more rough than scientific', but the Wanderers soon got on top and with two goals within three minutes of each other, and a third five minutes into the second half, they won the match 3-0. The teams were:

Wanderers: *Goalkeeper* – William Dallas Ochterlony Greig (Brighton College); *Full-backs* – Alfred Hugh Stratford (Malvern), William Lindsay (Winchester); *Half-backs* – Frederick Brunning Maddison

(Marlborough), Francis Hornby Birley (captain) (Winchester); *Forwards: Right* – Charles Henry Reynolds Wollaston (Lancing), George Hubert Hugh Heron (Mill Hill); *Centre* – Charles Francis William Heron (Mill Hill), John Hawley Edwards (Shifnal Grammar School); *Left* – Thomas Bridges Hughes (Winchester), Jarvis Kenrick (Lancing).

Old Etonians: *Goalkeeper* – Quintin Hogg; *Full-back* – James Edward Cowell Welldon; *Half-backs* – Albert Childers Meysey-Thompson, Hon. Edward Lyttelton; *Forwards: Right* – Herbert Percy Alleyne, Alexander Bonsor; *Centre* – Julian Russell Sturgis (Eton), Hon. Alfred Lyttelton; *Left* – Arthur Fitzgerald Kinnaird (captain), Charles Maude Meysey-Thompson.

Royal Engineers Matches

1st Round	10 November 1875	High Wycombe	won 15-0 at Chatham
2nd Round	14 November 1875	Panthers	withdrew
3rd Round	29 January 1876	Swifts	lost 1-3 at Chatham

1st Surrey Rifles Match

| 1st Round | 25 October 1875 | Wanderers | lost 0-5 away |

105th Regiment Matches

| 1st Round | 6 November 1875 | Crystal Palace | drew 0-0 at Aldershot |
| Replay | 20 November 1875 | Crystal Palace | lost 0-3 at The Oval |

Scots Guards

Henry Edward Stirling Home Drummond-Moray

Henry Drummond-Moray played in goal for Old Etonians in the replay of the 1875 FA Cup final. He served with the Scots Guards, and was a Member of Parliament for Perthshire.

Drummond-Moray was born in Edinburgh on 15 September 1846, the son of Colonel Charles Stirling Home-Drummond-Moray (1816–91), 9th of Blair Drummond, and 19th of Abercairny, and his wife, Lady Anne

Georgina (1817–99), a daughter of Charles Douglas, 6th Marquess of Queensberry. They had married on 11 December 1845. Henry had an older sister named Caroline Frances and a younger brother named William Augustus (later captain, 1852–1939). The family also owned land and property at Ardoch House in Braco near Dunblane. Drummond-Moray was a cousin of the Duke of Atholl, and also of the Earl of Mansfield.

Henry was educated at Eton College, and entered the Scots Guards in 1866.

He was called up to play for Old Etonians in the 1875 final replay, when he played in goal, but his usual position was at half-back.

On 23 January 1877, he married Lady Georgina Emily Lucy (1848–1944), a daughter of Francis Seymour, 5th Marquess of Hertford. Lady Georgina later received the Order of Queen Elisabeth of Belgium, which was awarded to people recognised for providing humanitarian and medical care to Belgian victims of the Great War.

Henry won a by-election in 1878 to become Conservative Member of Parliament for Perthshire. However, in the 1880 General Election, while war was raging in Afghanistan, he lost his seat to the shipping magnate Sir Donald Currie, who donated the Currie Cup for South African rugby a decade later.

Lieutenant Colonel Drummond-Moray retired from the Scots Guards in 1880, and on inheriting his father's estates at Blair Drummond in 1891 he dropped the name of Moray to reflect his ancestral links. The family are still associated with the Scots Guards to this day.

He became involved in local affairs as an administrator, among which were convenor of Perthshire County Council, president of the Perthshire Unionist Association, and a Justice of the Peace. He was known to be a fair and considerate landowner

He had been suffering with heart trouble for some years, but his health appeared to be improving enough for him to attend the local council's Western District committee meeting held in Dunblane. However, he suffered a fatal heart attack and died at Blair Drummond House on 16 May 1911, aged 64. He was buried at Kincardine-in-Mentieth, near Blair Drummond. The 'Moray Albums' of family photographs can be seen in the Edinburgh Libraries, Museums and Galleries collection. Henry Drummond was happy to allow local people to take walks on his land, and part of the estate is now used as the Blair Drummond Safari and Adventure Park near Stirling.

Chapter 8

The 1876–77 Season

Thirty-seven teams entered the sixth staging of the FA Cup, with three army teams entering for the second time. The Universities of Oxford and Cambridge progressed well in the competition, while Maidenhead did not enter for the only time in their history.

No fewer than seven teams withdrew from playing their first- round matches, including Old Etonians. The Royal Engineers played Old Harrovians at Chatham. As the name suggests, the Old Harrovians were old boys from Harrow School, who had recently changed their name from Harrow Chequers. The army team won 2-1, with Lieutenant Herbert Rawson getting on the score sheet once again. The 1st Surrey Rifles and the 105th Regiment made FA Cup history when they contested the only ever all-military match in the history of the competition, with the 105th Regiment winning 3-0. Five-hundred spectators attended. There were wins for Clapham Rovers, Upton Park, Great Marlow, Rochester, South Norwood, Swifts, Forest School from Epping and Pilgrims from Clapton.

In the second round, the Royal Engineers beat Shropshire Wanderers 3-0 at Chatham, with Lieutenants Robert Hedley getting his name on the score sheet. The 105th Regiment had the misfortune to be draw against the in-form Oxford University in Oxford, and 1,204 spectators watched them lose 6-1. Sheffield FC put seven past South Norwood, Wanderers put six past Southall Park and other teams who progressed were Cambridge University, Rochester, Upton Park and Pilgrims from Clapton.

In the third round the Royal Engineers entertained Sheffield FC at Chatham, and Lieutenant Herbert Rawson scored the only goal of the game. After receiving byes in the previous two rounds, Queen's Park withdrew from their game against Oxford University. Cambridge University and Wanderers also progressed, as did Upton Park after a replay against Great Marlow.

In the quarter-finals the Royal Engineers travelled to Parker's Piece at Cambridge University, where they lost by the only goal of the game. Oxford University beat Upton Park by the only goal in 180 minutes of play, and the Wanderers received a bye.

Both university teams reached the semi-final for the only time in their history, where Oxford received a bye into the final, and Cambridge lost to the Wanderers by the only goal of the game.

Wanderers 2 Oxford University 1

(after extra time)

Wanderers had reached the final without having a goal scored against them, and 3,000 spectators turned up at Kennington Oval to watch the match on 24 March 1877. The referee was S.H. Wright of Great Marlow. Charles Wollaston, Arthur Kinnaird and Francos Borley were all playing in their fourth final.

The weather played a prominent part in the action as usual. Rain and sleet made the conditions hazardous, and there was a strong breeze. After fifteen minutes, Arthur Kinnaird caught the ball from a corner and, faced with the wind and sleet, he stepped back over the line and a goal was given. Wanderers equalised, and the score at normal time was 1-1. During extra time Wanderers scored a second goal to win the Cup. However, sometime later the own goal was annulled and the score appeared in the records as a 2-0 win for Wanderers. It was eventually realised that without the goal the extra thirty minutes would not have been necessary and the score should have been recorded as 1-0 for Wanderers. Eventually the original score of 2-1 to Wanderers was reinstated. The teams were:

Wanderers: *Goalkeeper* – Hon. Arthur Fitzgerald Kinnaird (captain) (Eton); *Full-backs* – Alfred Hugh Stratford (Malvern), William Lindsay (Winchester); *Half-backs* – Francis Hornby Birley (captain) (Winchester), Frederick Thomas Green (Winchester); *Forwards*: *Right* – Thomas Bridges Hughes (Winchester), Charles Henry Reynolds Wollaston (Lancing); *Centre* – George Hubert Hugh Heron (Mill Hill), Henry Wace (Shrewsbury); *Left* – Charles Ashpitel Denton (Bradfield College), Jarvis Kenrick (Lancing).

Oxford University: *Goalkeeper* – Edward Hugh Alington (Hertford); *Full-backs* – Owen Robert Dunell (Trinity), William Stepney Rawson (Christ Church); *Half-backs* – Evelyn Waddington (Oriel), James Henry

Savory (Trinity); *Forwards*: *Right* – Philip Hosken Fernandez (Trinity), Edward Hagarty Parry (captain) (Exeter); *Centre* – Henry Shirecliffe Otter (Christ Church), Alexander Hay Tod (Trinity); *Left* – Arnold Frank Hills (University College), John Bain (New College).

Royal Engineers Matches

1st Round	28 October 1876	Old Harrovians	won 2-1 at Chatham
2nd Round	9 December 1876	Shropshire Wanderers	won 3-0 at Chatham
3rd Round	20 January 1877	Sheffield	won 1-0 at Chatham
4th Round	17 February 1877	Cambridge University	lost 0-1 at Parker's Piece

1st Surrey Rifles Match

1st Round	11 November 1876	105th Regiment	lost 0-3 away

105th Regiment Matches

1st Round	11 November 1876	1st Surrey Rifles	won 3-0 at home
2nd Round	14 December 1876	Oxford University	lost 1-6 Oxford

Chapter 9

The 1877–78 Season

Forty-three teams entered the seventh competition, with three military teams involved again. William Lindsay, who played in all three Wanderers cup wins of 1876, 1877 and 1878, having scored the winning goal in the 1877 victory, came from a military family who were involved in one of the most dreadful atrocities in the history of the British Empire. Born in Benares, some of his family were British officers serving with the Bengal Native Infantry in the Indian Army. Fortunately, William was sent home to study not long before the outbreak of the Indian Mutiny, during which most of his family were murdered in the notorious Cawnpore massacres of 1857.

The Royal Engineers should have played Highbury Union in the first round but the Highbury club withdrew. On the following Saturday, 3 November 1877, they played the Wanderers at The Oval, in a rehearsal of the final, and the Wanderers scored twice in the last five minutes to win 4-0. At Camberley, 1st Surrey Rifles won their second game in the competition by beating Forest School 1-0. The 105th Regiment lost to Old Harrovians 2-0 on the same day, one of the goals being scored by Morton Betts. It was the last game the 105th would actually play in the FA Cup. The first Cup match ever to be played in the north-west region of England took place on 7 November 1877, when Darwen defeated Manchester FC 3-0; and the first-ever FA Cup tie to be played in Nottinghamshire saw Notts County draw with Sheffield FC on 3 November 1877. Wales was represented for the first time by Druids of Ruabon near Wrexham, who won. Maidenhead put ten past Reading Hornets, and there were also wins for Reading FC, Oxford University and Cambridge University, Upton Park, Clapham Rovers, Great Marlow, High Wycombe, Remnants, Swifts and Hawks. Sheffield FC and Pilgrims got through after replays. Hubert Heron scored four of the nine the Wanderers put past Panthers, in a tie played at Sandhurst.

In the second round, the Royal Engineers were drawn to play Pilgrims FC, who had reached the third round the previous year and were knocked out by Wanderers. Not much is known about this team. They were based in Clapton, and it may be that they were named after Pilgrims Road in that area, where the present Clapton Club once played. In 1891 an article in a journal called *Forest's Sporting Notes* reviewed a copy of the *1874 Football Annual*, under the heading *An Old Football Annual*, in which the author asks: 'What has become of such giants as Gitanos, Harrow Chequers, Pilgrims and Woodford Wells.' The match took place at Chatham, and Lieutenant Robert Hedley scored a hat-trick in a 6-0 victory.

Old Harrovians took their second military scalp by beating 1st Surrey Rifles 6-0 at Harrow. One of their goal scorers was Patrick 'Frank' Hadow, who won the Wimbledon Lawn Tennis Championships in the following year.

Wanderers scored another nine goals, their victims on this occasion being High Wycombe, and there were wins for Oxford University and Cambridge University, Upton Park, Barnes, Clapham Rovers, Remnants and Sheffield FC.

For their third-round match the Royal Engineers were drawn to play Druids FC. Druids had been founded in about 1872 by David and George Thompson at Ruabon near Wrexham, by the amalgamation of several local clubs; one of the clubs being a military unit called the 2nd Denbighshire Volunteers. The Football Association of Wales was founded in Ruabon in March 1876, and Ruabon were drawn to play Shropshire Wanderers on 14 October 1876, as the first Welsh club ever to enter the FA Cup. However, when their goalkeeper and founder, David Thompson, died suddenly on 14 September 1876, the club withdrew and wore black armbands as a mark of respect for the rest of the season. Druids travelled down from north Wales to Chatham, where they suffered an 8-0 defeat. Lieutenant Robert Hedley scored another hat-trick, as did Lieutenant George Alfred Tower, while Lieutenants Charles Haynes and Morgan Lindsay scored one each. Wanderers defeated Barnes FC, Oxford University beat Clapham Rovers, and after two drawn games and extra time Old Harrovians beat Cambridge University.

The Royal Engineers drew Oxford University in the quarter-finals, which produced an epic tie. The teams drew 3-3 at Chatham and this was followed by a 2-2 draw at the Parks in Oxford, with the Engineers' goals coming from Lieutenants Francis Bond and Charles Haynes, who both saw active service in the Zulu War a year later. The tie was finally decided when Royal Engineers ran out winners 4-2, with goals from

Lieutenants Francis Bond, Horace Barnet and Oliver Ruck. Wanderers beat Sheffield FC, and Old Harrovians defeated Upton Park.

Only four days later the Royal Engineers had to face Old Harrovians in the semi-final. They gained revenge for the defeats the men of Harrow had inflicted on the two other military teams by defeating them by the odd goal in three. Lieutenant Horace Barnet scored again and Lieutenant Charles Mayne got the winner. The Wanderers also reached the final, having lost only their first match of the season, and a couple of weeks before the final they had gone to Camberley and put nine past 1st Surrey Rifles with only one in reply.

Wanderers 3 Royal Engineers 1

The final was held at The Oval on 23 March 1878, before 4,500 spectators, the largest crowd to date. Because of their form, the Wanderers were firm favourites, with the Royal Engineers at 4 to 1, and if Wanderers won the rules stated that they were allowed to keep the trophy. The Royal Engineers felt hard done by, having to play so many games in such a short space of time; and to add to their grievances Wanderers had gained a bye straight from the semi-final into the final. The referee was Segar Richard Bastard of Upton Park, and the umpire for the Engineers was Beaumont Griffith Jarrett of the Old Harrovians, who the Engineers had beaten in the semi-final. The Engineers team included two Welsh-born players in Oliver Ruck and Morgan Lindsay.

The Engineers lost the toss for a fifth time, and the Wanderers immediately went on the attack. After two near misses by Jarvis Kenrick, the man who had scored the first-ever goal in the FA Cup while playing for Clapham Rovers back in November 1871, he put the Wanderers ahead after only five minutes. Thus he had scored in consecutive finals.

After fifteen minutes of play, the Wanderers goalkeeper, James Kirkpatrick, the oldest man on the pitch, was involved in a rough scrimmage. He managed to get the ball away but he found that he had broken his left arm. Nevertheless, he decided to carry on playing. On the twenty-minute mark, Lieutenant Morris took a strong, well-directed throw-in, and a pack of Engineers ran the ball over the line for the equaliser. No individual player has ever been given the credit for this goal.

After a strong attack by the Wanderers that nearly resulted in a goal, they won a free kick. This was taken by Lord Kinnaird, and after a short scrimmage Jarvis Kenrick scored his second goal, to make the score 2-1 at the break.

Just after the restart Lieutenant Hedley had a goal disallowed for offside. After sixty-five minutes, the same Lieutenant Morris who had assisted the Engineers' goal made an unfortunate miss kick and the ball fell at the feet of George Heron, who passed it to Jarvis Kenrick to score a third for the Wanderers. It was the first time more than three goals had been scored in a final, even including replays.

The Times for 25 March 1878 reported:

> The series of ties which have been played during the winter for the above challenge cup were brought to a close on Saturday last at Kennington Oval, when the final tie between the above clubs was played. The weather was fine and about 3,000 spectators were present.
>
> Play began at 20 minutes to 4 o'clock, when the military having lost the toss, Hedley kicked off from the eastern goal. At the outset the play was pretty even, but at length the splendid passing of the Wanderers told its tale through the agency of Kenrick and Wace. The sappers now mettled up and before long a goal was kicked for them out of a loose scrimmage, the ball having been well thrown in by Morris. The scores were thus level, and each side redoubled their efforts. Prior to half-time the excellent play of the Wanderers resulted in a second goal for them.
>
> After the change of ends, the Engineers struggled in a most determined manner. Hedley kicked the ball between the posts, but the goal was disallowed as the 'offside' rule had been violated. Soon after this a splendid piece of play on the part of Kenrick and Heron secured a third goal for the Wanderers. This proved the last score of the match, and at the call of 'Time' victory rested with the Wanderers by three goals to one. As this celebrated club has now won the Cup thrice in succession it becomes their absolute property.

Lord Arthur Kinnaird was playing in his fourth consecutive final, and Charles Wollaston won his fifth FA Cup final; a record that was equalled by Lord Kinnaird in 1882. The record was beaten when Ashley Cole won his sixth FA Cup while playing for Chelsea in 2010. He was on the winning side again in 2012, and played in a total of eight finals. Lord Kinnaird played in no fewer than nine FA Cup finals.

The rules stated that as Wanderers had won the trophy three times in succession they were entitled to keep it. However, they handed it back to the Association on condition that it was never to be won outright by any club. Unfortunately, the Little Tin Idol was stolen from a shop window in Birmingham in 1895 while Aston Villa were the holders. Luckily, the Cup winners of 1893, Wolverhampton Wanderers, had been given miniature replicas of it as souvenirs and a new trophy was made based on these. A number of culprits owned up to the crime over the years, and the famous Peaky Blinders gang was known to operate in the area where the Cup was stolen. The teams were:

Wanderers: *Goalkeeper* – James Kirkpatrick (Privately); *Full-backs* – Alfred Hugh Stratford (Malvern), William Lindsay (Winchester); *Half-backs* – Arthur Fitzgerald Kinnaird (captain) (Eton), Frederick Thomas Green (Winchester); *Forwards: Right* – Charles Henry Reynolds Wollaston (Lancing), George Hubert Hugh Heron (Mill Hill); *Centre* – John George Wylie (Shrewsbury), Henry Wace; *Left* – Charles Ashpitel Denton (Bradfield), Jarvis Kenrick (Lancing).

Royal Engineers: *Goalkeeper* – Lieutenant Lovick Bransby Friend; *Full-backs* – Lieutenant James Henry Cowan, Lieutenant William George Morris; *Half-backs* – Lieutenant Charles Blair Mayne, Lieutenant Frederick Crofton Heath-Caldwell; *Forwards: Right* – Lieutenant Horace Hutton Barnet, Lieutenant Henry Edzell Morgan Lindsay; *Centre* – Lieutenant Charles Edward Haynes, Lieutenant Robert Shafto Hedley (captain); *Left* – Lieutenant Francis George Bond, Lieutenant Oliver Edwal Ruck.

Royal Engineers Matches

1st Round	27 October 1877	Highbury Union	withdrew
2nd Round	8 December 1877	Pilgrims	won 6-0 at Chatham
3rd Round	30 January 1878	Ruabon Druids	won 8-0 at Chatham
4th Round	15 February 1878	Oxford University	drew 3-3 at Chatham
Replay	27 February 1878	Oxford University	drew 2-2 at the Parks, Oxford
2nd Replay	12 March 1878	Oxford University	won 4-2
Semi-final	16 March 1878	Old Harrovians	won 2-1

Final	23 March 1878	Wanderers	lost 1-3 at The Oval

1st Surrey Rifles Matches

1st Round	7 November 1877	Forest School	won 1-0 at Camberley
2nd Round	22 December 1877	Old Harrovians	lost 0-6 away

105th Regiment Match

1st Round	7 November 1877	Old Harrovians	lost 0-2 unknown

Royal Engineers Players

Charles Edward Haynes

Charles Edward Haynes played in the 1878 FA Cup final, and saw two tours of active service in South Africa.

Haynes was born in Hampstead in Middlesex (now Greater London), on 8 July 1855, the son of a successful builder named William Haynes and his wife, Mary Ann (formerly Spragg). By the time of the 1851 census William had retired at the age of only 48. Charles entered the Royal Military Academy, from where he passed out and was commissioned as lieutenant in the Royal Engineers on 28 January 1875.

Lieutenant Haynes was described as an unselfish centre-forward, a style that helped him get into the Royal Engineers football team that reached the Cup final in 1878. However, his football career was cut short before the end of the year.

On 2 December 1878, he left Chatham with the 2nd Field Company destined for South Africa and active service in the Zulu War. They landed at Cape Town on 28 December, and arrived in Durban on 4 January 1879. He was attached to the column commanded by Colonel Charles Pearson. The Regimental History states: 'The disastrous commencement of the campaign [the massacre at Isandlwana] seriously jeopardised the safety of the column under Colonel Pearson, which, having crossed at the mouth of the Tugela, had advanced northward as far as Ekowe.' They encountered and defeated a Zulu army at Inyezane on

114

22 January 1879, the same day as the battle at Isandlwana, and reached Eshowe on the following day.

The Regimental History continued:

> The garrison being cooped-up within the space occupied by their lines, and the whole of the country between Ekowe and the Tugela being in the hands of the Zulus, communication with the rear was completely cut off. Under these circumstances Lieutenant C Haynes, RE, who was at the base on the Tugela, suggested the possibility of flashing signals to the beleaguered force. His idea was somewhat scouted by the authorities; still he was permitted to make the effort. The difficulty lay in the improbability of attracting the attention of those within the fort. When all was ready, signalling was begun, and was continued with patience day by day whenever a gleam of sunshine was available. For a whole week no indication was obtained that the flashes were observed, and it was not till long after a less persevering man would have abandoned the trial that the first answering gleam was obtained. It was an unpleasant and anxious task watching on an exposed hill-top for so long, but the reward of success was great, and Haynes had the gratification of receiving the personal thanks of Lord Chelmsford for his ingenuity and patience.

After the relief of Eshowe, Haynes was with the 2nd Company when it marched north to join the 1st Division under Colonel Evelyn Wood VC, for the advance on Ulundi. His War Office papers state: 'Served in the Zulu War from 4 January to 31 December 1879; in the 2nd Company, RE. He established the communications between Forts Tenedos and Eshowe by means of sun-flashing. Present at the battle of Ulundi, 4 July 1879.' He was twice mentioned in despatches, and received the South Africa Medal with 1879 clasp.

Bechuanaland Expedition in South Africa, 1884–85

Haynes's next tour of active service was also in South Africa in 1884–85. British forces under Sir Charles Warren, a Royal Engineer acting as a Special Commissioner for the British Government, launched an expedition into Bechuanaland (Botswana since 1966) in December 1884, to enforce British power in the region after encroachments by the

German-backed Ndebele from the Kalahari Desert and infiltration by the Transvaal Boer semi-independent states of Stellaland and Goshen. The Tswana Country was a vast area of grassland, savannah and desert, and among the troops who moved north from the Cape were three observation balloons, the first time the apparatus had been used on active service. Lieutenant Haynes was attached to the 7th Field Company. The Boers withdrew without bloodshed, and to avoid a problematic link between the Boers and the German lands of South-West Africa, they annexed Bechuanaland as a Protectorate on 31 March 1885. For his services Haynes received the Cape of Good Hope General Service Medal with Bechuanaland clasp.

In 1890 he married Elizabeth Maude, the daughter of Sir Henry Edward Williams KCB, and they had three sons.

Haynes was promoted captain on 28 January 1886, and to major on 1 October 1894 and lieutenant colonel in 1901. After becoming a colonel in 1907 he was on the Coast Defence, Eastern Command from 1908 to 1912, when he retired. He was appointed Commander of the Bath (CB) during the awards for King George V's coronation announced on 19 June 1911.

He was recalled for service during the Great War, and on 25 November 1915 he entered the France and Flanders theatres of war, for which he received the three general service medals.

Haynes's home was at Roborough House on Furze Hill Road in Torquay, and he died at the Mount Stuart Nursing Home in Torquay, on 29 October 1935, aged 90.

His brother, Captain Alfred Ernest Haynes of the Royal Engineers, who had served in Egypt in 1882, and was on active service with him in Bechuanaland, was killed in action at Chief Chingaira Makonis Kraal on 3 August 1896 while commanding 43 Company RE during the Mashonaland Rebellion in Rhodesia, and is commemorated by a brass plaque in Rochester Cathedral. His son, Charles Cecil (born in 1891), after getting wounded while serving with the Devonshire Regiment at La Bassée in 1914, became a flight commander with 62 Squadron, Royal Air Force, and another son, Henry John (born in 1891), became a commander in the Royal Navy, receiving the DSO and DSC during the Second World War.

Haynes's set of miniature medals were sold at auction on 2 April 2003 and his original set of medals were auctioned on 5 July 2011.

Francis George Bond

Francis Bond played in the 1878 FA Cup final and went on to have a highly distinguished military career, seeing active service in the Zulu War, in Egypt, on the North-west Frontier of India at Hazara and Tirah, in the Boer War and during the Great War.

Bond was born at Marlborough in Wiltshire on 10 August 1856, and he was baptised at St Mary the Virgin Church in Marlborough on 21 September of that year. He was the eldest son of the Reverend Frederick Hookey Bond (1821–97) and his wife, Mary Isabella (formerly Delafosse, 1833–1916). His father was the headmaster of the Marlborough Royal Free Grammar School from 1853 to 1876. His paternal grandfather was Rear Admiral Francis Godolphin Bond RN (1765–1839), and he was related to a Royal Navy commander who served with Captain Bligh on HMS *Bounty*, and therefore Francis was intended for a career in the Royal Navy. He was a cousin of Sabine Baring-Gould, who was the author of numerous hymns such as 'Onward, Christian Soldiers'.

Bond began his education at his father's school before attending Marlborough College, for whom he played rugby, and went to the Royal Military Academy. The family moved to Bath in the year he was commissioned as lieutenant in the Royal Engineers on 8 August 1876.

Playing at inside-left during the Royal Engineers games in the 1877–78 campaign, he scored at least two goals in the two matches against Oxford University in the quarter-finals, and it was said that he: 'Did good service for the Engineers in the cup ties, keeping well on the ball and rarely missing a shot.' However, his football career was soon cut short.

When reinforcements were requested for active service in the Zulu War in 1879, Bond and Lieutenant Rich sailed to South Africa with the C or Telegraph Company, 30th Field Company, RE, taking part in the re-invasion of Zululand. His War Office Papers state: 'He served in the Zulu War from 13 May to 24 November 1879. Employed on Line of Communications in Zululand and Natal in connection with the field telegraphs and signalling. Also in creating and maintaining the Utrecht–Wakkerstroom telegraph line in the Transvaal.' For his service he received the South Africa Medal with 1879 clasp. He was a talented artist, and made two coloured sketches of the scene at Rorke's Drift, and at the Buffalo River.

At St Jude's Church in Kensington, on 1 February 1881, Bond married Alice Maud Vivian (1857–1944), the daughter of the Right Reverend William Forrest, who took the service and was assisted in the ceremony by Lieutenant Bond's father. They had four sons between 1881 and 1894, three of whom joined the army. The second son, Lionel Vivian (1884–1961), served with the Royal Engineers, becoming a lieutenant general and being knighted for his services in the two world wars.

Bond was posted for active service in the Egyptian Campaign, taking part in the actions at Kassassin on 28 August 1882 and the decisive battle at Tel-el-Kebir on 13 September 1882. His War Office Papers state: 'Employed in connection with field telegraphs under Maj-General G Graham VC. Also in charge of Poucers attached to 4th/2nd Staff of Cavalry Division under General Drury-Lowe; Sir G Wolseley in chief command. Present at the reconnaissance to Kassassin, Sep 9, and Tel-el-Kebir.' For his service he received the Egypt Medal with Tel-el-Kebir clasp and the Khedive's Bronze Star.

He was promoted to captain on 2 February 1887 and posted to the North-West Frontier of India, where, on 4 February 1890, he was initiated into Freemasonry by joining the Beauchamp Lodge at Roorkee, achieving high office in the District Grand Lodge of Freemasons in the Punjab.

Hazara Expedition on the North-West Frontier of India, 1891

Bond took part in the Hazara or Black Mountain Expedition from 12 March to 17 June 1891 as the field engineer with the 4th Company of Bengal Sappers and Miners, attached to the 1st Brigade. Hazara lies on the banks of the Indus River on the North-West Frontier of India. This was the fourth occasion that British forces had launched an expedition to engage the Hassanzai, Akazai and Chagarzai tribes of Pathans totalling about 8,000 men, led by Hashim Ali, the Khan of Isazai. It was more of a demonstration of British military might and determination, and was typical of an almost continuous series of expeditions into tribal areas. The aim of the force was to converge from three directions on the main village of Thakot. As the force moved through the mountains, they were constantly engaged by the enemy, usually by sniper fire into the camps at night from a distance. This kept the British on constant alert. It was a massive task to haul the bigger guns up the steep mountains to shell the villages and seek out the leaders. The tribes eventually submitted, which was the usual outcome of similar expeditions. For his service Captain Bond was mentioned in despatches, and received the Indian General Service Medal with Hazara clasp.

Tirah Campaign on the North-West Frontier of India, 1897–98

Having been promoted to major on 29 March 1895, Bond was employed at the School of Infantry at Roorkee in India in 1896, and then he received orders for active duty in the Tirah campaign. This was perhaps the hardest-fought of all the British Army's expeditions in the unstable and hostile mountainous regions of the North-West Frontier of India. The main reason for the expedition was a show of force to subdue several uprisings in the region and deter the tribes, especially the Afridi, from continually marauding into British India. A famous action during the campaign was the storming of the Dargai Heights on 20 October 1897, for which four Victoria Crosses were awarded.

Major Bond served from 2 October 1897 to 6 April 1898, where he was wounded in the left hand in the Khyber Pass on 1 January 1898. His War Office Papers state: 'Commanded 5th Company, Bengal Sappers and Miners with Peshawar Column. Afterwards in the 5th Brigade with the Force under Brig-Gen Hammond VC, and at the operations in Khyber Pass and Bagar Valley; 15 December 1897 to 15 February 1898.' For his service Major Bond received the India Medal with Tirah clasp. The India Medal had replaced the Indian General Service Medal in 1895.

Bond saw active service during the Second Boer War in South Africa as Deputy Assistant Adjutant General (DAAG) of the 4th Division. He was chief staff officer in the Eastern Transvaal, being mentioned in despatches. For his service he received the Queen's South Africa Medal with three clasps, and he was appointed Companion of the Bath (CB) during King Edward VII's birthday honours on 26 June 1902.

He was promoted to the local rank of lieutenant colonel on 1 January 1902, 'whilst specially employed at the Headquarters in South Africa'. He was made lieutenant colonel in the Royal Engineers on 27 July 1902, while he commanded the Queen's Own Sappers and Miners from 1902 to 1904. Bond was made substantive colonel on 27 July 1905, while being employed as assistant quartermaster general in the Punjab from 1904 to 1906. He became deputy quartermaster general in India from 1906 to 1908, and was given the temporary rank of brigadier general on 18 April 1908, while he was employed as director general of the Military Works in India from 1908 to 1911. He retired as honorary brigadier general on 10 August 1913.

Bond was recalled for administrative duties during the Great War as an assistant director of Quartering at the War Office; serving as director from 1917 to 1919. He received several honours for his services in the Great War: on 3 June 1918 he was created Companion of the Order of St Michael and St George (CMG), on 31 October 1918 he was Knight of Grace in the Order of the Hospital of St John of Jerusalem in England, he was appointed Knight Commander of the Most Excellent

Order of the British Empire (KBE), and he received the American Distinguished Service Medal on 12 July 1919.

He joined the Army and Navy Lodge of Freemasons at Aldershot on his return from India in 1913. After the war he was employed by the Ministry of Pensions, with the role of organising hospitals for the care of the disabled. Bond suffered a severe heart attack in February 1928, and remained unwell until his death at his home of Stowe in Brackendale Road, Camberley, on 15 August 1930, five days after his 74th birthday. He was buried with military honours at St Michael's Church in Camberley.

General Sir Bindon Blood said of Bond: 'I have watched Frank Bond's progress and his many important and brilliant services to the country, including his work in the Great War. To the end, he was the same as always: a soldier and a gentleman, a pattern to us all.'

Lovick Bransby Friend

Lovick Friend played in the 1878 FA Cup final, was present at the battle of Omdurman during the Mahdist uprising of 1898 and served in high administration in Ireland and during the Great War.

Friend was born at Penhill on Halfway Street in Sidcup, Kent, on 25 April 1856, the fourth son in the very large family of a merchant named Frederick Friend and his wife, Fanny, the daughter of G. Tyrrell and his wife, Frances. He grew up at Woollett Hall in North Cray, in the London borough of Bexley, which his father bought in the mid-1850s and remained the family home until late in the nineteenth century. It is now a mental health care facility known as Loring Hall, a Grade II listed building. Friend was educated at Cheltenham College, and at the Royal Military Academy, where he won a prize for artillery before he was commissioned as lieutenant in the Royal Engineers in 1873.

'... always cool, and a sure kick', Friend was considered to have a safe pair of hands as he played in goal at football and was wicketkeeper and right-hand batsman for the Royal Engineers, for whom he scored 198 runs against Band of Brothers in 1885. He kept wicket for Kent County Cricket Club, played for Hong Kong in 1880 and occasionally for South Northumberland from 1887 to 1891. He also represented the MCC in 1891. In the six first-class matches he played for Kent his highest score was 72, and he made two catches.

Much of Friend's military career was served in administration. He was an instructor at the Royal Military College at Sandhurst, 1883–84, and he was promoted to captain in 1885, when he was appointed secretary for the Royal Engineers Experimental Committee from 1885 to 1889. At this time he served in the West Indies, where he trained the Fortress Company. He was appointed major in 1893.

Major Friend was posted to Egypt in 1897, and served as a staff officer in charge of organising supplies. He became attached to the Intelligence Department, being present at the decisive battle of Omdurman on 2 September 1898, where he was an aid to General Sir Herbert Kitchener, the commander of the British forces. The battle was notable for the famous charge of the 21st Lancers, in which Lieutenant Winston Churchill took part.

Battle of Omdurman in the Sudan, 1898

Several factors led Prime Minister Lord Salisbury to send an expedition to the re-conquest of the Sudan. He could see the need to secure the upper reaches of the River Nile to protect it from French encroachment, and additionally there was pressure to take revenge for the humiliation caused by the failure to relieve General Gordon at Khartoum during the Nile Expedition. General Sir Herbert Kitchener, who had reorganised the Anglo-Egyptian Army of 15,000 men, and armed with the most modern military equipment of the time, began his advance up the Nile to smash the Khalifa and his Dervish warriors, supported by a gunboat flotilla on the river.

After a victory over Dervish forces at Atbara on 8 April 1898, Kitchener pushed his men relentlessly on towards Khartoum, 200 miles away. When dawn rose on 2 September 1898, he had reached Omdurman near Khartoum. He had positioned his men in an oval shape with the rear defended by the wide waters of the Nile, supported by artillery and reserves – and he waited. Dervish banners began to appear on the hills, and the thump of war drums filled the air. The Dervishes made a suicidal frontal attack that was doomed to failure. Murderous fire from machine guns, rifles and artillery scythed wave after wave of them down before any of them got within 300 paces. It was more of an execution than a battle, and when the shattered warriors turned and fled they left behind a staggering 11,000 dead, 16,000 wounded and 4,000 prisoners. Kitchener's soldiers had suffered fewer than fifty casualties.

For his service in the campaign, Major Friend received the Queen's Sudan Medal with the Atbara and Khartoum clasp, the Turkish Order of Osmanieh, 4th Class and the Turkish Order of the Medjidieh, 4th Class (*London Gazette*, 23 September 1902), and he was mentioned in despatches.

He remained in the region, becoming director of works and stores for the Egyptian Army from 1900 to 1904, was employed for the Egyptian

Public Works in 1905, and was assistant director on fortification works, 1906–07. On returning to Britain in 1908 he was appointed Companion of the Bath (CB), and he was appointed to the command of Scottish Coast Defences from 1908 to 1912. Friend was appointed major general in charge of administration at the Irish Command in Dublin in 1912, becoming commander-in-chief in Ireland in 1914. He was replaced following the Easter Rising in 1916. He was on the Privy Council of Ireland in 1916.

During the Great War Friend served as the president of the Claims Commission for the British Army in France from 1916 to 1918. He was a Commander of the French Legion of Honour, and a Commander of the Belgian Ordre de la Couronne, and he received the Croix de Guerre (Belgium). He was created Knight Commander of the Order of the Bath (KCB) in 1919. A number of his papers and letters concerning the Curragh Mutiny in 1914 and the role of Ireland in the Great War are held at the Bodleian Library in Oxford, and the British Library in London.

Friend retired from the British Army in June 1920, although he continued to serve as chairman of the French Committee of the Disposal Board. During his retirement he spent some time in South Africa and Australia. His home was at 7 Park Place in the St James district of London, and he died in a nursing home at 20 Glazbury Road in West Kensington, London, on 19 November 1944, aged 88.

James Henry Cowan

James Cowan played in the 1878 FA Cup final, and later saw service in the Second Boer War.

According to the British Olympic Association, Cowan was born in Brentford, but other sources say Chiswick, on 28 September 1856, the eldest son of William Cowan, LLD, JP, and his wife Selina, daughter of W. Deeming.

He was educated at Edinburgh Academy, Cheltenham College and at the Royal Military Academy. From there he was commissioned as lieutenant in the Royal Engineers in February 1876, having won the Sword of Honour, and been awarded the Pollock Medal in July 1876. The medal was given out twice a year to the most distinguished cadet at Addiscombe or Woolwich on passing the biennial examination for a commission.

After going through the submarine mining course at Chatham, Cowan was posted to Malta with the 33rd (Submarine Mining) Company, and then he was employed at the War Office from 1885 to 1887; first in the Submarine Mining and later in the Fortifications branches. He then became instructor in fortification at the Royal Military Academy.

He played rugby for the RMA while he was there. He was comfortable either as a full-back or a half-back, and it was noted that he '... never misses his kick; very difficult to pass'.

Cowan was most prominent in rifle shooting. While at Cheltenham he won the Spencer Cup at Wimbledon, and he shot for the Old Cheltonians in the Public Schools' Veterans Trophy forty-one times, leading them to ten victories. From 1891 he shot six times for the Scottish team in the Elcho Shield. In 1893 he was one of the founders of the Army Rifle Association, and that year he won the Gold Jewel at the Army Championships. From then until 1905, with a break when he was serving in South Africa and China, he always gained a high place. Just before he went to South Africa, Cowan was a member of the team that represented Britain at The Hague in 1899. He shot thirteen times for the Army Eight, and was captain from 1908 to 1913. He was a member of the successful British Olympic shooting squad for the 1908 London Games, which was held at the Bisley Rifle Range near Camberley. He was placed equal sixth in the Running Target, single shot, and tenth in the Running Target, double shot.

In 1880 Cowan married Alice, the daughter of the commanding Royal Engineer at Chatham.

He was promoted captain in 1887, and major in 1895. Major Cowan then saw active service during the Second Boer War in South Africa, 1899–1902. For his service he was mentioned in despatches and received the Queen's South Africa Medal with Cape Colony, Transvaal and Laing's Nek clasps.

In July 1901 he was appointed commanding engineer at Weihaiwei in China. After the Russians had leased Port Arthur from China in 1898, the British Government responded by pressuring the Chinese to lease nearby Weihaiwei to them, and the British fleet took possession on 24 May 1898. The British used it as a summer anchorage for the Royal Navy's China Station, and Major Cowan was employed in keeping it maintained. He returned to Britain in the following year.

He was a member of the Ordnance Committee from 1902 to 1905. He was commanding Royal Engineer at Chatham in 1906–07, and having been promoted colonel in 1908, he became assistant director of fortifications and works at the War Office from 1908 to 1913, when he retired from military service.

On the outbreak of the Great War Cowan returned to the War Office to superintend the provision of rifle ranges for the Territorial Army and continued the work for the duration of hostilities. During this employment he arranged for the construction of 200 rifle ranges in Britain, including those for the Royal Flying Corps, and no accidents were recorded at his ranges during the whole of the war period. For his service he was appointed Commander of the Bath (CB) in the New Year Honours' List of 1917.

On his retirement at the end of the war Cowan settled at Moffat in Dumfriesshire, and also had property at Boghall in Linlithgow. He owned about 1,300 acres of land, and there are records that he leased some to the Pumpherston Oil Company (Scottish Shale) to mine for oil. His usual breakfast was two apples and a glass of milk, and it was noted: 'He was always wonderfully fit and active, and when nearing 80 thought nothing of cycling 50 miles a day.' He also retained good eyesight, and his last appearance for the Old Cheltonians was just before his 79th birthday, when he scored nine consecutive bulls but dropped his last shot.

Colonel Cowan died at Moffat on 7 August 1943, aged 86.

William George Morris

William Morris played in the 1878 FA Cup final. He saw active service in South Africa, and later gained a reputation in scientific circles.

Morris was born in the Malagaum Camp near Kumpa in the Bombay Presidency of India, on 12 February 1847, the eldest of two sons in a family of six children born between 1847 and 1855, to Lieutenant Colonel William John Morris (1809–70) of the Bombay Army and his wife, Georgiana (formerly Cunningham, 1824–1900). The family home was in Brighton.

William attended Cheltenham College and the Royal Military Academy, from where he was commissioned as lieutenant in the Royal Engineers on 10 July 1867.

On 27 April 1871, Morris married Edith Sofia (1849–1917) at St Margaret's Church in Bowers Gifford, Essex, where Edith's father, the Reverend William Tireman, was the parish priest. They had three sons and a daughter between 1874 and 1878. Having been made a widow in 1939, his daughter, Winifred, married Major General George Henry Addison, whose father, George William Addison, had played for Royal Engineers in the 1872 and 1874 FA Cup finals.

Morris was aged over 30 when he played in the 1878 FA Cup final, when his 'excellent' and 'well-directed' throw-in led to the only goal scored by the Royal Engineers.

He was assistant instructor in Surveying at the School of Military Engineering at Chatham from 1877 to 1882, during which time he was promoted to captain on 9 October 1879.

Morris was involved in the study of geodetics, the branch of mathematics that deals with measurement and representation of the Earth, and he was in charge of the Transit to Venus Expedition to Brisbane in Australia in 1882, which was sent out to observe the passage of Venus across the face of the sun, and which would allow scientists to obtain new data concerning the distance between the Earth and the sun. However, they were unsuccessful due to thick cloud cover.

Morris received further promotion to major on 31 December 1886, while he was in charge of the survey of South Africa from 1883, and he was promoted to lieutenant colonel on 14 July 1893. He returned to Chatham in 1894 in command of the Training Battalion for one year, and then he was appointed assistant commandant at Chatham from 1895 to 1898. During this time he was promoted to colonel on 14 July 1897.

He was appointed colonel on the staff of the Royal Engineers in South Africa on 22 July 1898. When the Second Boer War began he was acting as district inspector based in Cape Town. During his employment there he and his staff arranged for the construction of lines of blockhouses across the war zone. It was recorded that he was disappointed that 'no use whatever was made of his unique knowledge of the topography of Cape Colony'. Nevertheless, for his service he was twice mentioned in despatches by Lord Kitchener for his 'special and meritorious service', and he was appointed Commander of the Bath (CB) on 29 November 1900.

Morris became superintendent of the Ordnance Survey of the Transvaal and Orange Free State in 1902. He retired from military service in 1904, but he remained at his current post in a civilian capacity. He retired in 1907, the year he was created Knight Commander, Order of St Michael and St George (KCMG), during the birthday honours.

Following Edith's death on 7 January 1917, when he was aged 70, he married Ethel Joan (1866–1956), the daughter of Robert Warren of Gosford Pines, near Othery St Mary in Devon. The marriage took place on 4 July 1917 at St Gabriel's Church in Warwick Square, London. Ethel was nearly twenty years his junior.

On his retirement he lived at a house named Fron Heulog in Betws-y-Coed, Caernarvonshire, before moving to a house named Islwn. He died at his home on 26 February 1935, two weeks after his 88th birthday, and he was buried at St Michael's Church in Betws-y-Coed.

Charles Blair Mayne

Charles Mayne played in the 1878 FA Cup final, and went on active service in Afghanistan in the same year.

Mayne was born at Vizagapatam (Vellore) in Madras, India, on 15 October 1855, the son of General Jasper Otway Mayne (1830–86) of the Royal Engineers and his wife, Adriana Amelia (1832–1909), the daughter of James Blair and his wife, Charlotte Cecilia. They had married in Harrow on 13 December 1854 and made their home at Bagshot in Surrey.

He entered the Royal Military Academy, from where he was commissioned as lieutenant in the Royal Engineers on 28 January 1875.

Described as '… a very useful half-back', he scored the second goal in the semi-final that got the Royal Engineers to the 1878 final.

Mayne was posted for active service in the Second Afghan War, where he took part in the opening battle of the campaign on 21 November 1878 at the Afghan fort of Ali Masjid, which stood overlooking the western end of the Khyber Pass and formed the border between Afghanistan and British India. For his service he was awarded the Afghanistan Medal with Ali Masjid clasp.

He was appointed honorary captain on 14 November 1881, and he was an Assistant Instructor in Surveying at the School of Military Engineering at Brompton Barracks in Gillingham, Kent, from 18 July 1882 to 15 September 1886, although the 1881 census records that he was already living in that establishment. He was promoted captain on 28 January 1886, and he was appointed professor of surveying, military topography and reconnaissance at the Royal Military College of Canada at Kingston in Ontario, Canada, from 16 September 1886 to 31 July 1893.

Mayne was the author of several publications concerning the military, the most notable works being entitled *The Defence of Plevna, 1877* and *Infantry Fire Tactics*, which was produced in 1888. While he was serving in Canada he married Victoria Amelia (formerly Moore) at St George's Cathedral in Kingston, Ontario, on 6 April 1893.

On his return to Britain he became secretary at the Royal Engineers Institute from 1 July 1894 to 30 September 1897, during which time he was promoted to major on 10 December 1894. Having been promoted lieutenant colonel in the Royal Engineers on 1 April 1901, he was made Assistant Inspector General of Fortifications at the War Office on 2 February 1903; and then Assistant Director of Fortifications and Works. His final promotion was to colonel on 31 December 1904.

Mayne was the executor to his mother's estate when she died in 1909, at Witwood in Camberley. He died at 3 Southwell Park Road in Camberley on 17 October 1914, two days after his 59th birthday, and he was buried at St Michael's Church in Yorktown, Camberley. He is also remembered on the Camberley War Memorial, where he is recorded as being a major in the Central India Horse, which was his brother's regiment.

His brother, Augustus Blair Mayne (born in 1860), was wounded in action during the Great War in 1917 and died of his injuries. Charles lost two of his sons to the Great War. Major Jasper Moore Mayne (born at Chatham in 1895) was killed in action in France in 1915 while serving with the Royal Artillery in the British Expeditionary Force. Lieutenant Victor Charles Moore Mayne (born at Chatham in 1896) was killed in action in France in 1916 while serving with the 1st Battalion, South Wales Borderers in the British Expeditionary Force.

Frederick Crofton Heath-Caldwell

Frederick Heath played for Royal Engineers in the 1878 FA Cup final, and later saw active service in Egypt, the Sudan and in South Africa.

Heath was born at Mersham House at Bitterne near Southampton, on 21 February 1858, the second son of five in the family of seven children born between 1854 and 1863 to Admiral Sir Leopold George Heath, KCB (1817–1907) and his wife, Mary Emma (formerly Marsh). They married in Malta on 8 December 1853. Admiral Heath was a veteran of the Crimean War, 1854–56, and of the expedition to Abyssinia (now Ethiopia) in 1868.

Heath entered the Royal Military Academy, from where he was commissioned as lieutenant in the Royal Engineers on 25 January 1877. Described as a half-back with a vigorous style, he played in his only FA Cup final the following year.

His first tour of duty was in the Egyptian Campaign in 1882, and for his service he received the Egypt Medal with Tel-el-Kebir clasp and the Khedive's Bronze Star. He remained in the region and took part in the Nile Expedition of 1884–85 **and** served with the 17th Company brought from Cairo to work on the Saukin to Berber railway. He was mentioned in despatches and received the Sudan Medal with Abu Klea clasp.

Heath was promoted captain on 25 January 1888 and he was promoted major on 12 August 1895.

In 1889 he married Constance Mary, the daughter of Colonel H. Helsham-Jones. They had two sons. Cuthbert Helsham (1889–1979) was a decorated Royal Navy officer, and Martin Frederick (1893–1915) was killed in action during the Great War.

Heath was posted for a third tour of active service during the Anglo-Boer War in South Africa, 1899–1901, where he was Assistant Adjutant

General (AAG) South Africa from 1900 to 1902. For his service he was mentioned in despatches, and received the Queen's South Africa Medal with two clasps and the King's South Africa Medal with 1901 and 1902 clasps

Having been promoted lieutenant colonel in 1903 and colonel in 1906, he was appointed AAG Royal Engineers at Army Headquarters from 1906 to 1908. He was inspector of Royal Engineers from 1908 to 1913, commanding the Scottish Coast Defences, 1913–14. At the time of the Great War he was director of military training at the War Office, 1914–15, general officer commanding the Portsmouth Garrison from 1916 to 1918, and general officer commanding the South-East Area, RAF, in 1918. He retired from military service at the end of the war, with the rank of major general.

Heath was appointed Commander of the Bath (CB) on 24 June 1910. In retirement he became a Justice of the Peace in the County Palatine of Chester.

Under the condition of the will of his uncle, James Stamford Caldwell, Heath was to assume the name Caldwell on the death of his wife, and Frederick's great-aunt, in order for him to inherit the Linley Wood Estate at Talke in Staffordshire, which they had owned since 1789. She died in 1913. General Heath died at Linley Hall on 18 September 1945, aged 87. The estate was sold at auction in 1949.

Henry Edzell Morgan Lindsay

Morgan Lindsay became the first Welsh-born player to appear in an FA Cup final, and later saw active service in the Transvaal, the Sudan, the Anglo-Boer War and the Great War.

Lindsay was born at Tredegar Park near Newport in South Wales, on 11 February 1857. He was the eldest son of Lieutenant Colonel Henry Gore Lindsay (1830–1914), of the Rifle Brigade, who later became chief constable of Glamorgan, and his wife, Ellen Sarah (1837–1912), the fourth daughter of Charles Morgan Robinson Morgan, who was Member of Parliament for Brecon and was created Baron Tredegar in 1859. Lieutenant Colonel Lindsay served in the Kaffir War in South Africa, 1852–53, in the Crimean War, 1854–56, and in the Indian Mutiny, 1857–58. One of Morgan's brothers, Lionel Arthur MVO OBE (1861–1945), followed his father as chief constable of Glamorgan, and his youngest brother, George Mackintosh (1880–1956), rose to the rank of major general and was an expert on mechanised warfare. The family also owned property and land at Glesnevin near Dublin.

Morgan was educated at the Royal Academy in Gosport and attended the Royal Military Academy, from where he passed out as temporary lieutenant in the Royal Engineers on 2 August 1876. This was later made permanent and backdated six months.

In addition to playing for the Royal Engineers at football, Lindsay was a member of the Marylebone Cricket Club (MCC), and he also played for I Zangari. He played for Glamorgan when they were not a first-class county, and he played for the South Wales Cricket Club. He represented the Royal Engineers in an engraving of 'Famous Footballers', which was issued by the popular *Boy's Own* paper, volume 4 of 1881–82.

Lindsay's first tour of active service was as a member of Number 1 Section, Field Telegraph, in the later stages of the Transvaal (First Boer) War in 1881. No medal was awarded for this campaign. He returned to England in September 1882, and later spent the October and November of 1873 at the Hythe School of Musketry in Kent. He joined the newly formed Postal Telegraph Service in May 1884, where he remained until February 1885.

Saukin Expedition in the Sudan, 1885

In 1883 the Sudanese religious leader, Mohammed Ahmed, proclaimed himself the Mahdi and provoked an uprising among his fanatical Dervish followers, who inflicted a number of defeats on Egyptian troops. The British Government had little desire to become involved yet again in the problems of the region. However, they realised that the east-coast port of Saukin would have to be secured if the evacuation of British subjects became necessary, and reluctantly authorised the deployment of a British expeditionary force.

Sudanese forces had laid siege to a number of garrisons and outposts containing Egyptian troops, and on 29 February 1884, a British force of 4,000 infantry and cavalry, with eight 7-pounder guns and six Gatling guns, advanced in the classic 'Brigade Square' formation to try to relieve the garrison at Tokar. They came upon 10,000 well-entrenched Dervishes led by Osman Digna near the village of El Teb, strengthened by a number of captured guns. However, the Dervishes' rear was unprotected, and the square marched against this vulnerable section of their lines. As the British advanced steadily, a mass of Dervish warriors sprang up and attacked the square on three sides. A brutal clash at close-quarters followed.

The Mahdi was eventually driven out and the British Government ordered the troops to withdraw, leaving behind a small detachment to garrison Saukin.

Morgan was placed in command of the 2nd Section, Telegraph Battalion, Royal Engineers, and was sent to take part in the Saukin Expedition of February 1885. He was present at the engagement at Tofrek on 22 March 1885, during which his fellow Engineers footballer Lieutenant Edwin Newman was killed in action.

He returned to England in June 1885. On 1 October 1886, he was appointed captain and adjutant with the Royal Monmouthshire Engineers Militia, but he resigned from the Royal Engineers on 2 October 1891 and became honorary major with his new unit on 30 December 1891.

At Pontypridd on 24 July 1889, he married Ellen Katherine, the daughter of a landowner named George Thomas. They had four boys and three girls born between 1891 and 1910. The three sons who were old enough to fight for their country were killed in action during the Great War. The eldest, George Walter Thomas (1891–1917), served with the Royal Artillery, and on transferring to the Royal Flying Corps was killed in a plane crash near Bristol in 1917. Archibald Thurston Thomas (1897–1918) was killed by a sniper in France in 1918 while serving with the Royal Monmouthshire Royal Engineers. Claud Frederic Thomas was serving with the Royal Artillery when he was killed while leading his battery in a rearguard action in France, just a week after Archibald. The youngest son, David Edzel Thomas (1910–68), was invested as an officer of the Most Venerable Order of the Hospital of St John of Jerusalem (O St J).

Morgan's third tour of active duty took him back to South Africa for the Second Boer War, in May 1900, in command of a company of Royal Monmouthshire Royal Engineers. They joined the regular Royal Engineers in the Orange Free State, where they were employed around Bloemfontein, repairing the roads, railways and bridges. In late 1900 the company was transferred to Kroonstadt, where Morgan was appointed deputy superintendent of Works and Office, commanding the troops maintaining the railways in the Orange Free State, and being responsible for the pay, clothing and discipline of the soldiers of all Corps employed on the Imperial Military Railways in the Colony. His rank of major was made permanent on 20 March 1901, with the honorary rank of lieutenant colonel awarded to him on 27 April 1901. The company was recalled to England in September 1901, and was disbanded on 14 October 1901. For his service Morgan was mentioned in despatches by General Kitchener (*London Gazette*, 29 July 1902) and he received the Queen's South Africa Medal with three clasps.

Although he was serving in South Africa, Morgan stood for Parliament as the Conservative candidate for the East Glamorganshire constituency during the 1900 General Election. His wife Ellen campaigned on his behalf, but he was unsuccessful. He was chosen again as the Conservative candidate for East Glamorganshire seat at the 1915 General Election, but the Great War caused this to be postponed. He was heavily involved in Glamorgan and Dublin civic affairs and administration. He became a member of both the Glamorgan County Council and the Caerphilly County Council in 1892, where he acted as the senior magistrate for the Caerphilly petty sessions division. He was deputy lieutenant for the County of Dublin and he was a Justice of the Peace for the County of Dublin, and for the County of Glamorgan.

Having been appointed commanding officer of the Royal Monmouthshire Royal Engineers, Morgan was appointed Commander of the Bath (CB) (civil division) in the 1911 Coronation awards. At the outbreak of the Great War, he remained in command of his unit based at Monmouth, although he travelled to the Western Front in January 1917. He relinquished his commission on 24 May 1917. The well-known garden designer Norah Lindsay was his cousin. She lived at Sutton Courtenay near Abingdon, and in 1919 Morgan was asked to design the war memorial there.

He was very involved in the administration of sport in South Wales, acting as president of the South Wales Football Association from 1890 to 1922, and with the Glamorgan Cricket League. He was a member of the committee of Glamorgan County Cricket Club, and helped with their fund-raising activities in 1921 as they moved to become the first and only Welsh county cricket club to gain first-class status.

Morgan began to establish horse-racing stables at his home. At first he trained horses for point-to-point races, and one of his better horses at this time was Brunette, which won the Glamorgan Hunt at Crossways near Cowbridge in 1890. He eventually turned his hand to training steeplechasers, and he had his first big success in 1906 when Creolin won the Scottish Grand National at Ayr. He trained Miss Balscadden to win the Welsh Grand National at Chepstow in 1926 and 1928, and in the following year he entered the horse for the Aintree Grand National, where it lived up to its 200-1 betting and failed to finish. His most notable success came at the 1933 Cheltenham Festival, when his horse Ego won the National Hunt Steeplechase with the amateur jockey Major General Reginald Harding, CB, DSO, of the 5th Royal Inniskilling Dragoon Guards, on board. He was a member of the National Hunt Committee, and his clients included the Welsh industrialist Sir David Llewelyn. He also had a cricket pitch and pavilion at his home and established his own boys' cricket team.

Morgan died at Ystrad Fawr, Ystrad Mynach in Glamorgan, on 1 November 1935, aged 78, and he was buried with full military honours in the family vault at Holy Trinity Church in Ystrad Mynach. At a memorial service soon after his death, the Bishop of Llandaff stated:

> Colonel Lindsay's name was held in respect and reverence by all who knew him. He was a great gentleman, a great Christian, and a great Churchman. He was a great gentleman not simply by reason of birth, education, and position, but by reason also of qualities he possessed that made him a gentleman. A gentleman was a man who thought of other people before himself, and Colonel Lindsay was one. People saw the integrity of his character, his kind deeds, and generosity as a Christian; and knew that those acts sprang from the grasp he had of eternal realities, the things of the spirit. His outward conduct revealed an inward conviction. He valued the Church not because it was an ancient institution, but because he found in the sacraments and ministry of the Church that which satisfied his soul.

Morgan's youngest daughter, Nesta Jessie (1898–1957), was appointed the Most Excellent Order of the British Empire (MBE) in 1944 for her work as commander of the Auxiliary Fire Service in the East End of London during the Blitz. His eldest daughter, Ellen Blanche (1893–1990), was awarded the British Empire Medal (BEM) in 1955 for her work with the Nottinghamshire Women's Voluntary Service. His family home of Ystrad Fawr was later acquired by Caerphilly County Council, and after being demolished it is now the site of Ysbyty Ystrad Fawr Hospital.

Robert Shafto Hedley

Robert Hedley scored hat-tricks for the Royal Engineers in the first and second rounds of the 1877–78 FA Cup competition, and was captain in the final; after which he was twice selected to play for England. He later lost his life by drowning at the age of 27.

Hedley was born at West Monkton near Taunton in Somerset, on 17 January 1857. The 1861 census records that he was the third of four children to a magistrate named Robert Hedley and his wife, Charlotte Catherine. They lived at Springfield House in West Monckton. A decade later he lived with his mother as the third of six children at Easby Hall at Easby near Richmond in North Yorkshire, a large house that they rented from the Jaques family.

He attended Reading School from 1871 to 1873, and in the school's first football season in 1871–72 he was chosen to play for them against Reading FC when he was aged just 15. He attended the Royal Military Academy, from where he passed out as a lieutenant in the Royal Engineers on 2 August 1876.

Reports suggest he was a bulky and robust centre-forward, and he answered a comment that he 'should study shooting at goal' by scoring three goals against Pilgrims in the second round of the 1877–78 competition, and another hat-trick in the third round against Druids. He was captain for the Royal Engineers in the final.

Hedley was a member of the Football Association Committee in 1878–79, and not long before his appearance in the 1878 FA Cup final he was selected to play for England against Scotland at Hampden Park in Glasgow on 2 March 1878, but he was injured and missed out. England lost 7-2. He was selected again for the England versus Scotland match at The Oval, on 1 March 1879, however, the game was postponed because of bad weather. He was only selected as a reserve for the rearranged match on 5 April 1879, which England won 5-4.

Hedley was posted to Ceylon (Sri Lanka), and on 29 January 1884 he was out boating at Trincomalee when he landed on a rock. His boat got loose and drifted away from him and he was forced to swim after it. It is not sure what happened next but his body was recovered by a search party that had set out to look for him. He was aged 27. His estate went to his father, who was living at 44 St George's Square in London.

Horace Hutton Barnet

Horace Barnet played at outside-right in the 1878 FA Cup final, scoring at least one goal in the earlier rounds, and one of the two goals that got the Royal Engineers into the final. Soon after the final he went on active service in the Afghan War. He later saw active service in Burma and during the Great War.

Barnet was born at 2 Leinster Gardens in Bayswater, London, on 6 March 1856, the son of an East India Company merchant named George Barnet and his wife, Frederica Sarah (formerly Salomons, 1830–1917). He had two younger siblings, Geoffrey (born in 1859) and Lilian (born in 1860). He attended Rugby School and entered the Royal Military Academy on 17 June 1873, from where he was commissioned as lieutenant in the Royal Engineers on 28 January 1875.

He also played cricket, and was a member of the MCC. However, his main asset seems to have been his speed down the wings, and he was known to be a good sprinter on the athletics track.

Soon after his appearance in the 1878 final, Barnet was posted to Bombay, from where he was sent for active service in the Second Afghan War of 1878–80, but he was invalided home with severe sunstroke.

While he was at the School of Military Engineering at Brompton Barracks, Barnet was picked to play for England when they thrashed Ireland 13-0 in Belfast on 18 February 1882, which is still a record England score. He also played for Middlesex, London, the South and as a guest for Corinthians. He was on the Football Association Committee in April 1883.

After six months on sick leave, Barnet served at the Chatham depot until 1883, after which he returned to India to join the railways department. He was promoted captain on 28 January 1886 while serving during the Burmese War, for which he was mentioned in despatches, and received the Indian General Service Medal, 1854, with 1885–87 and 1887–89 clasps.

In 1890 Barnet married Leonora Rose (formerly Monckton, born at Agra in India on 3 February 1857), and they had a son named Dennis George, who was born at Allahabad in India on 21 July 1893 and christened at Quetta.

At the time of the 1891 census he and his wife were living with his mother at 26 Montagu Square in Marylebone, London. He joined the Indian Military Works Department, where he remained until his retirement. He became a major on 24 October 1894, and he spent much of his time at Quetta, where he was Executive Engineer, and he helped to build the garrison church.

Barnet also served in Allahabad, Multan, Calcutta, Barrackpore and Hansi, becoming commanding Royal Engineer at Lucknow. His last appointment was as Commanding Royal Engineer at Meerut. During this time he was promoted lieutenant colonel on 1 October 1901, and he retired with the rank of colonel in 1909. While serving in India he became a noted big-game hunter.

Barnet's wife had died in 14 April 1902, aged only 45, and at the time of the 1911 census he was a widower and retired colonel, living with his widowed mother at 16 Young Street in Kensington, London, where they employed three servants.

He was recalled for service during the Great War, when he was employed with the Intelligence Branch at the War Office.

On 31 May 1935 Barnet received the dreadful news that the town of Quetta, including the garrison church, had been destroyed in an earthquake. He died in his flat at 9 Lincoln House in Basil Street, Knightsbridge, London, on 29 March 1941, aged 85.

Oliver Edwal Ruck

Oliver Ruck played in the 1878 FA Cup final, and later saw service in the Transvaal (1st Boer) War.

Ruck was born at Pennal in Merionethshire, on 27 June 1856, being a younger brother of Richard Matthews Ruck, who played in the 1875 Cup-winning team. His father was a gentleman farmer named Laurence Ruck (1820–92) and his mother was Mary Anne (formerly Mathews). His parents were of Welsh extraction, and could trace their ancestry to Owain Glyndŵr, the last King of Wales. Laurence had moved from Wales when he inherited his uncle's estate of Cranbrook Manor House at Newington in Kent.

He was a brother of Amy Roberta 'Berta' Ruck, a romance novelist; an uncle of Bernard Darwin, the grandson of the botanist Charles Darwin, who became a respected golf writer; and a brother-in-law of James, Baron Atkin, the newspaper editor and judge.

Oliver was educated at a private school and then attended the Royal Military Academy, from where he was commissioned as lieutenant in the Royal Engineers on 28 January 1875. He played at outside-left for the Royal Engineers in the 1878 FA Cup final.

Ruck's only tour of active service came when he was posted to South Africa for the Transvaal (First Boer War) in 1881. He was promoted to captain on 28 January 1886, major on 3 November 1894 and lieutenant colonel on 7 October 1901.

He married his brother Richard's stepdaughter, Eleanor Annie 'Eve' (1854–1941), the daughter of Thomas Humphrey Pedley (1806–71) and his wife, Mary Constance (formerly Gully, 1832–1914), and they had two children: Mary Dorothy, born in 1885, and Laurence Humphrey, born in 1888.

At the outbreak of the Great War, Laurence Ruck became a lieutenant in the Worcestershire Regiment, and was killed in action at the battle of Neuve Chapelle on 11 March 1915, aged 26. He left an amount of money to his friend, Edda Bell, who was the Aberdyfi ferryman. He used the money to buy a new ferryboat, which he called *The Hero*.

Oliver became a well-known archaeologist and wrote papers and articles on the subject. He died at his home of Brynderw in Aberdyfi (Aberdovey) in Merionethshire, on 24 July 1934, aged 77.

Chapter 10

The 1878–79 Season

Forty-three teams were in the running for the eighth competition, and although Shropshire Wanderers had reached the semi-finals in 1875, this was the first year when the southern clubs became wary of the skills and determination shown by teams from the north.

The Royal Engineers opened their campaign with a 3-0 first-round win over Old Foresters at Chatham. The 105th Regiment should have played Minerva, of Ladywell in London, but they were deployed for service in Ireland and had to withdraw. The only game they ever won in the competition was against 1st Surrey Rifles, and this was their last attempt to take part.

After two gruelling Cup final defeats in 1875 and 1876, which both went to replays, the Old Etonians had withdrawn from the Cup in 1876–77 and had not even entered for the 1877–78 tournament. However, Major Marindin was instrumental in reviving them in October 1878, and they defeated Wanderers 7-2 in their first match back in the tournament.

Among the other results, Old Harrovians scored eight against Southall Park, Oxford University put seven past Wednesbury Strollers – the first club from the Birmingham area to enter the competition, Forest School beat Rochester 7-2, Eagley lost to Darwen in the first-ever Cup match played in Bolton. The first-ever all-Nottingham FA Cup derby match saw Forest beat County 3-1, the match having to be played at the Beeston Cricket Ground because Trent Bridge was unavailable (see Appendix I).

It was a short campaign for the military teams as the Royal Engineers travelled to the Parks at Oxford University for their second-round match and lost 4-0, the first time they had not got beyond this stage. Clapham Rovers trounced the Forest School 10-1, and there were wins for Cambridge University, Barnes FC, Old Harrovians, Nottingham Forest, Remnants and Minerva. Old Etonians won at Reading.

The first signs that northern teams were on the rise came in the third round in the form of Darwen FC, and although neither of the teams involved were from the military the tie warrants inclusion here. Darwen were drawn to play a team from Slough called Remnants, which was made up of former public schoolboys. The game was played in a hotbed of old boys amateur football on the home ground of Swifts near Slough town centre, the towers of Eton College standing tall just down the road. The game was played on 30 January 1879, while the Zulu War was raging in South Africa. The northerners shocked the amateurs by winning by the odd goal in five; the old boys took note. Old Etonians beat Minerva, and there were wins for Nottingham Forest and Oxford University. Clapham Rovers won 1-0 against Cambridge University.

In the quarter-finals, Clapham Rovers beat Swifts 8-1, and Nottingham Forest beat Oxford University 2-1. The Southern clubs breathed a sigh of relief when Darwen was drawn to play the Old Etonians. What chance would a bunch of unknowns from the factories of Lancashire have against the players from Eton, and they converged on The Oval on 13 February 1879 to watch the northerners get thrashed.

The match nearly didn't take place. Darwen's club funds had been stretched to their limit with travelling expenses to get to the game at Slough, and the club could not afford the cost of the journey all the way to London. However, the people of Darwen came to the rescue and enough funds were raised by public subscription.

The tie turned out to be an extraordinarily nail-biting affair, and at first it seemed the amateurs were going to get their wishes as the Old Etonians led 5-1 with fifteen minutes to go. Then an own goal made it 5-2 and the Darwen players seemed to get a second wind. They scored three goals to draw level at the final whistle, and with the impetus in their favour they suggested to play extra time. However, the tired old boys rejected the offer, and a replay was arranged for 8 March 1879 at The Oval.

The Lancashire people came to the rescue again and a second public fund raised £175, which was a large amount in those days. The Football Association contributed £10, and even the Old Etonians chipped in with a fiver. Darwen were once again equal to the task and forced a 2-2 draw after extra time. A second replay was arranged.

However, after three long journeys south, the Darwen players had to return to a week's work in industrial Lancashire, and then endure a fourth long, wearisome trip back to The Oval on the following Saturday. Consequently the Old Etonians won 6-2.

In the semi-final, 600 spectators at Kennington Oval watched Old Etonians defeat Nottingham Forest by the odd goal in three, and Clapham Rovers achieved their place in the final by way of a bye.

Old Etonians 1 Clapham Rovers 0

Charles Alcock was in charge of his second final at The Oval on 29 March 1879, and 5,000 spectators watched Old Etonians beat Clapham Rovers with a sixty-fifth-minute goal from Charles Clerke with a 'clever' shot. Edgar Lubbock was playing in his fourth final, and Arthur Kinnaird in a record-breaking sixth. The Clapham team was very young, with at least four teenagers in the squad, and they did well to keep the experienced Old Etonians to a single goal. James Prinsep was aged 17 years 245 days, and was the youngest player to appear in a Cup final until Curtis Weston came on as substitute for Millwall in the 2004 final at the age of 17 years 119 days; although Prinsep remains the youngest to play in a full match. The teams were:

Old Etonians: *Goalkeeper* – John Pervis Hawtrey; *Full-backs* – Edward Christian, Lindsay Bury; *Half-backs* – Arthur Fitzgerald Kinnaird (captain), Edgar Lubbock; *Forwards*: *Right* – Charles John Clerke, Mark Hanbury Beaufoy; *Centre* – Harry Chester Goodhart, John Barrington Trapnel Chevalier; *Left* – Norman Pares, Herbert Whitfield.

Clapham Rovers: *Goalkeeper* – Reginald Halsey Birkett; *Full-backs* – Robert Andrew Muter Macindoe Ogilvie (captain), Edgar Field; *Half-backs* – Norman Coles Bailey, James Frederick McLeod Prinsep; *Forwards*: *Right* – Frederick Lawrence Rawson, Arthur John Stanley; *Centre* – Edward Frederic Growse, Cecil Edward Keith-Falconer; *Left* – Herbert Shelley Bevington, Stanley Winckworth Scott.

Royal Engineers Matches

| 1st Round | 9 November 1878 | Old Foresters | won 3-0 at Chatham |
| 2nd Round | 7 December 1878 | Oxford University | lost 0-4 at the Parks, Oxford |

105th Regiment Match

| 1st Round | 8 October 1878 | Minerva FC | 105th withdrew |

5th Northumberland Fusiliers

Cecil Edwards Keith-Falconer

Cecil Keith-Falconer played for Clapham Rovers in the 1879 FA Cup final. He was killed in action at Belmont during the Second Boer War.

Keith-Falconer was born at St Leonard's Forest near Horsham in West Sussex on 11 October 1860, the oldest of three sons in the family of nine children born between 1858 and 1878 to Major Charles James Keith-Falconer (1832–89), of the 4th Light Dragoons and 10th Hussars, and his wife, Caroline Diana (1838–1920), the daughter of Robert Aldridge. He was a grandson of the 7th Earl of Kintore. His father fought in the Crimean War, and although the 4th Light Dragoons took part in the Charge of the Light Brigade, it seems that Major Keith-Falconer was not on duty that day.

Cecil was educated at Charterhouse School, where he played for their football XI in 1877–78, and in their cricket XI. On leaving he continued to play for Old Carthusians, and he also played for Swifts at Slough.

Keith-Falconer joined the army in 1881 with the Sussex Militia, transferring to the 1st Battalion, 5th Northumberland Fusiliers, in January 1883. In 1887 he was appointed ADC to the Governor and Commander-in-Chief Sir Henry Loch, in Victoria, Australia, from 1887 to 1889, and ADC to Governor Loch when he transferred to the Cape of Good Hope from 1889 to 1892.

On 13 April 1890 he joined the British South African Police in command of C Troop of the Pioneer Column in their march into Mashonaland. For his service he received the British South Africa Company Medal with Mashonaland clasp.

Keith-Falconer was promoted captain on 1892, and passed out of the Staff College with honours. From 1895 to 1898 he was attached to the Sudanese Battalion, with which he took part in the Dongola Expedition of 1896, under General Kitchener. He was appointed brigade major in March 1898, and served with General Hector Macdonald at the battles of Abu Hamed, Burbur and Atbara, and during the battle of Omdurman. He was three times mentioned in despatches and was promoted lieutenant colonel in November 1898. He received the Queen's Sudan Medal with Firket, Sudan 1897, Abu Hamed, Atbara and Khartoum clasps.

On 24 June 1899, Keith-Falconer married Georgina Sarah, the daughter of John Henry Blagrave, of Calcot Park near Reading, and the family home was at 25 Granville Place, Portman Square in London.

He received orders for active service in the Second Boer War in South Africa. He was on a reconnaissance patrol with Colonel Gough of the 9th Lancers at Luipers Kop near Belmont on 10 November 1899 when he was killed in action. A newspaper recounted: 'The report states that Colonel Keith-Falconer was killed while reconnoitring near the Orange River. Three other officers were wounded. Later particulars have been received concerning the death of Colonel Keith-Falconer. It appears that he was killed while trying to turn the flank of the enemy, and to discover their laager.' Another report said: 'A small British force attacked 700 Boers. It appears that Colonel Keith-Falconer left cover in order to assist a wounded officer. He had hardly moved a yard into the open when he was fired upon by the enemy and shot dead.'

He is buried in the cemetery on the banks of the Orange River. For his service he received the Queen's South Africa Medal with Cape Colony clasp. His medals were sold at auction in 1994.

* * *

Three Royal Engineers officers had played in the 1875 and 1878 FA Cup finals and later saw active service in the Anglo-Zulu War of 1879. As the war was raging in South Africa, the *Sheffield Telegraph* published several letters that had come from soldiers serving in the campaign. This made the people of Sheffield and West Yorkshire fully aware of the dreadful situation the men were experiencing in South Africa.

In an effort to try to raise funds for the widows and families of men who had lost their lives in the Zulu War, a Mr Brewer of Fartown in Sheffield decided to get together a team of players from the area to play charity matches. Football was extremely popular in the city, this being increased by the Royal Engineers' tour of the region in 1873.

In order to make the project as authentic as possible, the players decided to wear Zulu regalia, and managed to get hold of Zulu weapons that soldiers had brought back from the conflict as trophies. They also adopted what they thought were Zulu names. Most of the names were genuine, such as Cetshwayo, the Zulu King; Sihayo, whose kraal was the first to be attacked when the British invaded; and Dabulamanzi, who led the Zulu attack on the garrison at Rorke's Drift'. However, one of them called himself Jiggleumbengo, which was pushing it a bit. The players even blackened their faces with cork, which would of course be frowned upon in modern times. They usually did a tour of the towns in which they were playing to promote interest in the matches, and Thomas Buttery, who was Cetshwayo, went among the spectators at the matches to sell programmes before kick-off. They also performed their version of a Zulu tribal dance to entertain the crowd, brandishing their assegais and shields.

As it happened, the real Zulus had gained some degree of notoriety in Britain after the initial phases of the war, when hundreds of British soldiers of the 24th (2nd Warwickshire) Regiment had been massacred at Isandlwana on 22 January 1879; and a party of soldiers of the 80th (South Staffordshire) Regiment had been massacred on the banks of the River Ntombe on 11 March 1879. Contemporary news reports from Nottingham, Dublin and Glasgow refer to black men being heckled, abused or even assaulted after being accused of being Zulus. However, it also meant that the word 'Zulu' invoked curiosity, which was exploited by the football team.

Some of the players were well-known footballers in the region. Thomas Buttery had played against the Royal Engineers during their Northern Tour in 1873, and on 14 October 1878 he appeared for Reds against Blues at Bramall Lane in the first-ever match aided by electric lights. Jack Hunter became an FA Cup winner in 1883, playing for Blackburn Olympic, the first 'working-class' club to win the trophy. James Lang played for Sheffield Wednesday, being employed by one of the club officials. This was a ploy that came to be known as Shamateurism.

The Zulus began their series of matches in Scarborough, before taking on a strong selected XI from Sheffield before 2,000 spectators at Bramhall Lane, which they won 5-4. Their first two games had generated considerable interest among the general public, which encouraged them to start a tour of other towns. Next came a match held in bad conditions on 24 November 1879 at the Recreation Ground in Chesterfield, which resulted in a 2-2 draw. A 2-1 win over Notts and Derby Lambs was followed by a 6-0 thrashing of Barnsley Victoria and District.

It was clear from the outset that the Sheffield Zulus were a popular team, which resulted in them receiving an invitation to play in Scotland. However, their exploits north of the border were not so successful. On 21 April 1880, they lost 7-0 to Queen's Park at Hampden Park in Glasgow, and 2,000 people turned up at Easter Park on Christmas Day 1880 to see them lose 6-0 to Hibernian.

It was a time when football was considered to be a recreational game, and it was frowned upon for players to be paid for appearances. The project eventually ran into controversy when FA officials started to get reports that the Zulus were being paid for their appearances. William Pierce-Dix, honorary secretary of the Sheffield FA and a well-known referee, was fiercely opposed to professionalism. The Football Association got involved and the Zulus were no more.

Chapter 11

The 1879–80 Season

Among the fifty-four names that went into the draw were Aston
Villa and Blackburn Rovers for the first time. However, after
Aston Villa and Birmingham FC received byes in the first
round, it was left to Charles Crump's Stafford Road of Wolverhampton
and the Wednesbury Strollers to play the first-ever FA Cup match
in the West Midlands, when Stafford won 2-0 in Wolverhampton on
8 November 1879.

The Royal Engineers continued to make good progress in the
competition. In the first round at Chatham they beat Cambridge
University 2-0, the university's last-ever FA Cup tie. In the second round
Lieutenant Charles Learoyd scored twice in a 4-1 defeat of Upton Park.
Lieutenant Hugh Augustus Lawrence Paterson scored one of the other
two goals. This round saw the first-ever all-Sheffield derby match,
when Sheffield FC fought out a 3-3 draw with Sheffield Providence on
15 December 1879, before beating them 3-0 in the replay; and the first-
ever FA Cup match played in Birmingham on 24 January 1880, when
Aston Villa beat Stafford Road 2-0.

In the third round the Engineers defeated Old Harrovians 2-0 at
Chatham, and in their last ever FA Cup match, Wanderers lost to Old
Etonians. It seems that the Villa committee did not realise the importance
of the competition. On being drawn to play Oxford University in the
third round, they chose to withdraw and play a Birmingham Senior
Cup match instead. Nottingham Forest trounced Blackburn Rovers 6-0.

For their fourth-round tie the Engineers travelled to Dulwich to
play Grey Friars, where Lieutenant John Arthur Tanner scored the only
goal of the game. Nottingham Forest and Sheffield FC played out a
2-2 draw in Nottingham. Sheffield refused to play extra time, and when
the situation was reported to the Football Association, they awarded
the match to Forest.

In their fifth round quarter-final the Engineers travelled to the Parks at Oxford University. Lieutenant Massy scored for the Engineers, but the result was a draw after extra time. In the replay at Chatham ten days later a vicar playing for Oxford scored the only goal of the game. Nottingham Forest reached their second semi-final in a row but lost by the only goal of the match against Oxford University before a crowd of 2,000 spectators. Clapham Rovers received a bye into the final.

Clapham Rovers 1 Oxford University 0

The final at Kennington Oval was played on 10 April 1880, and Major Francis Marindin took charge for his first time. Six thousand spectators watched the game, the highest FA Cup final attendance to date. Clapham had managed to retain most of the defensive players from the previous year, and Clopton Lloyd-Jones had scored in every cup game for Clapton, but the Oxford defence managed to keep him out and extra time seemed imminent. However, six minutes from time, Francis Sparks of Clapham made a good run on the wing and crossed the ball. The Oxford full-back Charles King intercepted it, but he miskicked the ball and it fell at the feet of hotshot Lloyd-Jones, who kicked it between the Oxford posts.

This was the last match Oxford University played in the FA Cup, and they were the last university team until Team Bath reached the first round proper in the 2002–03 competition. However, they were not the last university team to enter the competition before 2002 because Caius College, Cambridge, entered in 1880–81 and 1881–82, but they withdrew both times before the matches were played. The teams were:

Clapham Rovers: *Goalkeeper* – Reginald Halsey Birkett; *Full-backs* – Robert Andrew Muter Macindoe Ogilvie (captain), Edgar Field; *Half-backs* – Vincent Edward Weston, Norman Coles Bailey; *Forwards*: *Right* – Harold de Vaux Brougham, Arthur John Stanley; *Centre* – Felix Barry, Francis John Sparks; *Left* – Clopton Allen Lloyd-Jones, Edward Albert Ram.

Oxford University: *Goalkeeper* – Percival Chase Parr (New College); *Full-backs* – Claude William Wilson (Exeter), Charles James Stuart King (Hertford); *Half-backs* – Francis Angelo Theodore Phillips (Balloil), Bertram Mitford Heron Rogers (Exeter); *Forwards*: *Right* – Reginald Thomas Heygate (captain) (Keble), Evelyn Henry Hill (Oriel); *Centre* – Francis

Demainbray Crowdy (Oriel), John Eyre (Keble and Christ Church); *Left* – John Birkbeck Lubbock (Balloil), George Borlase Childs (Magdalen).

Royal Engineers Matches

1st Round	13 November 1879	Cambridge University	won 2-0 at Chatham
2nd Round	23 December 1879	Upton Park	won 4-1 at Chatham
3rd Round	4 February 1880	Old Harrovians	won 2-0 at Chatham
4th Round	18 February 1880	Grey Friars	won 1-0 at Chatham
5th Round	5 March 1880	Oxford University	drew 1-1 (aet) away
Replay	15 March 1880	Oxford University	lost 0-1 at Chatham

Royal Engineers Players

Hampden Hugh Massy

Hugh Massy scored two goals for the Royal Engineers in the FA Cup in 1880, and later was killed in action during the disastrous engagement on Spion Kop.

The British India Office Register of Births and Baptisms states that he was born in Calcutta on 11 August 1858 to Cork-born Surgeon Hampden Hugh Massy (1820–95) of the 2nd Dragoon Guards, and his wife, Dublin-born Mary Rebecca (formerly Irwin, 1828–95). He was baptised at St Paul's Cathedral, Fort William in Calcutta, on 18 September 1858.

His father was a surgeon with the 17th Lancers, and attended to the wounded of the regiment as they returned from the Charge of the Light Brigade at Balaclava during the Crimean War. At the outbreak of the Indian Mutiny he transferred to the 2nd Dragoon Guards, who were heavily involved in the operations during the siege and relief of Lucknow. He wrote pamphlets on military surgery, and his set of miniature medals were sold at auction on 2003. Hugh junior had an older brother named William George (1857–1941), who became a captain in the Royal Dublin Fusiliers; and another brother named Edward Charles (1868–1946), who became a colonel in the Royal Artillery. His set of eight miniature medals were sold at the same auction as his father's in 2003.

Hugh was educated at Cheltenham College and at the Royal Military Academy, from where he passed out as lieutenant in the Royal Engineers on 9 October 1877. He married Ethel Katherine (1863–1945), the daughter of Lieutenant General, Sir John Fryer, KCB, of Rothley Grange in Leicester. He was promoted to captain in 1888, and major in August 1896. Both his parents died in Bournemouth in 1895.

On the outbreak of the Second Boer War in South Africa, Major Massy received orders for active service with the 17th Field Company of Royal Engineers with General Buller's Natal Field Force, tasked to go to the Relief of Ladysmith. On 24 January the force reached Spion Kop, and Buller ordered it to be seized. Two-thousand British soldiers scrambled courageously up the steep slopes, but when they reached a plateau at the top they found that they could only dig-in a couple of feet in the rocky surface. A thick mist hid the surrounding terrain from them and when it cleared they discovered that they were exposed to devastating sniper fire from Boer commando units situated on a higher summit. The British were mowed down mercilessly, and after the battle a line of 700 corpses huddled together moved many Boers to tears.

Major Massy was involved in the construction of entrenchments when he was killed by a sniper bullet. For his service he was twice mentioned in despatches (on 30 March 1900 and 8 February 1901) for his gallant conduct. He also received the Queen's South Africa Medal with Cape Colony and Relief of Ladysmith clasps. His name appears on the family tomb at St Andrew's Church at Kinson in Bournemouth, and on the South African Memorial Arch at Brompton Barracks in Chatham.

Charles Douglas Learoyd-Cockburn

Charles Learoyd played as a forward for the Royal Engineers in the early 1880s, being twice selected for England. He saw active service in three theatres of war in the Sudan and Burma.

Learoyd was born on 23 October 1859, in Huddersfield, West Yorkshire, the youngest of four children of Charles William Learoyd and his wife, Isobel. They lived at Hare Dell in Huddersfield, and his father was a woollen manufacturer of Learoyd Brothers and Company. In 1881 he and his three siblings were still living at home, which was now at Headlands House in Huddersfield, and they employed four servants.

Charles was educated at Worksop and at the Royal Military Academy, from where he was commissioned as lieutenant in the Royal Engineers on 18 December 1878.

He was selected as a reserve to play for England against Scotland at Hampden Park on 13 March 1880, which Scotland won 5-4. Two days later he was picked to play against Wales at the Racecourse Ground in Wrexham, but he had to withdraw through an injury. Lieutenant Wilson of the Royal Engineers also withdrew because of injury. Charles was also a good cricketer.

Learoyd's first tour of active duty was with the Saukin Expedition in 1884. He remained in the Sudan, where he took part in the Nile Expedition in 1885, and from there he was posted for active service in the Third Burma War, from 1885 to 1887.

He was promoted captain on 19 March 1889, major on 24 March 1897, brevet lieutenant colonel on 29 November 1900 and lieutenant colonel on 1 October 1904.

On 5 October 1893, Learoyd married Mary Clayton, at St Mark's Church in Surbiton, Surrey. She was the daughter of W.Y. Cockburn JP DL. They had two sons. The England Football Online website records that in 1915 he was 5ft 6in tall and weighed 11st 3lb. He was appointed Commander of the Order of the British Empire (CBE).

After he married, Learoyd and his wife seem to have moved about the country quite a lot. From 1911 he was living with his wife and son, John Cockburn, at Stackley House in Great Glen (Glen Magna), Leicester; in 1919–20 he resided at Whiteshoots Cottage in Bourton-on-the-Water, Gloucestershire; by 1931 he was based at Redlynch Park near Bruton in Somerset; and by 1939 he signed himself with the surname Learoyd-Cockburn and was living at Calcott Park Golf Club near Reading.

Mary died in 1932, while Learoyd himself died at Syresham House in Brackley, west Northamptonshire, on 29 December 1946, aged 89. Probate went to his sons, John Cockburn Cockburn, a retired army colonel. A coloured oil-on-canvas portrait of Charles was painted by the artist William Logsdale (1859–1944).

Learoyd's sons deserve a mention here. Colonel John Cockburn Cockburn fought in the Second World War with the Argyll and Sutherland Highlanders. He was awarded a Distinguished Service Order (DSO), and was appointed a Member of the British Empire (MBE). Commander Richard Cockburn Cockburn served during the Second World War with the Fleet Air Arm. On 25 July 1941, he was serving with 808 Squadron flying Fulmar aircraft on board HMS *Ark Royal*, protecting convoys between Gibraltar and Malta.

Twelve Italian bombers were detected approaching the convoy and Cockburn led a mixed detachment of Fulmars to intercept them. The Italians were driven off, but three Fulmars in the thick of it were shot down, including Cockburn's. For his gallantry he was awarded the DSO. The action was such that one of his fellow airmen was recommended for a posthumous Victoria Cross. Richard Cockburn was in his 100th year when he died in Kent.

One of Charles' nephews was Wing Commander Roderick Learoyd, who was awarded the Victoria Cross for a low-altitude attack on the Dortmund–Ems Canal in Germany on 12 August 1940.

John Arthur Tanner

John Tanner played for the Royal Engineers in the 1880s. He was killed in action while serving in the Great War.

Tanner was born on 27 February 1858, at Tidcombe in Wiltshire, the son of John Tanner and his wife Marion, of Poulton in Marlborough, Wiltshire.

He was educated at Wellington College from August 1868 to July 1875 and then at the Royal Military Academy, from where he was commissioned as lieutenant in the Royal Engineers on 19 June 1877; at the same time as Lieutenant Hugh Paterson.

He served in the Mahsud Waziri Expedition on the North-West Frontier of India in 1881, with the 6th Company, Bengal Sappers and Miners. He then saw active service in the Sudan, initially assigned to the Indian Labour Corps for the Saukin Expedition in 1884. He took part in the Nile Expedition, where he was present at the engagement at Tofrek on 22 March 1885. After the battle he was assigned to F Company, Bengal Sappers and Miners, to replace an officer killed in the battle.

In 1916 Tanner married Gladys H., the daughter of C.T. Murdoch MP, of Buckhurst in Wokingham, and they lived at the Manor House in Finchampstead, Berkshire.

He went to France in September 1915 as a Commander of the Royal Engineers attached to the 22nd Division. Later that year he was promoted to brigadier general, and was posted as chief engineer with the VII Corps in the Third Army. He served during the Somme Offensive in July 1916, and in the battle of Arras in 1917. He was killed in action at Ficheux on 23 July 1917, aged 58, and he was buried at the Bucquoy Road War Cemetery in Ficheux. His name also appears on the Pas de Calais Memorial, and on the war memorial in St Mary's Churchyard, Eversley, Hampshire.

Hugh Augustus Lawrence Paterson

Hugh Paterson was a prominent player for the Royal Engineers in the 1880s.

He was born on 6 April 1858, at Nyanee Tal in West Bengal, India; the oldest of six sons in a family of twelve children born between 1858 and 1883 to Major General Adrian Hugh Paterson (1825–99), of the Indian Army, who had served in the Sutlej Campaign of 1845–46 and in the Indian Mutiny of 1857–58. He served as inspector general of police in Bengal. His mother was Georgiana Jessie Turnbull (1838–85), the second daughter of Brigadier General Hugh Sibbald CB, who was murdered by rebels at Barielly on the outbreak of the Indian Mutiny when he was shot in the chest by one of his orderlies while he was riding to the parade ground.

Paterson attended the Royal Military Academy, from where he was commissioned as lieutenant in the Royal Engineers on 19 June 1877, at the same time as Lieutenant John Tanner.

He died on 18 November 1919, aged 60, at 4 Albany Mansions in Marina, near the sea front at Bexhill-on-Sea, East Sussex.

Chapter 12

The 1880–81 Season

For the first season there were no Wanderers or university teams from Oxford or Cambridge. After a goalless draw against Remnants at Chatham in the first round, the Engineers travelled to Slough for the replay and won 1-0. Blackburn Olympic entered the tournament for the first time, but they lost at Sheffield FC by the odd goal in seven. Clapham Rovers scored fifteen against Finchley, Darwen put eight past Brigg Town from the North-East and Upton Park scored eight without reply against Mosquitoes of Dulwich. Caius College of Cambridge University became the first individual university college to enter the FA Cup, but they were drawn against Nottingham Forest and withdrew. The first all-Bolton derby match took place on 30 October 1880, when Astley Bridge beat Eagley 4-0.

In the second round, the Engineers played Pilgrims for the second time, and Lieutenant Massy scored the only goal of the game. The Cup ties were beginning to look more familiar to modern football enthusiasts, as Aston Villa beat Nottingham Forest, and Sheffield Wednesday put four past Blackburn Rovers.

The third round brought together Rangers of Clapham and the Royal Engineers, in a tie to be played at Kennington Oval. Among the players for Rangers was Frederick Wall, who would become the secretary of the Football Association from 1895 to 1934, and despite a heavy 6-0 defeat he remembered how his team had savoured the opportunity to meet such a successful club at such a famous venue and that they enjoyed every moment of it.

The Engineers' campaign came to an end at Charterhouse, when the Old Carthusians scored twice without reply; their opening goal being scored by Teddy Wynyard of the King's (Liverpool) Regiment.

In the quarter-finals Darwen scored sixteen goals against Romford (1876), and as Old Etonians and Old Carthusians were the only other teams to progress, there would be yet another bye from the semi-final into the final, which was given to Old Etonians. Old Carthusians defeated Darwen 4-1 to reach the final, with Teddy Wynyard getting on the score sheet again.

Old Carthusians 3 Old Etonians 0

This was the only final the Old Carthusians reached and it was played before 4,500 fans at Kennington Oval on 9 April 1881. The referee was the same William Pierce-Dix of Sheffield who had been instrumental in causing the demise of the Sheffield Zulus. The Old Carthusians team included two players who were associated with the army, namely James Prinsep of the Essex Regiment and Edward Wynyard of the King's (Liverpool) Regiment, who scored the first goal to beat Old Etonians 3-0 in what was the only final between two public school 'old boys' teams. Both men went on to receive bravery medals from the Royal Humane Society. Having celebrated his 18th birthday the previous day, Walter Harry Norris of Epsom took over from Bob Sealy-Vidal as the youngest player to win the FA Cup, while playing for Old Carthusians. He kept this record for nearly a century until 1980, when Paul Allen won the Trophy with West Ham United at the age of 17 years 256 days. The teams were:

Old Carthusians: *Goalkeeper* – Leonard Francis Gilett; *Full-backs* – Elliot Graham Colvin, Walter Harry Norris; *Half-backs* – Joseph Vintcent, James Frederick McLeod Prinsep; *Forwards: Right* – Walter Edward Hansell, Lewis Matthew Richards; *Centre* – William Robert Page, Edward George 'Teddy' Wynyard; *Left* – Edward Hagarty Parry (captain), Alexander Hay Tod.

Old Etonians: *Goalkeeper* – John Frederick Peel Rawlinson; *Full-backs* – Charles Windham Foley, Thomas Harvey French; *Half-backs* – Arthur Fitzgerald Kinnaird (captain), Bryan Farrer; *Forwards: Right* – William Joseph Anderson, John Barrington Trapnel Chevalier; *Centre* – Reginald Heber Macauley, Harry Chester Goodhart; *Left* – Herbert Whitfield, Philip Charles Novelli.

Royal Engineers Matches

| 1st Round | 13 November 1880 | Remnants | drew 0-0 at Chatham |
| Replay | 20 November 1880 | Remnants | won 1-0 away |

2nd Round	9 December 1880	Pilgrims	won 1-0 at Chatham
3rd Round	9 February 1881	Rangers	won 6-0 at Chatham
4th Round	19 February 1881	Old Carthusians	lost 0-2 away

King's (Liverpool) Regiment

Edward George 'Teddy' Wynyard

Teddy Wynyard scored the first goal for Old Carthusians when they won the FA Cup in 1881. He was an exceptional all-round sportsman, who later saw active service in Burma.

Wynyard was born at Saharanpur in Uttar Pradesh, in the North-Western Provinces of India, on 1 April 1861, the eldest of two sons, and third child of six, born between 1857 and 1880 (including twins) to William Wynyard JP, of Northend House in Hursley near Winchester, Hampshire, who served with the Bengal Civil Service as a judge at the High Court of Allahabad. His mother was Henrietta Ellen, the daughter of Sir Henry Willcock, a diplomat of Castelnau House in Mortlake. Teddy and the family faced a number of dangers while in India during the 1857–58 Mutiny. His mother died in 1868, and the 1871 census records that the family lived at 32 Onslow Gardens in South Kensington, London, where they employed a number of servants. His father remarried in 1874, his stepmother being named Isabella Sophia (formerly Ward).

Wynyard was educated at Woodcote House Prep School in Windlesham, Surrey, at Charterhouse School from 1874 to 1877, and at St Edward's Boarding School in Oxford until 1879. He was over 6ft tall and stockily built, and played rugby at St Edward's: 'He was a glorious three-quarter, fast and strong, and could turn on a sixpence when in full cry. Had he not gone into the army he would have reached the top in the rugger world.' As centre-forward for Old Carthusians, he was variously described as 'a heavy forward' with 'plenty of dash; makes himself obnoxious to the opposing backs'. He played hockey for Hampshire, and he became very keen on golf, playing regularly at Camberley Heath. He formed his own team of cricketers, mostly composed of well-known players, which he called the Jokers, and appointed himself Chief Joker.

However, Wynyard's favourite sport was cricket. He played for Hampshire as a right-handed batsman from 1878 to 1908, becoming captain from 1896 to 1899. During 1893–94 he scored three consecutive centuries. The club became a first-class county in 1894, joining the County Championship in the following year. In 1896 Teddy scored 1,038 runs, the second highest average of the season, including 268 against Yorkshire; and in 1899 he scored 1,281 runs, including a sixth-man partnership of 411 with Robert Poore against Somerset.

His first Test series was three matches against Australia in England in 1896, which England won 2-1. He was asked to go on the tour of Australia in 1897–98, but he had to decline because of Army duties, and he had to decline a second time to go on a tour to Australia in 1907–08 for family reasons. He played in the five Test matches in South Africa in 1905–06, which South Africa won 4-1, and in the three 1907 Test matches in England, which England won 2-0. He was a member of the MCC, whom he captained on tour to New Zealand in 1906–07 and was on the committee from 1920 to 1924. He went on several other tours, including to Egypt and the United States, and on the tour to the West Indies in 1904–05 he topped the batting averages with 562 runs. His last tour was to Canada in 1923, aged 62, when he headed the bowling figures with his underarm lob.

Wynyard was commissioned as lieutenant in the 1st Warwick Militia in 1881 and transferred to regular service in the 8th King's (Liverpool) Regiment in May 1883. He was posted to India with his unit, taking part in the Third Burma Expedition of 1885–87. The regimental history records: 'On 12 June 1885, in Upper Burma, a large force of rebels under Oo Temah were beaten off after attacking a small force of the 8th King's Liverpool Regiment, and 2nd Bengal Infantry. They were followed and found entrenched strongly in a walled pagoda, which was carried by assault.' General Sir Robert Low KCB, in his despatch, stated: 'Owing to the bold leading of a handful of tired men by Lieutenant Wynyard, after the death of Captain Dunsford of the 2nd Bengal Infantry, a position of considerable danger was averted, and as a result of this success order was restored in the surrounding district.' General Sir George White emphasised Lieutenant Wynward's part in the action in his despatch. For his service he was specially promoted to a company of the 41st Welsh Regiment, twice mentioned in despatches and received the Indian General Service Medal with Burma, 1885–87 clasp. He was created a Companion of the Distinguished Service Order (DSO), which was published in the *London Gazette* on 25 November 1887, stating: 'Edward George Wynyard, Lieutenant, Liverpool Regiment; for service during the recent operations in Burma.' He transferred to the Welsh Regiment as captain on 19 March 1890.

Wynyard spent some time tobogganing in Switzerland, and on 9 December 1893, 'at great personal risk, he attempted to rescue a Swiss peasant [flower seller] from drowning in the lake at Davos'. In 1895 he was awarded the Royal Humane Society's Medal for his bravery. He became the tobogganing champion of Europe at Davos in 1894.

He was adjutant of the Oxford University Volunteers, 1899–1900 and instructor in military engineering at the Royal Military College at Sandhurst from 26 December 1899 to August 1902, when he returned to his regiment. He retired from military service the following year.

Wynyard had an imaginative sense of humour. While he was at Sandhurst he arranged a cricket match with W.G. Grace's XI, but the famous batsman contacted Teddy and told him he could not play. In those less technical times he discovered that, although his cadets had heard about Grace's long black bushy beard, none of his cadets had ever seen him. After he got someone to make him up to look like Grace, he walked out onto the pitch. After imitating Grace's batting style and hitting several runs he got deliberately hit on the head and retired hurt, and nobody spotted the deception. He surprised both teams at lunch when he appeared without his cap and false beard, declaring 'I think I have spoofed you all this time!'

In 1914 Wynyard married Sarah Louise (1879–1972), the daughter of James Gooderham Worts (1853–84) of Toronto, Canada, and Mary Louise (formerly Elliott). They had a son, born on 23 May 1918.

On the outbreak of the Great War he joined his old regiment as major, being attached for duties with the Army Ordnance Corps until May 1915. He transferred to the Middlesex Regiment in November 1916, becoming commandant at Thornhill Labour Camp at Aldershot from 1916 to 1919. He retired in April 1919, and was awarded the Order of the British Empire (OBE) military division.

Wynyard played twice for Corinthians in 1893, and scored five goals, and he was president of the Old Carthusians Cricket and Football Club from 1913 to 1919. He continued to play golf into the 1930s. He was a member at Beaconsfield Golf Club, was an honourable life member of the Royal Wimbledon Club from 1930, and an honourable life member of the Oxford Graduates' Golfing Society from 1931.

He died at the Red House in Knotty Green, Beaconsfield, Buckingham-shire, on 30 October 1936, aged 75, and he was buried in the Old Holy Trinity Churchyard at Penn. Sarah Louise died on 24 November 1972, in her 96th year, and she is buried with him.

Essex Regiment

James Frederick McLeod Prinsep

James Prinsep was the youngest footballer to appear in an FA Cup final until 2004. He played in the finals of 1879 and 1881, and he saw active service in the Nile Expedition of 1884–85.

Prinsep was born at Aligarh in India on 27 July 1861, the son of James Hunter Prinsep of the Indian Civil Service and his wife, Christine Louisa (formerly White).

He was educated at Charterhouse School, 1874 to 1878, and then at the Royal Military College at Sandhurst; he played on the football teams at both establishments. He was commissioned as lieutenant in the Essex Regiment in 1880. This unit was formed in 1881 by the amalgamation of the 44th (East Essex) Regiment and the 56th (West Essex) Regiment.

On the football pitch Prinsep was described as being '... always cool, very strong on his legs, and combining plenty of strength with great accuracy; kicks splendidly and with judgement, seldom makes a mistake. Can kick the ball in any position, and passes it admirably to his forwards.'

He also played at half-back for Clapham Rovers, Old Carthusians, The South, and The Rest versus England. He played a full international against Scotland in 1879, and he was selected to play in 1881–82 but he was unavailable.

Prinsep took part in the Nile Expedition, and on 23 December 1884 he was on the river at Shaban Rapids near Kanneck, when Private G. Wheeler, a non-swimmer, fell into the water and was continually disappearing under the surface as he struggled for air. Major Prinsep dived in and swam back about 30yd to where Wheeler was struggling and held on to him until help arrived. For his bravery he received the Royal Humane Society's bronze medal.

On 19 December 1885, he was on the Nile near El Sabon when he saved the life of a Sudanese sailor who had fallen into the water. For this act of gallantry he received a clasp to his Royal Humane Society's bronze medal.

Prinsep remained in Egypt after the campaign and served as a major in the Egyptian Army from 1885 to 1890. He joined the Egyptian Coast Guard Service from 1890 until his death, reaching the rank of sub-inspector general. He owned property in Alexandria, and his home in Britain was at 46 Thurloe Square.

On 27 July 1891, he married Evelyn Elizabeth Campbell at St Stephen's Church in Kensington, London. Evelyn had been born in India and her father was also employed with the Indian Civil Service. A daughter named Evelyn was born in Alexandria in 1892, and a son named Caradoc was born there in the following year.

While his wife was pregnant with their third child, Prinsep took a year's leave of absence, and decided to spend some time with his relations at Nairn. Although he had been suffering with a bad cold, he played a game of golf on a wet day, and the illness turned to pneumonia. After fighting the illness for seven weeks, he died of blood poisoning and kidney failure on 22 November 1895, aged 34. He was buried in Nairn.

Chapter 13

The 1881–82 Season

In the first round the Engineers defeated the Kildare Cub based at Kensal Green in London at Chatham 6-0, and then received a bye into the third round. Regions were zoned, and it is not surprising that the North-Western District, which included four teams from Blackburn and four from Bolton, produced the first Blackburn FA Cup derby match on 29 October 1881, between Blackburn Rovers and Blackburn Park Avenue, to be played on the Leamington Ground. Such was the reputation of Rovers that the local press had already written-off the Park Avenue team, and Rovers justified their doubts with a 9-1 win (see Appendix I). Darwen beat Blackburn Olympic 3-1 on the same day. In the first-ever FA Cup tie played on Merseyside on 5 November 1881, Bootle of Liverpool beat Blackburn Law by the odd goal in three. An interesting note is that the Bootle club was compelled to play two games in one day, and after the FA Cup tie they drew 1-1 with Preston North End in the Lancashire Association Challenge Cup (see Appendix I). The two Bolton Derby matches took six games to decide, with the tie between Astley Bridge and Turton going to a third replay. No fewer than five teams from Sheffield had entered, and three progressed to the next round.

Caius College of Cambridge entered for a second time, but they scratched from the game they should have played against Dreadnought of West Ham. However, they were the last university club to enter the competition for more than 120 years, until Team Bath in 2002.

For the third round the Engineers were faced with the holders of the trophy, Old Carthusians, at Charterhouse. However, the Engineers rose to the occasion, and with a goal from Lieutenant Godfrey Williams, and a gift goal from the Charterhouse team, they went through. Aston Villa and Notts County fought out a three-match epic, with Villa eventually going through.

In the fourth round at the Old Foresters ground, the Royal Engineers lost by the odd goal in three, with the Engineers' goal coming from

Lieutenant William Kincaid. There were several local derby ties, in which Sheffield Wednesday beat Sheffield Heeley, Wednesbury Old Athletic defeated Aston Villa, and Blackburn Rovers beat Darwen. In the fifth round Great Marlow defeated Old Foresters 1-0 at the Dolphin Ground in Slough, after they had played a goalless draw at The Oval.

In the semi-finals, Old Etonians easily dispensed with Great Marlow 5-0 in front of 6,000 spectators at The Oval (see Appendix I). The first semi-final match to be played outside London took place at St John's Rugby Ground at Fartown in Huddersfield, where Blackburn Rovers and Sheffield Wednesday fought out a goalless draw. The replay took an FA Cup semi-final to the north-west of England for the first time, when Blackburn Rovers became the first northern club to reach the FA Cup final when they won 5-1 at the Brantingham Road Ground in Whalley Range, Manchester, which is still used for football matches to this day. Ten-thousand spectators watched the game, so football was likely to return there at some time.

Old Etonians 1 Blackburn Rovers 0

In the final, Lord Kinnaird of Old Etonians equalled Charles Wollaston's record of five FA Cup wins, and celebrated the occasion by standing on his head in front of the pavilion. James Forrest of Blackburn Rovers equalled the record in 1891. Ashley Cole played for Arsenal and Chelsea in eight finals. He equalled the record number of wins while playing for Chelsea in 2009, and he won winner's medals in 2010 and 2012 for a new record total of seven. Blackburn Rovers travelled to London with a formidable reputation. They had won 31 and drawn 4 of their matches, scoring 192 goals with 33 against.

The Sportsman reported: 'The whistle of the referee put an end to the game,' which was the first time a referee's whistle was mentioned in a Cup final report. Blackburn Rovers had not been beaten all season, and although they were the losing side on this occasion, it was the last time an old boys' unit won the trophy, which would go up to Blackburn for the next four seasons. The teams were:

Old Etonians: *Goalkeeper* – John Frederick Peel Rawlinson; *Full-backs* – Thomas Harvey French, Percy John de Paravacini; *Half-backs* – Arthur Fitzgerald Kinnaird (captain), Charles Windham Foley; *Forwards*: *Right* – William Joseph Anderson, John Barrington Trapnel Chevalier; *Centre* – Reginald Heber Macauley, Harry Chester Goodhart; *Left* – Arthur Tempest Blakiston Dunn, Philip Charles Novelli.

Blackburn Rovers: *Goalkeeper* – Roger Howarth; *Full-backs* – Hugh McIntyre, Fergus Suter; *Half-backs* – Frederick William Hargreaves (captain), Harold Sharples; *Forwards*: *Right* – John Duckworth, James Douglas; *Centre* – James Brown, Thomas Strachan; *Left* – Geoffrey Avery, John Hargreaves.

Royal Engineers Matches

1st Round	5 November 1881	Kildare	won 6-0 at Chatham
2nd Round	Bye		
3rd Round	20 December 1881	Old Carthusians	won 2-0 at Charterhouse
4th Round	21 January 1882	Old Forester	lost 1-2 away

Royal Engineers Players

William Francis Henry Style Kincaid

William Kincaid was a regular scorer for the Royal Engineers in the early 1880s, and he took part in three campaigns in the Sudan and in South Africa.

Kincaid was born on 3 July 1861, the only child of John Henry Kincaid MA JP of Dublin, and his wife, Isabella, the daughter of Charles Style. They had married in Dublin in September 1859.

William was educated at the Royal Military Academy, where he was awarded the Pollock Medal in July 1880, and he was commissioned as lieutenant in the Royal Engineers on 27 July 1880.

After Home service mainly at Chatham, Kincaid was posted for active service on the Nile Expedition in the Sudan, 1884–85. He was promoted captain on 1 October 1889, and was selected for active service during the Dongola Expedition of 1896, where he was employed as assistant adjutant general to the infantry division.

Dongola Expedition in the Sudan, 1896

The first phase of the re-conquest of the Sudan under General Kitchener was the occupation of Dongola. At Firket on 7 June 1896, an army of Dervishes under the Emir Osman Asraq was defeated. The advance continued and reached Dongola on 15 October 1896. Hafir is on the west bank of the Nile, and the decisive battle of the campaign was fought and won there.

In his despatch from Dongola sent on 30 September 1896, General Kitchener stated:

The detachment of the Royal Engineers performed most valuable service during the whole period of the operations, and I have pleasure in recording my high opinion of the zeal, energy and resource displayed by one and all under, at times, exceptionally difficult circumstances. The detachments attached to the Mazim Battery took part in all operations against the enemy during the campaign, and were always well to the front; their commanding officer, Captain Lawrie RA, speaks in the highest terms of their good service and excellent conduct on all occasions, and I have great pleasure in endorsing his opinion of their efficiency and great utility throughout the operations.

For his services Captain Kincaid was awarded the Queen's Sudan Medal with Firket and Hafir clasps. He remained in the Sudan, being promoted to brevet major on 10 November 1896. He was present at the battle of Omdurman on 2 September 1898, and for his further service he was awarded the Abu Hamed, Sudan 1897, the Atbara, Khartoum and Gedaref clasps. He was promoted to lieutenant colonel on 16 November 1898.

Kincaid saw active service during the Second Boer War in South Africa, where he served in support of the 7th Infantry Division, mainly in the Orange Free State. He was mentioned in the despatches of Lord Roberts of 28 February 1900, who stated: 'As to Paardeberg, the work of Colonel Kincaid and the 7th Company of Royal Engineers in the last rush forward was brought to notice.' For his service he was awarded the Queen's South Africa Medal and the King's South Africa Medal with 1901 and 1902 clasps.

On 13 June 1904 Kincaid married Rosamund, the daughter of John James Hamilton Humphries, of Camus in County Tyrone, Ireland, and his wife, Elizabeth.

He was appointed Commander of the Bath (CB military) during King Edward VII's birthday honours' list of 29 June 1906. He was a member of the United Services Club. He served as Assistant Quartermaster General Administrative Staff, Aldershot Army Corps, from 1903 to 1907, and on the outbreak of the Great War he served in the same capacity from 1915 to 1919. Lieutenant Colonel Kincaid died on 19 December 1945, aged 84.

Chapter 14

The 1882–83 Season

In the Royal Engineers' first-round match at Chatham they played
Woodford Bridge from East London and won 3-1, with goals
from Lieutenants Edwin Newman, Riccardo Petrie and William
Stafford. This round saw the first-ever FA Cup tie to be played in
Liverpool, when Liverpool Ramblers drew 1-1 with Southport on
21 October 1882, and on 4 November 1882 the Druids and Oswestry
Town played the first all-Welsh FA Cup tie. There were some high-
scoring matches: Blackburn Rovers defeated Blackpool St John's 11-1,
Blackburn Olympic beat Accrington 6-3, Eagley of Bolton beat Bolton
Olympic 7-4, Bolton Wanderers defeated Bootle 6-1 and Etonian
Ramblers beat Romford (1876) 6-2.

In round two, also played at Chatham, the Engineers trounced
Reading with hat-tricks from Lieutenants William Kincaid and William
Stafford, and one each from Lieutenants Charles Godby and Oliver Ruck.
In other high-scoring ties, Blackburn Olympic defeated Lower Darwen
8-1, and Nottingham Forest beat Sheffield Heeley 7-2. Darwen gained
revenge for the town by beating Blackburn Rovers by the only goal of
the game, but it would be the last game Rovers lost in the FA Cup until
4 December 1886, a total of twenty-one consecutive wins. They were
beaten in a replay at Blackburn by Renton, one of four Scottish clubs to
enter the competition that year.

The Engineers received a bye in the third round. It is likely that
teams were beginning to take more notice of Blackburn Olympic, as
they added to their total goals of fourteen so far in the competition by
beating Darwen Ramblers 8-0. Old Etonians defeated Rochester 7-0.

In the fourth round, the Royal Engineers were yet again drawn to
play Old Carthusians, who had beaten them on the way to winning the
competition two years earlier, at Charterhouse. Although Lieutenants
William Kincaid and Morgan Lindsay scored for the Engineers, Old

Carthusians replied with six. Blackburn Olympic and Old Etonians both gained relatively tame two-goal wins.

As might have been expected by the turnout for the previous season's semi-final replay match, the FA gave the tie to the Whalley Range ground again, but this time a southern public school team was involved and only 2,500 spectators turned up to watch Blackburn Olympic play Old Carthusians. To add to the poor attendance, it seems the game was delayed because nobody had thought to bring a ball with them and an official had to go and borrow one. Hence, the ground was never used again. Olympic won 4-0, and in the other semi-final Old Etonians beat Notts County 2-1 at Kennington Oval.

Blackburn Olympic 2 Old Etonians 1

(after extra time)

The final was played at Kennington Oval on 31 March 1883 in front of 8,000 spectators, and the referee was Charles Crump of Wolverhampton. Lord Kinnaird was playing in a record ninth FA Cup final (not counting two replays), a record that still stands. The nearest player to it since has been Ashley Cole, who played in his eighth final in 2012 but has since retired. In addition to that four Etonians were making a third final appearance, and it was the fourth final for Harry Goodhart and John Chevalier.

The Olympic team spent some time in Blackpool in special training for the final, and they travelled south on the previous Thursday having arranged to stay at Richmond to avoid the tedious journey so close to the game. The team included six men who worked in the cotton industry in Blackburn, including James Ward, who, having celebrated his 18th birthday three days earlier, became the second youngest player ever to win the FA Cup. He was a full-back like Walter Norris, and became the Olympic's only capped player. The Etonians team was the same as for the previous final, except Herbert Bainbridge replaced Philip Novelli on the left wing.

Old Etonians used the benefit of Cup-final experience and led 1-0 at half-time, but in the second half the fitness created by the pre-match training of the Olympic players began to show. They also started to rough it up and intimidate the Etonians, having a least twice charged from behind, which was frowned upon even in those times, and the

Etonians began to lose men to injuries. Arthur Dunn went off with a knee injury after about fifteen minutes of the second half had been played, and the Etonians carried on with ten men. Five minutes later, a picture framer named Alfred Matthews equalised. Harry Goodhart and Reg Macauley of the Etonians were also injured when time was called, but they elected to play on during extra time. Three minutes into the second half of extra time saw a Liverpool-born cotton spinner named James Costley put Olympic ahead. There was no further score when time was called.

All previous presentations had been made at the winning club's annual dinner, but for the first time Major Marindin presented the Cup and medals to the players on the stand adjoining the pavilion. The teams were:

Blackburn Olympic: *Goalkeeper* – Thomas Hacking; *Full-backs* – James Ward, Samuel Alfred Warburton (captain); *Half-backs* – Thomas K. Gibson, William Astley, John Hunter; *Forwards*: *Right* – Thomas Dewhurst, Alfred Matthews; *Centre* – George Wilson; *Left* – James Costley, John Yates.

Old Etonians: *Goalkeeper* – John Frederick Peel Rawlinson; *Full-backs* – Thomas Harvey French, Percy John de Paravacini; *Half-backs* – Arthur Fitzgerald Kinnaird (captain), Charles Windham Foley; *Forwards*: *Right* – William Joseph Anderson, John Barrington Trapnel Chevalier; *Centre* – Reginald Heber Macauley, Harry Chester Goodhart; *Left* – Arthur Tempest Blakiston Dunn, Herbert William Bainbridge.

As the trophy was being paraded around the streets of Blackburn, the Olympic captain, Sam Warburton, stated that the Cup would have a good home in Lancashire and that it would never go back to London. That particular cup never did. It was won by teams from Lancashire and the Midlands in the following seasons, and after Aston Villa won it in 1895 it was stolen from the window of William Shillcock's Football Works boot and shoe shop at 73 Newtown Row in Aston, Birmingham, on 11 September of that year and was never seen again. The area was the hunting ground of the notorious Peaky Blinders gang. In fact, the FA Cup never went south again during the reign of Queen Victoria, with non-League Tottenham Hotspur winning it in 1901 after her death earlier that year.

Royal Engineers Matches

1st Round	21 October 1882	Woodford Bridge	won 3-1 at Chatham
2nd Round	29 November 1882	Reading	won 8-0 at Chatham
3rd Round	Bye		
4th Round	25 January 1883	Old Carthusians	lost 2-6 away

A number of Royal Engineers players warrant extra mention here. Although the glory days of the club were behind them, they continued to represent their regiment until active-service commitments made it impossible for them to do so.

Royal Engineers Players

Edwin Montague Browne Newman

Edwin Newman was a prominent member of the Royal Engineers football team in the early 1880s. He was killed in action at the engagement at Tofrek during the Nile Expedition in the Sudan.

Newman was born in late 1861, the eldest son of Walter Newman (1836–94) of the Royal Artillery, and Emma Montague (formerly Browne, 1844–1930). Walter came from Yeovil, and served in the Crimean War and in the Indian Mutiny. A series a letters he wrote to his then girlfriend, Emma, are preserved at the National Army Museum in London. They married in Plymouth in early 1861 and had three children.

Edwin was educated at Wellington College. In the summer of 1879 he passed fourth for entrance into the Royal Military Academy at Woolwich, where his father had once attended. He was commissioned as lieutenant in the Royal Engineers on 26 July 1881, and after representing his regimental football team, he was ordered for active service in the Sudan with the 24th Field Company, Queen's Own Sapper and Miners.

Battle of Tofrek in the Sudan, 22 March 1885

The Regimental History recorded:

> On the receipt of the intelligence of the fall of Khartoum in England, the first impulse on all sides was to persevere in the war, recapture the place, and effectually punish the Mahdi.

With this view a railway was to be laid down from Saukin to Bereber, and Lieutenant-General, Sir Gerald Graham was appointed to command the troops necessary to protect its construction.

About 20 miles of railway were laid under great difficulties. The enemy were on the alert, and it was necessary as the line advanced, to construct posts to protect those at work on it, as well as the railway itself. It was in one of the advances made for this purpose by a party under the command of Sir John McNeill, that on 22 March a furious and unexpected onset was made by the Arabs at El Tofrek whilst a zareba [thorn fence] was under construction. The result was a serious loss of life before the enemy were repulsed.

Lieutenant Newman was posted for active service with the Nile Expedition, where he was attached to A Company, Madras Sappers and Miners, in the Indian Corps sent from Cairo. He was killed in action at Tofrek on 22 March 1885 and buried in one of the communal graves with his fellow comrades who had been killed during the battle, which was close to McNeill's zareba where they died.

Charles Godby

Charles Godby was a prominent player for the Royal Engineers in the early 1880s, and he served two tours of active duty in the Sudan.

Godby was born in Lewisham in 1863, and he was educated at the Royal Military Academy, from where he was commissioned as lieutenant in the Royal Engineers on 1 October 1882.

He was posted for active service in the Nile Expedition, and was at the battle of Tofrek on 22 March 1885 where Lieutenant Newman was killed. He returned for engineer duties in the Sudan in 1889.

Godby was promoted captain on 4 May 1891, major on 25 January 1900 and lieutenant colonel in 1911. While stationed at Portsmouth in 1913 he attended the funeral of Major Charles Watkins of the Royal Engineers, held on the Isle of Wight.

He was recalled for active service during the Great War as temporary brigadier general, and he was chief engineer of the IX Corps in the British Expeditionary Force. For his service he was awarded the Distinguished Service Order (DSO); the Most Distinguished Order of St Michael and St George (CMG) in the New Year Honours' List for 1 January 1917; he was made Commander of the Bath (CB) in the June

1918 birthday honours; and on 27 October 1919 he was awarded the Croix de Guerre. He retired from military service in 1919. Godby died in Surrey in 1956.

Riccardo Dartnell Petrie

Riccardo Petrie was a prominent player for the Royal Engineers during the early 1880s. He went on to see active service in Balochistan, Burma, Lushai, China and during the Great War.

Petrie was born in Callao, in the Callao Province of Lima in Peru, on 15 September 1861. He was the second son of three in the family of seven children born between 1852 and 1872 (two of them were born while sailing across the Pacific Ocean), to an Angus-born ship owner named George Petrie (1822–99) and Penelope Mary Abelita (formerly Dartnell, 1834–1913), who was born in Cork. They had married at Callao on 12 February 1851.

Riccardo was educated at the Royal Military Academy, from where he was commissioned as lieutenant in the Royal Engineers on 23 February 1881. At that time the family were living at 1 De Vere Gardens in Kensington, a twenty-two-room house where they employed six servants; and at the time of the 1891 census his parents were staying at the Hotel Metropole on the King's Road in London. They were living at the same house for the 1901 and 1911 censuses.

In 1884 Petrie saw active service during the Zhob Valley Expedition in Balochistan, on the North-West Frontier of India, and his second tour of active service was in the Third Burma War from 1885 to 1889, after which he was promoted captain on 17 December 1889. He took part in the Chin-Lushai expedition of 1889–90, and after being promoted to major on 10 May 1899 he saw active service during the Boxer Rebellion in China in 1900.

Boxer Rebellion in China, 1900

In 1900 a secret society of Chinese militants trained in martial arts known as the Righteous and Harmonious Fists – from which the world's press conjured up the name 'Boxers' – was established. Their grievances stemmed from two causes: mounting resentment for the attitude of superiority shown by Westerners towards the Chinese, and a fear that the Chinese Empire was going to be partitioned among European powers. After the Boxers began their violent attacks on the 'foreign devils', the revolt spread so rapidly that Empress Dowager Yehonola, the power behind the Chinese throne, who shared the same sentiments and feelings as the Boxers, decided to support the rebellion as a means of ending foreign domination.

When the Boxers incited a riot in Peking in May 1900, an international relief force of more than 2,000 men set out by rail from Tientsin the next day, but in a ludicrous failure they actually got lost and had to return to Tientsin. A second relief force of 17,000 men from eight countries including Britain – the Eight-Nation Alliance – commanded by the competent British General Alfred Gaselee, set out to march against the Boxers in Peking, on 4 August 1900. German soldiers had been told by the Kaiser: 'Anybody who falls into your hands must be destroyed!' and the international army acquired a fearsome reputation. As they advanced, Boxer resistance melted away and the four largest national contingents moved swiftly on to Peking.

In Peking the British Legation was under siege. Boxer rebels had already murdered the Japanese and German foreign ministers and they were outside the walls shouting 'Sha! Sha!' ('Kill! Kill!'). The remaining diplomats and foreign engineers were in great peril. However, the Boxers only made one all-out assault in fifty-four days, and on the following day the relief force arrived and stormed the gates to put an end to the revolt.

In 1906, at the age of 45, Petrie married Jessie Inez Natalia, daughter of B. Horace Wood of Claremont, in Natal, South Africa.

He saw service as a brigadier during the Great War, being appointed Commander of the Bath (CB) in 1915. Petrie died in Buenos Aires, Argentina, on 27 December 1925, aged 64.

Bruce Bremner Russell

Bruce Russell was a prominent left-back in the Royal Engineers squad during the early 1880s, and he was capped for England in 1883.

Russell was born in Bayswater in Kensington, London, on 25 August 1859, the eighth of nine children to John Alexander Russell (1814–82), an East India Company merchant, and his wife, Laura Condie (formerly Pattison, 1828–76). At the time of the 1861 census the family were living at 32 Pembridge Gardens in Kensington, London, and they employed six servants.

He attended the Worthing House School on the Chapel Road in Broadwater, Worthing, and was educated at the Royal Military Academy, from where he was commissioned as lieutenant in the Royal Engineers on 18 December 1878.

With an Irish father and a Scottish mother, Russell could have played football for three of the home countries. However, he chose to play for 'his' own home country. He was picked to play for England against Scotland at Hampden Park on 11 March 1882, and for England against Wales at the Racecourse Ground in Wrexham on 13 March 1882, but he had to withdraw because of injury. England lost both games. In what should have been his third cap, he played left-back for England against Wales at Kennington Oval on 3 February 1883, a game that England won 5-0.

On 10 May 1892, after being trusted by Russell with the power of attorney for the transfer of certain property, 'but did convert the same to his own use', his solicitor, William Charles Galloway, pleaded guilty to the offence on 26 July 1892, and he was sentenced to five years' penal servitude.

Russell was promoted major on 18 January 1897, and on 9 October 1909, he was placed on half-pay after completing five years' service as a regimental lieutenant colonel, becoming colonel a week later. He was recalled for service during the Great War, where he was awarded the Distinguished Service Order. He retired from military service on 1 January 1918.

At the time of the 1911 census Russell was head of the household, living in The Mount at Glen Magna in Leicester. He had one boarder and three servants. On 21 November 1922 he left the port of Liverpool on board the *Castalia* bound for Bombay, although he was still officially living at The Mount.

Russell was still single in 1939, and living at 49 Wilbury Road in Hove, Sussex, with his sister, Alma, and two servants. He died at his home on 13 May 1932, aged 82.

Chapter 15

The 1883 to 1890 Seasons

Although the Royal Engineers had got to the third round and beyond in every season from 1872 to 1883, except for 1878–79, their performances in the FA Cup declined rapidly and they only got beyond the first round one more time, which was during the 1887–88 tournament; the last time they reached the first round proper. They entered in 1888–89 but were eliminated in the first qualifying round.

In the first round of the 1883–84 competition, played on 10 November 1883, they were beaten by Windsor Home Park 5-3 at Windsor. In the opening round of the 1884–85 tournament they were thrashed 10-1 at Great Marlow, on 8 November 1884, and went out of the Cup in the first round for the third consecutive season when Old Foresters came to Chatham on 31 October 1885 and went away with a 5-1 victory. Having re-entered the competition, the 1st Surrey Rifles lost 12-0 to Clapham Rovers on the same day.

By this time three clubs used the Great Lines at Chatham as their home ground, and a history of the Corps recorded:

> It may be added that before the advent of professionals, football grounds were generally unenclosed and the RE at Chatham played on the Great Lines, a ground [pitch] being marked out for each match. Other local clubs also used a ground [pitch] on the Lines and in 1883–84 [it was actually 31 October 1885] three matches in the first round for the Association Cup were in play simultaneously on the Lines the local teams being RE [versus Old Foresters]; Chatham [versus the former holders, Old Carthusians]; and Rochester [versus Reading].

The 1886–87 season was the last time two military teams played in the first round proper of the FA Cup, but they both went out at that stage. On 23 October 1886, the 1st Surrey Rifles had nine goals put past them by Upton Park, and on the following Saturday the Royal Engineers lost to Old Etonians by the only goal of the game.

The 1st Surrey Rifles had only ever won two games and scored three goals in the competition, and in their last three appearances in the competition they had twenty-seven goals scored against them. Consequently, they never took part in the competition again. The 1887–88 tournament produced a mini tri-competition for the Great Lines clubs. On 15 October 1887, the Royal Engineers beat Rochester 5-0 – their last ever victory in the FA Cup – and Chatham defeated Luton Town 5-1. In the second round played on 5 November 1887, Chatham beat the Royal Engineers 3-1.

This season's tournament provided the highest score in FA Cup history when Preston North End beat Hyde 26-0. The prolific Scottish marksman James 'Jimmy' Ross scored seven.

The 1888–89 season saw the Royal Engineers' last game in the FA Cup. In the first qualifying round, played on 6 October 1888, they lost 5-1 to Crusaders.

The Crusaders Club of London was founded in 1863, and the club had been represented at the meeting when the Football Association was established. They played in white shirts and shorts with red socks, and their home ground was in Brompton. Their team roster included two English and two Welsh international players, and Edgar Lubbock, who had been in four finals: playing for Wanderers when winning the first-ever final in 1872, Old Etonians when losing to the Royal Engineers in 1875 and Wanderers in 1876, before winning the Cup in 1879.

Chapter 16

The 1890–91 Season

The last military club to reach the first round proper of the Football Association Challenge Cup was the 93rd Highland Regiment during the 1890–91 Season. In October and November 1890 they played four qualifying matches against Luton Town, Watford Rovers, Swindon Town and Ipswich Town, scoring twenty goals against three. In the first-round proper match, played on 17 January 1891, they travelled to the North-East, where they lost 2-0 to Sunderland Albion. They entered the FA Cup for 1891–92 and were drawn to play at Bedminster, but they withdrew from the fixture before it was played.

A team by the name of the Crystal Palace Engineers also entered the 1890–91 FA Cup, and the 1st Highland Light Infantry entered the 1891–92 competition, but after wins over Maidstone and Millwall Athletic, they lost to Casuals 4-1.

93rd Highland Regiment Players

James John 'Jock' Fleming and John 'Sandy' McMillan

Jock Fleming was born at Leith near Edinburgh in September 1864, and Sandy McMillan was born in 1869.

Fleming played for Vale of Leven, based in the town of Alexandria in West Dumbartonshire. The club reached the Scottish Cup final seven times between 1877 and 1890, winning the trophy three times running from 1877 to 1879. They beat the mighty Glasgow Rangers on two of those occasions and the 3rd Lanarkshire Rifle Volunteers on the other.

Fleming and McMillan entered the Princess Louise's (Argyll and Sutherland Highlanders), and joined the football club, which was commonly known as the 93rd Highland Regiment FC. McMillan rose to the rank of sergeant. They formed the backbone of the team, with McMillan's firm play at centre-half and Fleming's element of aggression up front as centre-forward.

After their cup run, the 93rd Highlanders played an exhibition match against Southampton St Mary's of the Southern League at the County Ground, and won 2-0. The committee at St Mary's were particularly impressed with Fleming and McMillan and signed them in readiness for the next round of the FA Cup.

They made their debut in the FA Cup second qualifying round against Reading at the Antelope Ground in Southampton, on 24 October 1891, and Fleming scored a hat-trick in a 7-0 victory. However, the Southampton committee had failed to sign their registration forms in time so, being considered to have fielded illegal players, Saints were expelled from the competition.

Nevertheless, Fleming continued to play in friendly matches at St Mary's until December, when they were both posted to India. Fleming left the army in May 1892 to pursue a football career. McMillan remained stationed at Umballa when Fleming returned to Britain. Sergeant McMillan died of enteric fever in the following year.

Fleming had a couple of seasons in the Football League, playing four games for Aston Villa in 1892, scoring two goals on his debut against Everton, and eleven games for Lincoln City of the League's newly formed Second Division, scoring five goals.

He returned to non-League football in Scotland in May 1893, playing mainly with Larkhill Saints in South Lanarkshire. He died in August 1934, a month before his 68th birthday.

A Selection of Newspaper Reports Concerning FA Cup Matches Featured in the Text

The report from the *Nottinghamshire Journal* of 18 November 1878, on the first Nottingham FA Cup Derby match:

Nottingham Forest v Notts Club Association Cup Tie

One of the most interesting matches of the football season in Notts was that played on the Beeston Cricket Ground, on Saturday last, between the Forest and Notts Clubs, who had both entered into competition for the Association Challenge Cup, and were drawn together in the first round of ties. The match was played at Beeston, in consequence of the Trent Bridge Ground being engaged for the purpose of a handicap, and the ground was partially enclosed in order that gate money might be charged. The trains leaving Nottingham at 2 o'clock were crowded with people, and there would be probably be five hundred persons on the ground, notwithstanding the inclemency of the weather, whilst many took their stand upon the platform of the station, whence a good view of the game was obtained.

Both teams were well represented, and a spirit of emulation as to which club was best worthy of representing the town on the football field contributed to make the game of a much more exciting character than usual. Owing to the recent rains the ground was in a very sodden condition, and as a matter of course the going was very heavy, while half a breeze blew from the station end of the ground towards the pavilion. The spin of the coin favoured the Notts captain, who elected to attack the pavilion goal during the first half-time, thus having the wind in his favour at the commencement of the match.

The following are the names of the players engaged, and it will be seen that the teams contained the best exponents of the winter game there are to be found in the neighbourhood of Nottingham.

Notts: E H Greenhalgh (captain and back), H Greenhalgh (goal), A T Dobson (back), G Seals and H Morse (half-backs), H Cursham and T Oliver (left forwards), A W Cursham and R J Greenhalgh (right forwards), G Cursham and the Reverend J R B Owen (centre-forwards).

Forest: S W Widdowson (captain and back), A H Smith and A C Goodyer (right forwards), J H Turner (centre-forward), F W Earp and W Luntley (left forwards), E Luntley and C J Caborn (backs), J Sands (goal), A J Bates (right half back), A M Holroyd (left half back) – Referee: Mr Wardle; Umpires: Mr A T Ashwell (Notts), Mr C J Spencer (Forest).

Widdowson set the ball a rolling at half past two o'clock, but it was out immediately on the right hand side, and the throw in falling to the eldest Cursham, he cleverly dribbled it to the top left hand corner, when it was put behind the goal line off a Forester, and the corner kick was entrusted to R J Greenhalgh. Nothing definite, however, resulted from his effort, and Earp who throughout the game played with remarkable cleverness and good judgment, carried the war into the Notts ground, but was well stopped by Dobson just when he appeared dangerous. Earp was not to be denied, however, and after an ineffectual try at goal, a foul was awarded to the Foresters, the free kick nearly resulting in a goal, the custodian being compelled to use his hands to avert Smith's shot.

Five minutes after the commencement of play a corner kick fell to Earp, who planted the 'leather' clean in front of the Notts goal, and it was neatly put through by Turner amidst loud cheering for the scarlet colours, the wearers of which were unmistakably the favourites with the spectators, although as much as 2 to1 had been laid against them before the start. When the play was resumed, Widdowson was applauded for some smart dribbling forward, the Forest captain, although put down as playing back, being general in the front rank of his men. The Notts men were thoroughly on their mettle, and Dobson having lifted the ball amongst his forwards; Owen, whose brilliant play in front of goal is so well known, got possession of it, and amidst shouts of 'well played' worked his way right in front of the Forest stronghold, but the shot failed. The next important point was the dribbling of Widdowson in the centre, and he having passed the ball to Earp, the little one again judiciously middled it and it was goaled by Goodyer with a smart kick, this second goal for the Foresters being again received with cheering. Two goals after fifteen minutes play.

Notts retaliated with a vengeance, the back play of Greenhalgh and Dobson, and the half-back play of Morse, being recognised by the spectators, but the forwards did not seem quite at home until at length H Cursham and Oliver got possession of the ball and the former's shot was cleverly frustrated by Caborn, who headed the ball out. H Cursham had another try at the goal immediately afterwards, but failed to score, and the game became faster than ever, Widdowson running in grand form, and carrying operations once more into his opponents ground. A W Cursham then gave the Foresters a taste of his quality by taking the leather right up the field in splendid style. He passed it on to Owen, who, with indomitable pluck, worked his way forward, and though regularly surrounded by scarlet jackets he forced the ball through a scrimmage and drew first blood for Notts, the feat being greeted with cheers.

The two elder Curshams again distinguished themselves in the centre of the ground, and Oliver also played in good form, but they could not get the leather past the Forest backs, the brothers Luntley and Caborn kicking with great precision and being mainly instrumental in preventing further scoring. Turner had another shot which went over the crossbar, and Greenhalgh (goal) having of course the kick-out, landed the ball well into the Forest part of the ground, where C Cursham, Oliver and Owen rendered very good service, and, the ball having been touched down behind the Forest goal line, Notts had the advantage of a corner kick, and a 'bully' occurred in front of the Foresters goal. Just when there seemed a great probability of the score being made even, Caborn with a rush headed the ball out of danger. The Foresters returned the compliment with another fierce attack on the railway end goal, and after some grand dribbling by Owen and A W Cursham further exchanges took place, but when half-time was called the score had received no addition.

After a few minutes interval, the Notts captain kicked-off against the wind, but the ball was returned directly, and Goodyer on the right hand side had a try, but the ball passed over the crossbar. Bates, now for almost the first time in the game, showed prominently, and stopped the forwards in two or three runs, but the ball was gradually worked nearer to the Forest goal, although not quite near enough to admit for a shot. Goodyer had another chance of scoring but he was placed offside, and Morse was applauded for some fine kicking. Harry Cursham made some very useful and clever screw kicks, whilst Owen also showed to advantage, the play about this time being decidedly in favour of Notts. Owen once more was cheered for his dribbling, whilst Holroyd distinguished himself by the manner in which he tackled Owen on several occasions, and more than once succeeded in getting the ball away from him.

A corner kick, which was entrusted to Widdowson, resulted in nothing, but Smith made a very good shot, which only just passed outside the posts, and not withstanding that the Notts back tried to get the ball away, Widdowson and Goodyer ran it well up the centre of the ground, and passed to Smith, who scored the third goal for the Forest in a very neat manner.

After this the game began to grow fast and furious, there being plenty of charging and rough play, but, with the exception of fine runs by H A and A W Cursham, together with Owen for the Notts; and Earp, Widdowson and Goodyer for the Forest, nothing particularly worthy of notice occurred, although the play was first in one goal and then in another. After an hour and a half's play the game resulted in the favour of the Foresters by three goals to one.

Both teams were cheered on returning to the pavilion. The Notts captain rendered invaluable service back, whilst the individual play of the two elder Curshams, Oliver, Owen and R J Greenhalgh was excellent, but they did not play well together. Dobson and Morse kicked in good style half-back, and the play of both goalkeepers is worthy of mention, neither's post being sinecure. Earp we have already mentioned, together with Goodyer, Widdowson and Smith, for their useful efforts forward. Caborn showed some improvement on his previous form this year, but Bates was not in such good fettle, as he was suffering from a severe cold, and we have seen Turner play better before. The brothers Luntley also deserve mention for their plucky play, and both teams may be congratulated upon playing a well-contested game.

Note: There were seven players on show in the match who gained international honours. Henry Alfred 'Harry' Cursham (1859–1941), one of the five sporting Cursham brothers, holds the individual goal-scoring record for the FA Cup with forty-nine goals in forty-four games, and he played eight times for England from 1879 to 1884, scoring five goals; he also played for Corinthians FC. His older brother, Arthur William (1853–85), was chosen to play for England on seven occasions between 1876 and 1883, although he withdrew from one of the matches. He was twice captain, and scored two goals. He died of malaria in Florida on Christmas Eve, 1885.

Ernest Harwood Greenhalgh (1849–1922) of Mansfield, played twice for England, in the first-ever official international match against Scotland in 1872, and again in 1873. Two of his brothers also played in the match. Harold Morse (1859–1935), of Birmingham, played for England in 1879, when they beat Scotland for the first time since 1873. He also died in the United States.

Arthur Copeland Goodyer (1854–1932) played for England against Scotland in 1879. He was the third player from the Cup tie to die in the United States. Edward 'Ted' Luntley (1857–1921), who was originally from Surrey, was selected on five occasions to play for England but he only appeared in two matches in 1880. John Sands (1854–1911) played in goal for England against Wales in 1880. He died suddenly while travelling on a tram in Nottingham.

* * *

The report from the *Blackburn Times* of 5 November 1881, on the first Blackburn FA Cup Derby match:

Blackburn Rovers v Park Road (Blackburn)

With the dispiriting prospect of a certain defeat before them, the only certainty being as to whether or not they would be able to score at all, the representatives of the Park Road Club and their formidable opponents in the first round of the English Association Challenge Cup competition, the Rovers, met on Saturday, on the Leamington Ground. Little interest centred in the match, not many more than a thousand spectators being present.

Brown kicked-off for the Rovers. During the first half the Rovers had the sun shining in their faces and did not play in their usual style. The Park Road men on the other hand, acquitted themselves better than was expected, and more than once prevented a goal from being registered against them when that seemed imminent.

Six minutes after the commencement of the match, Brown, to whom the ball was passed by J Hargreaves and Avery, scored the first goal. Two or three attempts to increase the score failed, but about twenty minutes from the start Douglas took the ball down the field, and after a little sharp play in the mouth of the visitors' goal, the ball was sent through by Avery and Brown. Strachan got kicked severely and limped badly for some time, and Avery similarly suffered in the second half. A determined attack was made on the visitors' goal, but without result, and while the ball was in the visitors' quarter of their left wing, the Rovers Umpire blew his whistle and the home team ceased play accordingly. The referee cried out 'Go on' and Nuttall, who had the ball at his toe, and none to oppose him, ran it to the Rovers goal and kicked it through before he could be overtaken, the ball passing too high to be stopped by Howarth. The goal was allowed, and at half-time the score was thus two goals to one.

After change of ends the play of the Rovers improved. As soon as the ball was set in motion it was taken into the visitors' quarters, and from a corner kick by Brown the third punt was scored. Another corner kick followed almost immediately, and when the leather was sent out into the centre of the field it was at once returned but struck the outside of the goal post. For some minutes the goal was seriously threatened, and twice in quick succession the ball was caught by the goalkeeper in his hands. Greenwood kicked the ball from the centre of the field into the mouth of the goal, and when it was knocked back by the goalkeeper, Avery returned it, and striking Wilson, it rebounded from him through the goal. Afterwards Brown worked the ball round to the right corner, and then passed it to Avery, who made a good try at goal, but the ball passed outside. Ultimately however, the attack resulted in the scoring of another point, the ball being headed through by Douglas from a kick by Brown; and after some nice passing by Douglas and Duckworth, Avery secured the sixth goal. Some time afterwards F W Hargreaves sent the ball to his brother, who passed it to Avery, and the latter shot it through the goal.

The most exciting piece of play occurred in the mouth of the visitors' goal five minutes from the call of time. Wilson several times knocked the ball with his hands, but despite his efforts and those of the backs, who played well during the game, Strachan secured the eighth goal, and a moment later F Hargreaves, with a long kick sent the ball against the top bar, but, rebounding onto one of the defenders, it shot through, making the Rovers victors by nine goals to one. The teams were:

Blackburn Rovers: *Goalkeeper* – Roger Howarth; *Full-backs* – Dr Haydock Greenwood and Fergus Suter; *Half-backs* – Hugh McIntyre and Frederick William Hargreaves (captain), Harold Sharples; *Forwards*: *Right* – John Duckworth, James Douglas; *Centre* – James Brown, Thomas Strachan; *Left* – Geoffrey Avery, John Hargreaves.

Park Road: *Goalkeeper* – W Wilson; *Full-backs* – J W Pickup and J Jefferson; *Half-backs* – T McQuirk and J Walmsley; *Forwards*; *Right-wing* – J Hartley, A Mackereth; *Centre* – J McQuirk and J Pemberton; *Left-wing* – J Nuttall, W Whalley.

The Umpires were W Duckworth (Rovers) and W Holden (Park Road), and the referee was Mr Mangnall (Eagley).

* * *

The report from the *Waterloo Times* of 12 November 1881 on the first FA Cup match ever to be played on Merseyside:

Sports and Pastimes

The Bootle (Association) Club had the courage to tackle two sets of opponents on Saturday on the home ground. The first match was with Blackburn Law to decide the preliminary round of the English Challenge Cup competition. By the time the captains had got their men on the ground a large quantity of spectators had gathered together to witness the contest.

At 3:30pm the visitors set the ball in motion, but the home team soon ran it over their opponent's goal line and got a corner kick, but failed to work the ball between the posts. The play for some time was mostly in the visitors' quarters until the forwards, by a splendid run, reversed the play, but the ball was soon returned and several attempts by the home team to score failed. The visitors were not so unfortunate in the attempt, as their forwards rushed up to the ground with the ball and a struggle took place close to the home team goal posts. The Bootle goalkeeper missing his kick, the visitors slipped the ball through and scored the first goal. The home team then worked hard to equalise the gain, but half-time was called without them gaining any success.

After a short interval the ball was re-started and the home team made a splendid run, sending the ball over the goal line. The visitors won after a successful run, Heaton prominently distinguished himself, and a few minutes after the same player made a good attempt to score, the ball striking the crossbar and rebounding into play and going into touch near the goal line. Turner threw in and Smith headed the ball through. Both sides now worked hard to gain the deciding point, but the Bootle showed the best play and secured the winning point, which was loudly applauded by the spectators. At the call of time the game stood – Bootle two goals to the Blackburn Law one. Heaton, Turner, Rayner, Rogers and Smith all played well for the winners. The teams were:

Bootle: *Goalkeeper* – S W Jones; *Full-backs* – F G Heaton (captain), R M Sloan; *Half-backs* – J Rogers, C Allsop; *Forwards:*

Right-wing – S G Smith, C O Rayner; *Centre* – Reverend A W Keeley, R E Lythgoe; *Left-wing* – G W Turner, P Bateson.

Blackburn Law: *Goalkeeper* – J Shaw; *Full-backs* – J Brogden, W Shaw; *Half-backs* – R L Rylands (captain), H Fecitt; *Forwards: Right-wing* – Barker, Pemberton; *Centres* – Willan, H Fecitt; *Left-wing* – Greenhalgh, Hacking.

After a short interval the Bootle team turned out to play Preston North End, and as night was drawing on with very little time to rest from their previous exertions, having tossed for choice of ends, Heaton kicked-off for the home team, the forward carrying the ball into the visitors' quarters and sent it over the goal line. The play for some time was chiefly in the Preston quarters, until the visitors made a splendid run, and, with some sharp work, forced the ball between the posts and secured the first goal.

After the ball was re-started, Smith, Rayner and Keeley made a fine run, but their shot at goal went wide. The home team now played well together, and compelled the proud Prestonians to act very much on the defensive. The Bootle forwards took the ball close up to their opponent's goal post, and after some smart scrimmaging passed it through, and at half-time the game stood at one goal each. After changing ends the game became very fast, and the spectators got up a large amount of excitement, both parties exhibiting good play, working hard for victory. The visitors made two good shots at the home goal, but Jones prevented them scoring.

Bootle then began to press their guests very hard, a proceeding which they did not seem to be in a hurry to appreciate, and eventually the game came to a draw, the visitors stopping it, and stating that they would lodge an objection on the ground that Bootle had not been prepared to play the game whilst the light was good. After a long consultation it was decided to carry the play out, and the ground was cleared, but very little of the game could be seen owing to the darkness. At the call of time matters were equal, each side having scored one goal. The two clubs will have to meet again, I suppose on the Preston North End ground, and let us hope the best team may win.

* * *

The report from the *Buckingham Free Press* of 10 March 1882 on that year's FA Cup semi-final:

Football Association Challenger Cup – Great Marlow v Old Etonians

The aspirations of the partisans of the Marlow Club, which have been hitherto encouraged by the remarkable good form displayed by the local club against teams widely known in the football world, received a summary check at Kennington Oval on Saturday. Having fought their way into the semi-final round of the Challenge Cup Competition, Marlow were drawn against the Old Etonians (the runners-up last year), the winners of this match having to settle the final supremacy with one of two redoubtable northern clubs; the Blackburn Rovers and the Sheffield Wednesday. General anticipation pointed to a close match, though most of the cognoscenti appeared to think that the Etonians would just pull it off, and the odds were a point or two in their favour. Nobody certainly was prepared for the collapse of the Bucks team which actually occurred.

The contending teams could find no fault with the weather, which was bright and not too hot, with little wind blowing; the ground, too, was in good order. The prospect of a good match brought together about a thousand spectators, a considerable proportion of whom, as the shouts for Marlow during the progress of the game testified, were supporters of the plucky country club. Marked difference on weight was apparent as the teams faced each other, Marlow being much lighter all round than their opponents.

Having won the toss the Etonians took the Crown Baths end, and at a quarter past three the ball was kicked-off by Marlow. It was vigorously returned, and the Etonians forwards, following up smartly, forced the play into their opponents' lines. This, however, only lasted a few moments; Milward and Flint on the left wing cleared their lines by a smart run, and the fight was transferred to the other end. The Marlow forwards now began to play with great dash, and but for the excellent back play opposed to them they must thus early have made their mark. R A Lunnon and Flint were repeatedly cheered for brilliant runs and neat passing, and their comrades backing up well and doing their share of work the Eton backs had a very lively time of it for a quarter of an hour. But they stuck to their work manfully, French and Paravicini were always on the spot, the former kicking with excellent judgment; Kinnaird showed his old bulldog perseverance, and Foley closely imitated his leader.

Gradually the fire of the Marlow attack diminished, and the Eton front division had an opportunity of showing their dribbling skill. The great inferiority of Marlow in their back play now showed itself alarmingly, Macauley, Anderson, Dunn and Goodhart penetrating several times almost unchecked to a dangerous proximity to the Marlow goal. About half an hour from the start Macauley broke through in the centre, and dribbled at a great pace straight for goal. The custodian unfortunately was divided between the two courses of staying between the sticks or charging out to meet the danger, and when he adopted the latter course it was too late, and Macauley drew first blood for his side.

With this reverse to stir them into action, the Bucks men once more returned to the attack, and twice Rawlinson had to use his hands, but the backing-up was by no means so close as it ought to have been and that cool and safe goalkeeper had no difficulty in disposing of the ball. Marlow were forced back more easily this time, and soon afresh disaster for them happened; a throw-in by Foley producing a loose scrimmage in front of goal, out of which Goodhart registered a second point for the Etonians.

Ends were soon afterwards changed. Marlow had now the advantage of what little wind was blowing, and their partisans hoped they would make a better show. But the rush with which they went off at the beginning seemed to have told on them, and Eton, playing up hard, pressed them sorely. An occasional spurt by the forwards relieved their lines, but the visits to Eton territory were only of brief duration. A very doubtful goal was allowed to the Etonians soon after change of ends, Dunn having, in the opinion of the majority of the spectators, been clearly off-side when he commenced his run.

The spirits of the Marlow team seemed to have been damped by this third misfortune; their forwards, too, had been considerably knocked about, Lunnon in particular being scarcely able to keep on, while Shaw had a nasty kick on the ankle. The Etonians consequently had it pretty much their own way for the remainder of the game, and the ball seldom passed the half-way line. Hewett made ample amends for his first and only slip, stopping shot after shot with great quickness and precision; twice, however, his watchfulness was successfully evaded, Goodhart administered the final kick in each instance, and when time was called the Etonians were the winners by five goals to nothing.

There can be no doubt that the weak back play of Marlow lost them the match. Their forwards were almost equal in pace to the Etonians, and they dribbled and passed better; and had they been more strongly supported the score would have been a very different appearance. On the other hand the winners were exceptionally powerful in the defensive department, leaving their forwards free to skirmish in front with no anxiety as to their own communications. Macauley probably did more work than any other player on the ground, and his turn of speed served him in good stead; Goodhart, Dunn, Anderson and Novelli also played hard. French was decidedly the pick of the Eton backs, his kicking being very sure; both the half-backs were also well on the ball. There was not a great deal to choose between the Marlow forwards; perhaps Milward and Flint and Lunnon before he was hurt showed to most advantage. Speller proved very useful behind; playing pluckily though lacking weight, while among the half-backs Morgan and J Flint did most towards checking the Etonian advance. The sides were as follows:

Old Etonians: *Goalkeeper* – John Frederick Peel Rawlinson; *Full-backs* – Thomas Harvey French, Percy John de Paravacini; *Half-backs* – Arthur Fitzgerald Kinnaird (captain), Charles Windham Foley; *Forwards*: *Right* – William Joseph Anderson, John Barrington Trapnel Chevalier; *Centre* – Reginald Heber Macauley, Harry Chester Goodhart; *Left* – Arthur Tempest Blakiston Dunn, Philip Charles Novelli.

Great Marlow: *Goalkeeper* – H R Hewett (captain); *Full-backs* – F Speller, E Horwood; *Half-backs* – J Flint, J Morgan, T Walker; *Right-wing* – R A Lunnon, R H Lunnon; *Centre-forward* – R Shaw; *Left-wing* – W Milward, E Flint.

Referee – M P Betts (Old Harrovians). *Umpires* – C Warner (Upton Park) and C W Alcock (Wanderers).

The Blackburn Rovers and Sheffield Wednesday Clubs met at Huddersfield on Monday, but the game resulted in a draw and the teams will come together again on the 15th inst. at Manchester.

Appendix II

Military Men in the Unofficial Internationals

Previous to the first official international match in 1872, there were five non-official internationals, all played at Kennington Oval, in which military men took part; although the teams are described as an England XI and a team of Scotsmen resident in England. England did not lose any of the matches, the results of which were:

5 March 1870 – England 1 Scotland 1
19 November 1870 – England 1 Scotland 0
25 February 1871 – England 1 Scotland 1
18 November 1871 – England 2 Scotland 1
24 February 1872 – England 1 Scotland 0

Henry Renny-Tailyour played in the first 1871 match, and Hugh Mitchell played in the second match of 1871 and in the 1872 match. Also in the teams were:

William Charles Butler (1844–1914) was the son of a Royal Navy captain, and was a member of the Barnes and Civil Service clubs. He was the only man associated with the military to play for England in the unofficial matches. He played in the first 1870 game and in the first 1871 game. He enlisted in the 3rd Battalion, Border Regiment, being promoted captain in 1884. He subsequently became a justice of the peace in Cumberland (now Cumbria), and held the office of Probate Registrar at the High Court of Justice in Cumberland.

Harold Stuart Ferguson MBE (1851–1921) played in the second 1871 game, representing the Royal Military Academy; and in the 1872 game, representing the Royal Artillery. He was the son of a physician to Queen Victoria, whose friends included Sir Walter Scott. He married the daughter of Colonel Hamilton Maxwell of the Bengal Staff Corps, who was a niece of Field Marshal Lord Roberts VC. Ferguson joined the Royal Artillery and by the mid-1880s he was a lieutenant in the Nair Brigade of the army of the Rajah of Travancore, and spent most of his life in India.

Robert Erskine Wade Copland-Crawford (1852–94) only missed the first 1871 game of the five matches. He was the son of a captain in the Royal Artillery. He was educated at Harrow School, and joined the 2nd Middlesex, or Edmonton Royal Rifle Regiment of Militia, soon being appointed sub-lieutenant. In January 1874 he joined the 60th Rifles, known since 1881 as the King's Royal Rifle Corps. Copland-Crawford saw active service in Afghanistan in 1878–80, where he was mentioned in despatches for his involvement in the battle of Ahmed Khel on 19 April 1880 and he took part in the march to Kandahar with Lord Roberts VC. He resigned his commission on 6 August 1884. He became a police officer in Sierra Leone, where he fell from grace for causing the death by flogging of a native servant.

John Wingfield Malcolm (1833–1902) played in the first 1870 game. He was the first and last Baron Malcolm of Poltalloch, CB, VD, and was the son of the 14th Feudal Baron of Poltalloch in Argyll. He became a captain in the Kent Artillery Militia and an honourable colonel with the Argyll and Sutherland Highlanders. Malcolm was twice married, and at the time of his appearance for Scotland he was Conservative Member of Parliament for Boston in Lincolnshire, one of two sitting MPs in the first 1870 match. The other was William Henry Gladstone, son of the Liberal Prime Minister. Malcolm later became MP for Argyllshire.

Bibliography and Research Sources

Aberdeen Press and Journal, 23 July 1914.

Aeronautical Journal, December 1935.

Alcock, Charles William (ed.), *The Football Annual*, 1868–1885.

Alcock, Charles William, *The Association Game*, 1890.

Ancestry.com, including the British Regimental Registers of Service, 1756–1900.

Andy Cherry (military researcher).

AngloBoerWar.com

Atteridge, Captain A. Hilliard, *The Dongola Expedition of 1896 – The Journal of the Royal United Services Institution*, 1897.

Bancroft, James W., *Zulu War VCs: Victoria Crosses of the Anglo-Zulu War, 1879*, 2018.

Bancroft, James W., *The Devil's Trap: The Victims of the Cawnpore Massacre During the Indian Mutiny*, 2019.

Bell's Life (various).

Blackburn Times, 5 November 1881.

Bonhams Auctioneers, 9 April 2013.

Bragg, Melvin, and Charlton, Bobby, *The Rules of Association Football, 1863*, 2006.

British Army Muster and Pay Rolls, TNA, Kew.

British India Office Register of Births and Baptisms.

British Newspaper Archive.

Brown, Tony, *The FA Challenge Cup Complete Results*, 2020.

Brown, Brigadier General W. Baker, *The History of the Corps of Royal Engineers (Volume IV)*, 1952.

Buckinghamshire Free Press, 10 February, 24 February and 10 March 1882.

Burke's Peerage and *Landed Gentry.*

Cavallini, Rob, *The Wanderers FC: Five Times FA Cup Winners,* 2005.

census returns, 1841–1921.

Collett, Mike, *The Complete Record of the FA Cup,* 2003.

Conolly, T.W.J., *Roll of Officers of the Corps of Royal Engineers, from 1660 to 1898,* 1898.

Creagh, General Sir O'Moore, VC, *The VC and DSO, Two Volumes,* 1920.

Davidson, J., *The Mahsud Waziri Expedition of 1881,* 1884.

Derbyshire Times, 24 December 1873.

De Santis, Lieutenant Colonel Edward, *Officers of the Royal Engineers, n.d.*

Durnford, Sir Walter, Bridgman, Viscount William Clive and Kenyon-Slaney, Violet, *Memoir of Colonel, the Right Hon. William Kenyon-Slaney, MP,* 1909.

Edwardes, Michael, 'North-West Frontier', *British Empire Magazine,* 1971.

england-football-online.

Evans, Richard, *Teddy: The Life and Times of Major E G Wynyard, DSO OBE,* 2018.

FA Cup Final Reports for 1872, 1874, 1875 and 1878, held at the Royal Engineers Museum.

FamilySearch.org.

FIBIS (Families in British India Society).

Field, 23 March 1872, 14 March 1874 and 13 March 1875.

Football Association.

forces-war-records.co.uk.

Foster, Joseph, *Alumni Oxonienses, The Members of the University of Oxford, 1715–1886,* 1886.

Frimley and Camberley Great War 1914–1918 Memorial.

The Game (8 vols), 1969–70.

Gardner, Brian, 'The Boer War', *British Empire Magazine,* 1971.

Gardner, Brian, 'The Empire at War', *British Empire Magazine,* 1971.

Gibbons, Phillip, *Association Football in Victorian England – A History of the Game from 1863 to 1900,* 2001.

Gibson, Alfred and Pickford, William, *Association Football and the Men Who Made It* (4 vols), 1905–06.

Gillan, Don, *The First FA Cup. The Story of the Inaugural FA Cup Tournament,* 2017.

Grace's Guide to British Industrial History.

Groves, Lieutenant Colonel Percy, *History of the 93rd Sutherland Highlanders, 1800–1895,* 1895.

Hanna, Colonel Henry Bathurst, *The Second Afghan War, 1878–79–80: Its Causes, Its Conduct and Its Consequences,* 1904.

Hart's Annual Army List.

Harvey, Charles (ed.), *The Encyclopaedia of Sport*, 1959.

Hibbert, Christopher, 'China Humiliated', *British Empire Magazine*, 1971.

Hicks, Jim, 'White Man's Grave', *British Empire Magazine*, 1971.

History of Submarine Mining in the British Army, RE Institute, 1910.

Illustrated Sporting and Dramatic News (various).

Imperial War Museum, 'Lives of the First World War'.

Jackson, Nicholas Lane, *Association Football*, 1900.

Jackson, Nicholas Lane, *Sporting Days and Sporting Ways*, 1935.

JWB Historical Archive.

Lamming, Douglas, *An English Football Internationalists' Who's Who*, 1990.

Legg, Stuart, 'From Suez to Khartoum', *British Empire Magazine*, 1971.

Liddell Hart Centre, Military Archives at King's College in London.

London Gazette, 8 February 1901 and 29 July 1902.

Mackenzie, John, *Austral Africa; Losing it or Ruling It. Being Incidents and Experiences in Bechuanaland, Cape Colony and England*, 1887.

MacKinnon, J.P., and Shadbolt, S.H., *The South African Campaign of 1879*, 1880.

Mitchell, Andy, *First Elevens: The birth of international football and the men who made it happen*, 2012.

Mitchell, Andy, *Arthur Kinnaird: First Lord of Football*, 2020.

Morning Post (various).

Morris, Donald, 'War on the Veld', *British Empire Magazine*, 1971.

Navy and Army Illustrated, 30 October 1896.

New Oxford Dictionary of National Biography, 2004.

News of the World Football Annual (various).

Nottingham Journal, 18 November 1878.

Nottinghamshire Standard, 26 December 1873.

Porter, Whitworth, and Watson, Sir Charles Moore, *The History of the Corps of Royal Engineers*, Vol. II, 1889.

Portsmouth Evening News, 10 March 1930.

'Red Earth', Royal Engineers Museum Publication, 1996.

Royal Engineers Journal, September 1900, December 1928, and June 1935 (including the memoirs of Major General Sir Richard M. Ruck, KBE, CB, CMG and Colonel Sir William G. Morris, KCMG, CB).

Royal Engineers Museum, Chatham.

Ruck, Major General Sir Richard M., *R.E. Football in the Early Seventies*, 1928.

Sandes, E.W.C., *The Military Engineer in India*, 1933.

Sandes, E,W.C., *The Royal Engineers in Egypt and the Sudan*, 1937.

Sandes, E,W.C., *Indian Sappers and Miners*, 1948.

The Sapper, various including September 1896.

Secure the Shadow: Images from Early Photographs.

Sheffield and Rotherham Independent, 9 December 1873.

Sheffield Daily Telegraph, 22 December 1873.

Smith, Paul, *Scotland Who's Who*, 2013.

Spiller, Ray (compiler), *Football Association Cup, 1871–1881*, 1985.

Sporting Life (various).

The Sportsman, 19 March 1872.

Summers, Paul, 'A Man Largely Ignored by History: Charles Edward Haynes', *Miniature Medal World*, 13 June 1918.

The Times, 25 March 1878, 24 April 1900, 25 and 30 April 1908.

Tyson, Dick, *London's Oldest Rugby Clubs*, 2008.

Vibart, Colonel Henry Meredith, *Addiscombe: Its Heroes and Men of Note*, 1894.

Wall, Sir Frederick, *Fifty Years of Football*, 1935.

Warsop, Keith, *The Early FA Cup Finals and the Southern Amateurs*, 2004.

Waterloo Times, Liverpool, 12 November 1881.

Weir, Colin, *The History of Oxford University Association Football Club, 1872–1998*, 1998.

Welch, Reginald Courtney, *The Harrow School Register, 1800–1911*, 1911.

Wellington Journal, 2 May 1908.

Who Was Who, 1916–1928 and 1929–1940.

Wisden's Cricketers Almanac.

Wolstenholme, Kenneth, *FA Cup Centenary Gift Book for Boys*, 1972.

Index

.